A BIRD'S EYE VIEW OF MURDER

JACQUELINE VICK

This is a work of fiction. Names are either a product of the author's imagination or are used fictitiously. Any resemblance to actual people living or dead, places, businesses, or events is entirely coincidental.

Frankie Chandler Pet Psychic Book 2

Copyright © 2014 Jacqueline M. Vick
All rights reserved.

ISBN-13: 978-1-945403-35-4 (Paperback)
ISBN-13: 978-1-945403-02-6 (Ebook)

To Foster, with love.

ONE

The Baking Channel's newly appointed Blue-Ribbon Queen, Elvira Jenkins, lay face down alongside the kitchen island, her arms outstretched as if she had caught her toes under the long rubber spill mat and flapped wildly to catch her balance before going down. It was possible she had fainted, or maybe she had a severe case of narcolepsy and had fallen asleep in the middle of the most exciting night of her life. Neither optimistic scenario explained the large, bloody spot on the back of her iron-gray head of curls.

On this same kitchen set a mere hour ago, Elvira's forceful personality had loomed large with the confidence of one who could always turn others around to her way of thinking, whether they liked it or not. Now, she seemed insignificant—her thick, strong arms flaccid and pale, her bulky shoulders no longer firmly set. It was almost as if someone masquerading as the woman had taken off an Elvira Jenkins costume and tossed it carelessly aside.

Since I was sprawled out on the floor right next to her, I had a good view of her formerly penetrating grey eyes that now stared without seeing. And the dried spot of drool at the corner of her mouth.

The lingering smells of cookies and burnt cornbread wafted in the air, olfactory leftovers from the taping of the Baking Channel's newest show, *Blue-Ribbon Babes*, and a dusting of flour coated the floor beneath her face.

"Meow! Meow! M-e-o-w!" A large bird shrieked from inside a cage tucked into a corner of the countertop, white feathers fluttering madly as if it were trying to take off in flight and leave behind the horrible scene below.

"I think I'm going to be sick," I said. And then I was.

TWO

The Baking Channel's live premiere of *Blue-Ribbon Babes* took place at Saguaro Studios off Beeline Highway, about fifteen miles from my home in Wolf Creek, Arizona. As I drove south toward Mesa, I listened to the chatter of my Aunt Gertrude, who had swept in two days ago from Wisconsin. I'd like to think she came to see me, but I knew the premiere was her sole reason for weathering airport security. Unfortunately, Auntie insisted I be her guest—she had two tickets—and I couldn't talk my way out of coming without maligning her favorite hobby, baking. Besides, I figured I owed her.

Aunt Gertrude a.k.a. Madame Guinevere was the reason I got into the pet psychic business. For as long as I could remember, she read tarot cards at her dining room table to a steady stream of locals, all dying to hear what their futures held. She taught me everything there was to know about cold reading people—watching their body language and gauging their reactions to leading questions in order to make spectacular predictions. I used the same technique on pet owners, and I had a pretty good business going until my ex-boyfriend Jeff told a buxom reporter all my secrets. After an exposé appeared in the Loon Lake Local, I fled from Wisconsin to Arizona to live near my best friend, Penny, who promised life would get better. I was still waiting.

"Your mother won at Bunco last week. The pot was pretty high. About a hundred bucks."

"Good for her," I said, distracted by my driving and my irritation over missing my dinner in the rush to get to the studio on time.

"I told her she should spend it on a new wardrobe." Auntie plucked at the collar of her purple-and-pink paisley print blouse, which matched her purple polyester pants and light purple-and-pink blended eye shadow. And her pink lipstick. Auntie doesn't dress up very often, but when she does, she puts the emphasis on bright. "Your mother doesn't wear enough color. Looks like a dishrag half the time. I guess God ran out of good taste after He made me."

"Not everyone can pull off Butterfly Pink," I said.

"True. Beverly does the best she can," she added in what I'm sure she considered a spirit of generosity.

I leaned forward to read the approaching street sign. Saguaro Drive. "We're here."

It only took twenty minutes to get to the studio from my house, but it took just as long to make it past the studio security booth. Once we made it onto the lot, we were at the mercy of orange-vested sadists who had no intention of ever letting us park. God forgive me, but I cut off a station wagon filled with old ladies to pull into an open slot.

"Hurry it up." Auntie grabbed my hand and trotted to a gigantic rectangular building marked Stage 3, where clusters of mostly women gathered around the side door and waited to enter the magical behind-the-scenes world of televised programming.

I sized up the group and decided "one of these things was not like the others" and that *one* was me. My sour expression—lips pressed together and eyebrows raised to show I was far above the thrill of taking part in a studio audience—contrasted with the other attendees' bright smiles and the excited, high-pitched chatter that filled the air.

Auntie noticed my look and said, "What's the matter with you? I've got some antacids in my purse if you need them."

It's fine to be a martyr, but not to get called on it.

"I've got a headache," I mumbled, which was true.

About a month ago, I'd discovered my ability to communicate with animals. Quite a surprise for a *fake* pet psychic. The "gift" had only brought me trouble, including my involvement in a murder that concluded with my inability to hear my furry friends. I'd re-billed myself as an animal behaviorist. The moment I'd tossed out my pet psychic business cards, my client list took a nosedive.

Today, I'd had one customer who felt I should use domination techniques on his Rottweiler. Though he'd never try it himself, he wanted me to pin the Rottie to the floor with my shoulder and show him who was the boss, *just like the guy on television.* Then I met with a woman who couldn't understand why a reward system of gumdrops had left her Chihuahua hyperactive. And toothless.

"You had a headache yesterday. You should get those looked into," Auntie said. "Might be early menopause."

Standing in front of us was a Hispanic woman who had white streaks in her black hair and the figure of a rectangle cinched tightly at the waist. Her companion, a tall, thin beanpole with dishwater-grey hair, wore a light green cotton dress and the same puckered expression as my Home Economics teacher in high school.

"Did I hear someone has a headache?" said the Hispanic woman. "I've got chewable baby aspirin." She dug them out and handed me two.

"Isn't that kind," Auntie said. "I'm Gertrude Pit." She reached into her purse, pulled out a deck of cards, and handed them around. I took one from her and gaped. These weren't Auntie's favored Rider Waite tarot cards. The symbols on the front of the one I held resembled a typical Magician card, but the back had a swirling multi-colored pattern with Auntie's name, phone number, website, and addresses for Facebook, Twitter, and Skype in the corner. Tarot cards that doubled as business cards. All that technology was hard to reconcile with Auntie's word-of-mouth kitchen table business.

"This is my niece, Frances," Auntie said.

The Hispanic woman nodded. "A beautiful name. Like St. Francis of Assisi."

The tall woman asked, "Isn't he the one who talked to animals?"

"Something like that," I said with a slight shudder. I leaned sideways to see if the line was moving at all. My gaze roved over the people, my mouth moving as I silently counted heads. We were twenty-ninth and thirtieth in line, but the old woman with a walker in the big group up front was going to slow down our progress.

"It *is* a beautiful name. Can you believe some people call her Frankie?" Auntie tsked. "Not very feminine."

"I'm Beatrisa," said the Hispanic woman, "but everybody calls me Bea." Bea pointed to the tall woman. "This is my friend, Jane."

Jane held her purse in front of her, clasping the handle in both hands. "Pleased to meet you," she said.

A short, plump woman in a blue-green floral big shirt,

black stretch pants, and enough jewelry to start her own mall kiosk spun around at the mention of the name Frankie. Her dangly earrings tinkled with the motion. She continued to stare at me until introductions were made before stepping up to join our group.

"Frankie. That's an unusual name," she said. "I seem to remember a pet psychic named Frankie Chandler helping the police with the murder last month."

"Murder!" Auntie's face turned red. "No one in our family has ever been involved in a murder! We're not that sort. Tell her, Sissy," she said, invoking the nickname she always used for me.

I avoided looking into my Aunt's sharp china-blue eyes. She'd see through me in a minute. Thing is, I hadn't given my family details about the murder or my role in solving it, because my mother already had me permanently fixed on her prayer chain. If I'd said anything about my surprisingly real ability to read the minds of animals, I'm sure she would have called for a full exorcism.

"Actually, the maid of a client was the victim. Everyone connected with the client was questioned. Nothing to do with me, really."

She cocked her head. "But I'm certain I read that you helped out with the investigation."

Auntie, quick to latch onto a compliment, puffed with pride. "Helped out? That sounds more like it. Our family is known for their ability to separate the facts from the phooey."

"We are?" I mumbled under my breath.

"I bet I could tell the Loon Lake police a thing or two about solving crimes. Not that we have that many."

"You're a pet psychic?" Jane peered down at me over her long, thin nose.

"I only take animal behavior appointments now."

I couldn't very well explain that after reading the mind of a dog in order to save two lives—one of them being the dog's—I had lost my ability, especially as I'd never told my family about my "gift" in the first place. It had been three weeks since I'd "heard" from my furry friends.

The tattle-tale's name turned out to be Lola. By asking her how she came to be at the *Blue-Ribbon Babes* premiere, I managed to switch the topic of conversation from murder to baking.

A girl dressed in the type of navy-blue uniform I usually associate with stewardesses stepped in front of us and waved her hands in the air.

"If I could have your attention." The chattering stopped. "My name is Linda." She gave us an enormous, pearly white smile. "Anyone who isn't here for the premiere of *Blue-Ribbon Babes* is in the wrong place."

The crowd applauded. I'm not sure why.

"You should all have a postcard invitation with you." She held up a sample. "Does anyone *not* have their invitation?"

Everyone had come to the party armed.

She swept her arm toward a thickset young man stationed at the door who did not look good in the male version of the uniform. "My fellow page, Mike, is that good-looking guy standing at the door. Say hello, Mike."

He waved, and then Linda turned serious and called out instruction in the clipped tones of a drill sergeant.

"You will hand Mike your postcard. You will wait for him to mark you off on the special invitation list. Then you will proceed through the doorway, where one of the other pages will walk you to the seating area. It's first come, first serve, but there's plenty of room for everyone, so please don't hurry." Her smile faltered. "And please don't push. We don't want any injuries." She paused long enough to let us imagine possible grim scenarios—overturned walkers and broken hips—and then, bright smile back in place, she said, "Welcome and enjoy the premiere of *Blue-Ribbon Babes!*"

The employees operated at maximum efficiency, and the line moved steadily forward. It was the third week of April. The day's temperature had only reached the low eighties, so the wait in the evening sun, though blinding, was comfortable.

"You never told me how *you* got invited to the premiere," I said to Auntie.

"I've won several competitions with my raspberry scones, you know. Word gets around."

That didn't make sense to me, but we were next in line to pass through the door, so I let it drop. Just as I stepped forward, a teenager, his jeans pulled down to expose pink-and-white striped underwear, cut in front of us.

"I've got to see Sonny Street," he mumbled through a curtain of bangs.

"You know, Sissy, when I was younger, showing your butt like that was an invitation to get it kicked. In fact, my toes are starting to itch."

He ignored Auntie's threats, but he did hike his pants up an inch or two.

Mike asked, "Are you on the list?"

"I don't know about *him*, but *we're* on the list, and we were next in line," Auntie huffed.

"I don't know, man, but I've got to see him." He curled a lip at Auntie in an Elvis-style sneer. His upper lip twitched from the effort, as if he still needed practice. "It's life-or-death."

"We're taping tonight." Mike checked his watch. "He's probably in makeup."

The teen snorted. "Makeup? What is he, a girl?"

The page gave him a stern look. "Come back tomorrow."

The teen threw up his hands. "Tomorrow's too late! I gotta see him *now!*"

Mike didn't budge, so the teen was forced to move off, grumbling and tugging his pants back down to a stylish level as he walked. Mike turned his attention back to us.

"Name please?"

He took our postcard and turned it over, found Gertrude Pitt on the list and then, reading the bar code across the top of the invitation, added a number three in a column next to her name.

"I wonder what that means," Auntie whispered. "Maybe they're going to have a giveaway, like they used to do on Oprah. I could use a new blender."

He handed us each a voting card and a pencil. The card had three check boxes next to Contestant #1, Contestant #2, and Contestant #3.

"Are the contestant's names secret?" Auntie asked.

"I don't think so." Mike said. He called out, "Next!" and motioned us inside.

As we stepped through the door, I got my first impression of a show biz stage. I'd imagined something out of *Singing in the Rain*, with eager young men bustling about in vests and ties, aspiring ingénues strutting like peacocks in the hopes of being discovered, and everything looking so shiny and clean that celebrities could burst into impromptu dances without fear of catching hepatitis from a rusty nail on the floor.

I wasn't prepared for a cold, musty, cement-floored room that had the ambiance of a warehouse. Instead of my nattily dressed young men, there were two guys in jeans and sweatshirts passing overhead on a wooden walkway.

Instead of a handy ladder for Gene Kelly to mount while wooing Debbie Reynolds, a forklift rested next to a pile of lumber, and the only one taking advantage was a grey mouse that skittered between the boards.

"It's dirtier then I expected. Kind of takes away my appetite."

"They won't be cooking on the floor," Auntie said. "Don't be such a Negative Nellie. I'm sure the actual set is much cleaner."

To our right, temporary drywall partitions formed a kind of maze. A different page led us through a few turns until the walls opened up into a large room. I took a long look at my first live television set.

"Not what I expected."

THREE

Call me naïve, but as I watched programs from the comfort of my home, I imagined the actual set would be, well, cozy. Cooking shows always looked as if they were filmed in the star's home, and though I knew that wasn't practical, I still thought the actual set would be an average-sized kitchen with some floor level chairs set up for optimum intimacy.

Instead, retractable metal bleachers, the same kind we had in our tiny high school gym in Loon Lake, lined the wall and faced a brightly lit kitchen that reminded me of a prom date getting the final touches on her makeup and hair. Crew members swarmed over it, polishing the blue refrigerator and testing the burners that sat in the middle of a white countertop. On the other side of a large window positioned in the back wall, a man adjusted a Ficus tree until a woman in the kitchen signaled that the plant was centered. Another man in shorts and a t-shirt stood on a ladder and adjusted a camera that pointed down toward the countertop below.

Two more men stood idly next to a second camera on a rolling stand to the right of the set. A third camera of the same type was aimed directly at the island, giving the view of the studio audience. It seemed excessive to me. After all, they were filming food. How much action were they planning to capture?

Next to this last camera, an African-American woman with shortly cropped hair and a headset resting around her neck looked to be the most popular person in the room. The surrounding crew members fluttered around asking questions, and she calmly gave answers and sent them on their way.

Fake walls stuck out on either side of the set, but where they ended, I could see into the cavernous warehouse behind. It felt like Mickey Rooney and Judy Garland had set up a stage in a very large garage.

"Here you are," the page said, directing us to mount the stands by a center stairway. They had marked the first row *reserved*, but we found seats halfway down the fourth row, scooted in and took our places. Auntie folded down the chair seat and settled her plump rump in place. She pulled a tissue out of her purse and dabbed at her bulbous nose, while her gaze searched the set for any interesting tidbits she could share with the gals back in Loon Lake. In deference to the show's name, she had tied a blue ribbon around her salt-and-pepper bun.

Once seated and facing the set, I noticed two 55-inch televisions suspended from the ceiling on either side of the kitchen set. Currently, they displayed the Baking Channel logo—a white chef's hat crossed by a spatula and a wooden spoon.

"I wonder if they plan on showing the Diamondbacks' game to keep the male audience members interested."

Auntie had other things on her mind. "Do you think anybody famous is going to show up?"

"I doubt it. It's not like this is a world premiere that

matters." I shifted my butt to try to get more comfortable on the thinly padded seat. "You said this was a live show, right? So that means, what, a half hour? My rear can't make it more than half an hour on this seat."

Auntie responded with a gurgling noise. She stared, mouth open, at a group of people who took their places in the front row.

"Who's that?" I asked. "Don't tell me the celebrities have arrived."

I didn't recognize any of them, but since I haven't watched a television series since ER, I'm not in the know.

"It can't be," she whispered.

"Spill."

She didn't answer, so I pointed and gasped. "Is that Rachel Ray? She looks much taller in person."

She broke out of her trance. "Where?"

"My mistake. Now tell me who those people are. You obviously know them."

She made a face. "How would I know someone all the way in Arizona? Don't be ridiculous."

But her eyes strayed back to the group. If she leaned forward another few inches, she would have nosedived into the third row. She seemed focused on one person in particular—a tall man wearing a jean jacket and a cowboy hat. His sideburns were snow white, and his face bore the creases of an outdoor type. Though he might have been seventy, he had features women would always admire— square jaw, full lips, good teeth.

Auntie hadn't looked at another man since Uncle Pitt passed away twenty years ago. I didn't believe she had a boyfriend on the sly. She's missing the sneaky gene necessary for a clandestine love affair. I realized with a cringe that I had come to think of her as a kind of lay nun.

I checked him out again with more interest.

He looked down with a fond smile at the woman at his side, who was in her late thirties. She had curly, unnaturally bright red hair which contrasted well with her navy-blue jacket. Her white blouse strained against a large bosom and exposed a touch of cleavage, giving her a huge dose of Sex Appeal. There wasn't anything lusty about the old man's gaze, as if he were trying to recapture his youth in the company of a woman more than half his age, so she wasn't his date. Maybe his daughter?

When three little girls climbed into the empty seats next to the woman, her smile faltered. I could relate. Kids wouldn't make the best seatmates at a baking show. They'd be bored out of their little skulls.

The man bent forward to adjust something at his feet, and all three girls squealed, abandoned their places, and crowded around him. I craned my neck to better see.

"You've got to be kidding."

He was having difficulty tucking a gigantic bird cage out of the way of passers-by. Inside, an enormous beast with white feathers paced sideways on some kind of tree branch, turning its head to-and-fro like an angry con memorizing faces, ready to exact vengeance if he ever broke free. One child stuck her finger in the cage. The redhead gently pulled her hand away seconds before the bird's beak snapped shut. After that, the girls lost interest.

The bird let loose a squawk when a loud voice announced over the sound system that we were in for the treat of our lives via comedian Sonny Street.

Curious to see who could warrant the urgent attention of the teenage boy with slouching pants, I watched with interest as a good-looking man in his early forties, dressed in a dark gray suit and a tie in the requisite blue, stepped in front of the audience and said, "Good afternoon ladies and —gosh! I guess it's mostly ladies!"

That segment of the audience responded with whoops.

He put a hand over his eyebrows and did an exaggerated search of the stands. Then he jumped back and pointed at an elderly man wearing a pink polo shirt.

"There's at least one gentleman in the audience. You, sir! Can you tell us why you came today?"

The man jerked a thumb at the woman seated next to him—a solid specimen who looked capable of nursing an entire clan through the chicken pox while baking cookies for the parish summer social.

"Had to. She doesn't drive."

The entertainer gushed, "That's beautiful! What a good husband he is. Let's give him a round of applause!" He suited actions to words.

The banter, accompanied by bad jokes that the audience ate up, continued for another twenty minutes, until Sonny wrapped up his act with a few instructions for the audience.

"Each of you received a card as you walked in. Hang onto it, because that's how you'll cast your vote for the Blue-Ribbon Queen during the last commercial break of the show. If anyone doesn't have a voting card, please raise your hand and one of the pages will take care of you."

A few hands went up, including Auntie's.

"You're holding a card," I said.

"I want an extra for a souvenir."

I pulled her hand down. "You'll have your memories. And photographs, if you brought your camera."

She foraged through her purse and pulled out a surprisingly sophisticated cell phone, but as she jabbed at the ON button, Sonny put the kibosh on audience photography.

"Pictures are not allowed during the taping," he said, "but a souvenir package including a photograph signed by the contestants will be mailed to each member of the studio audience. And please, folks," he held out his hands in an imploring gesture, "remember to turn off your cell phones. This is a live show, so no do-overs."

The lights over the audience dimmed, and the same deep, male voice that introduced Sonny Street echoed through the room accompanied by a drum roll. The hanging televisions came to life, giving the audience a view of what the audience members watching from their living room sofas would see. I guess that was in case we got bored watching the live version.

"Ladies and gentlemen, the Baking Channel, sponsored by Cocolite Chocolate Chips—a low calorie treat used by responsible bakers—and the Scotch Girl Flour Company— To make it with class, bake with the Lass—is pleased to present the premiere episode of *Blue-Ribbon Babes*! And now, coming to you live from Saguaro Studios in sunny Arizona, here's your host, Heather Ozu!"

A petite Asian woman wiggled out in a tight-fitting orange dress with a mandarin collar. Her outfit stopped just short of sexy because a full-length white apron with *Blue-Ribbon Babes* embroidered on it in cursive letters covered her front, though the cinched waist emphasized her curves. She wore her short, black hair stylishly spiked except for long bangs that sported a blonde streak. When she reached an "X" taped to the floor dead-center in front of the kitchen counter, she waggled her long, orange talons at the audience to acknowledge their applause.

"Good afternoon, and welcome." She spoke with a slight accent, but it was Valley Girl, not Japanese. When the fresh wave of applause died down, she continued reading from large cue cards held by a scrawny crew member.

"*Blue-Ribbon Babes* is a brand-new show that's dedicated to those hard-working women who somehow find time in between raising a family and taking care of the household to enter county and state fairs...and win!"

More cheers and applause.

Auntie nodded. "It is an underrated profession."

"Which one? Housewife, mother, or contestant?"

"Yes." She shifted in her seat and leaned forward to better hear our host.

"Every show will feature a Blue Ribbon winner who will show you exactly how to make her prizewinning recipe at home, so you can wow your friends and family at that next holiday party or reunion! But this first show will feature three *Blue-Ribbon Babes*! That's right. We have an entire hour of live entertainment, just for you!"

"An hour?" I groaned. "We're stuck here for an hour?"

Auntie squashed my complaint with a sour look.

"Now, to add some extra excitement today," Heather continued, turning toward the camera to her right, "we're depending on participation from our viewing audience. At the end of the final demonstration, call the toll-free number at the bottom of your screen and vote for your favorite contestant. That's 888-555-2583, or 888-555-BLUE. And make sure you vote, because the winner will receive a check for $2,000 and claim the title of Blue-Ribbon Queen!"

Voices formed a chorus of oohs and aahs. I noticed they hadn't given the option to text, but I guess they knew their audience. My mother couldn't operate a cell phone if her life and the lives of her loved ones depended on it, though considering Auntie's fancy phone, maybe there actually were seniors who didn't break into tears at the site of a computer screen.

"Let's first meet those talented folks responsible for today's show. Our producer, Bert Hamilton!"

A tall man in a business suit turned and nodded in response to scattered applause. The hanging television screens gave us a close up of Bert scratching his nose after he thought the cameras were off him.

"Next to him, that beautiful woman is the show's director, Natasha Young!"

After a nudge from Bert, the African-American woman, deep in conversation with her headset, turned and waved, first to the camera, then to the audience.

"Now let's meet our first contestant! Donna Pederson comes to us all the way from Billings, Montana."

"Billings, Montana." Auntie murmured. "They really know how to bake there."

"How would you know? Have you ever been there?"

"It's common knowledge. If you have to drive six hours to get to the grocery store, you tend to favor homemade."

I stared. "Six hours? Are they driving in covered wagons?"

"Shh!"

"She's the three-time winner of the Special Diet Division at the Montana State Fair, and she's twice been named the People's Choice." Heather rubbed her flat stomach. "I'm always eager for new diet recipes, so let's welcome Donna and find out what she's going to make for us today!"

A slim, mousy-haired lady stepped out from behind the kitchen set and greeted Heather with the hesitancy of a bunny rabbit in a room full of beagles. When asked to tell the viewers about herself, Donna quietly recited a resume that included mother of three, a graduate of UCLA, and professional nutritionist.

She lost me at nutritionist. Thoughts of steamed fish and boiled, skinless chicken breasts filled my head, and my taste buds rebelled.

"Now," Heather said, "tell us what you have in store for us. My stomach's growling!"

"Mine, too," I hissed at Auntie. "But for real food. They are serving snacks at the reception after the show, right?"

"Hold your horses," she responded. "An hour's not that long."

Donna clasped her hands together, her only show of excitement so far. "Today, I'll be mixing up a batch of Chocolate Chip Miracles."

"Miracles, huh?" Heather raised her hands to encourage applause. Once the audience responded, she leaned her head in as if to share a private confidence. "What's the miracle part?"

"They're gluten free!"

Donna's grand announcement met with a smattering of polite clapping. Her hands clenched into fists, and her entire body went rigid. She seemed to sense this was the moment when she would either lose the audience to her flour-friendly competitors or make a grab for gluten-free respect. As timid as she looked, Donna wasn't going down without a fight.

She raised her trembling voice and proclaimed, "I use a mixture of rice and tapioca flours!" This didn't impress the audience. In a last-ditch effort, she pumped her fists in the air and cried, "And then I add Cocolite Chocolate Chips for some kick!"

At the mention of a sponsor, Heather raised her hands over her head and clapped. The audience responded in kind. Then she beamed into the camera. "We'll just have to see for ourselves when we try the finished product. Why don't you begin?"

From under the counter, Donna pulled out a tray already lined with several bowls of pre-measured ingredients.

"They measure everything out beforehand so they don't waste time," Auntie informed me, as if she were a baking show expert.

Donna proceeded to mix and chatter. Uninterested in the variety of flours available or cooking temperature variations, I settled back for a snooze.

Auntie poked me. "Did you see what she did there? She added tapioca flour instead of regular flour."

"Yeah. I got it. That's what makes them gluten free."

"There are actually people who can't eat gluten, poor souls. Life is so unkind. It makes me want to cry."

"They're not confined to cages. Nasty children don't poke them with sticks. They just can't eat certain things."

"Still, it's sad not to be normal," Auntie sniffed, getting in the last word.

Donna finally pulled a pan of cookies from the oven and presented one to Heather on a spatula. The host took a delicate bite and raved about how light and fluffy they were.

"I can't even tell that these don't use regular flour." She shrugged her shoulders, amazed. "They taste just like normal cookies!"

Donna winced at the host's choice of adjective. I'll give Heather credit. She made an immediate correction.

"Wait. Let me change that. They—taste—simply—amazing!"

Donna left the stage held in much higher esteem than when she'd arrived. As soon as the show cut to a commercial, a crew member swept all signs of her treats under the far end of the counter. We weren't spared the commercials, though they played on the hanging television sets without sound so as not to compete with Sunny Street.

In the stands, pages passed pre-baked batches of Donna's delights down each row. Audience members took one, sampled, and made notes on his—or more likely, her—voting card.

I popped a cookie in my mouth and chewed. "The chocolate chips are waxy."

"They're fine."

"I think they're waxy."

"You're so critical. The woman did her best with a difficult recipe. And she probably had to use the sponsor's chips. Don't blame her."

"So, I should give her a pity vote?"

Auntie conceded that the cookie wasn't up to her standards when she said, "If I had known about this competition, I would have sent in my recipe for Lemon Blueberry Buckle."

I balled up my napkin, and as I waited for the page to pass our row with the garbage bag, I heard a click. "What was that?"

"Nothing." Auntie shoved her hand into her lap, under her purse. I lifted the edge.

"That's your cell phone, isn't it? Were you taking pictures? You're going to get us thrown out of here," I said. "I wouldn't mind that, but there would probably be an embarrassing scene."

She dropped the phone into her purse and tucked it between her feet. "I don't know what you're talking about. I was looking for a cough drop, and then I decided to make sure my phone was turned off."

After Sonny Street waved and returned to his chair on the sidelines, we were subjected to the next guest—a Hispanic Betty Crocker wannabe in a bright pink dress, appropriately named Betty, who insisted on scrubbing the countertops in between each step. She radiated a frenzied joy while she stirred up Cajun Cornbread in a cast iron skillet, using Scotch Girl cornmeal. The woman next to me took copious notes.

Betty encountered a little trouble when she got distracted by a handprint-removal mission at the refrigerator and left the cornbread on too long. It slid out of the pan and onto the plate without a problem, but the edges were dark brown.

Heather chewed her sample with determination. Unable to talk, the host smiled, and still chewing, gave two thumbs up.

Of course, the samples that the audience members got were precooked, so our cornbread came with perfectly browned edges. I'm not a big fan of cornbread, but Betty had put in plenty of canned corn and cheddar cheese, so she moved ahead of the Chocolate Chip Miracles on my voting card.

We came to another commercial break, so I took the opportunity to stand and stretch.

"These seats aren't very comfortable."

"At least they have seats," Auntie said in the same tone grandparents use when they tell you they used to walk ten miles in the snow to get to school. "I once stood through an entire pinewood derby event just so I could cheer on your cousin Will from the sidelines. That was the year that wacko woman attacked the scouts for not letting in girls. Parents came from three counties to show their support for the boy scout troop. There weren't any chairs left by the time I got there. Even the girl scouts showed up with a banner that said *What's wrong with us?* They hurt so bad; I had to soak my feet in Epsom salts for an hour that night. Now that was a real pain."

"It's not a competition." For good measure, I added, "And I'm not soaking my butt in Epsom salts.

From my standing position, I had a good view of the entire room. Crew members loaded the baking supplies for the next guest under the counter, wiped down the appliances (though Betty hadn't left much for them to do in that arena) and generally straightened things up. The used utensils went back under the counter opposite of where the new items were placed.

Sonny Street suddenly shot out from behind the scenery, a scowl on his face as he jogged to his position in front of the crowd. By the time he started his first joke, the music cued a return to the final segment.

"I guess someone needed a potty break," Auntie snickered. Sonny just had time to ask if everyone was having a good time before Heather Ozu began to read from the cue cards again.

"Our third baker has blue ribbons from as far away as Loon Lake, Wisconsin."

"Loon Lake?" I sat up and poked Auntie's side. "I wonder if it's anyone we know?"

"She's currently a resident of Fountain Hills, Arizona," Heather continued. "Please welcome Elvira Jenkins."

Auntie gasped, and her entire body went rigid as a plump woman with the size and confidence of a navy ship steamed out from behind the back wall. Her curly steel-colored hair reminded me of when Grandma used to sleep in rollers and then forget to pick out the curls. When she grabbed Heather's hand and pumped the life out of it, the host winced.

Auntie, in an unconscious imitation, grabbed my hand and squeezed. Hard.

"Ow!"

She let go. "Sorry about that. I'm just excited." But she spoke with the flat tones of a zombie.

Heather opened her mouth to speak, but Elvira slapped two meaty hands on the counter, leaned forward and let loose with, "Yee-ha! I'm here to show you ladies how the country gal's do it!"

The audience, none of them looking particularly countrified, went wild.

Heather seemed torn between the benefit of an engaged crowd and a desire to assert her host status.

"Tell us about—" she began, but Elvira stampeded right over her.

"By the time I whip this Lemon Blueberry Buckle into shape, it'll float right off the plate."

"Lemon Blueberry Buckle? That's a coincidence," I whispered. Not a happy coincidence, if Auntie's body language was anything to go by. Her lips clamped together, her hands bunched into fists, and her concentrated stare should have bored a sizzling hole right through Elvira Jenkins' forehead.

"What type of ingredients should ambitious bakers have on hand to make a buckle?" Heather asked.

"There's the fruit, of course. I don't think there's anything better than what you get at the farmers' market, but you can use frozen if it's not the right season."

"Your buckle isn't gluten free, is it?"

Elvira threw back her head and let loose a full belly laugh. "I may be old fashioned, but I use flour."

The host winked at the audience. "I suppose Scotch Girl Flour is high on your list?"

"Never used it. Gold Treat flour is what's in my pantry."

Heather's smile faltered. "But you could use Scotch Girl."

"What I always say is, if it ain't broke, don't fix it. But I realize you have sponsors to satisfy, so go ahead and say Scotch Girl will work if you think it will." Elvira looked straight into the camera. "But don't blame me if your buckle turns out like lead."

Heather's frantic gaze went to Bert, who stood, arms crossed, next to the cue card holder. The producer closed his eyes in a pained expression. Heather's panic showed in 55-inch color on the screens above us. Natasha Young made frantic signals to one of the cameramen, probably to suggest he move the camera from the host's face. It wasn't necessary. Ever the pro, Heather plastered on a smile and forged ahead.

"All that fruit just cries out for ice cream, right?" Heather gushed. "I'm sure those of us who love chocolate could melt some Cocolite Chocolate chips for a little yummy sauce. Chocolate goes with blueberries. You can even buy chocolate-covered blueberries in your specialty shops."

That last bit sounded desperate. Even I, who considers chocolate a food group, thought the combination sounded ghastly.

With a superior sniff, Elvira said, "I've never used Cocolite products, but then I'm very careful to avoid ingredients that are filled with chemicals, which foods labeled lite often are."

"See?" I poked Auntie. "I told you those chips were waxy."

The look Heather Ozu gave Elvira Jenkins should have dropped the old lady where she stood, but then Heather, perhaps putting the show before her personal feelings, or maybe realizing that an angry expression emphasized her frown lines, put on a sweet smile and melted into the background, which allowed Elvira Jenkins to take over the show.

The host got her own back when she sampled a forkful of Lemon Blueberry Buckle. She blinked and swallowed hard. "Interesting! That wraps it up for our guests today. After the commercial break, we'll come back and find out who will reign as the Blue-Ribbon Queen!"

When they cut away, Elvira rounded on the host, her cheeks flushed crimson red. "You deliberately blew off my buckle!"

Heather put her balled fists on her tiny hips. "How dare you diss our sponsors!"

Elvira picked up a square of buckle with her spatula. "The truth is the truth, honey. Look at this baby. It's perfect."

Heather's voice lowered to a growl, which didn't affect the volume. I could hear her just fine, as could the rest of the audience members, who leaned forward as one.

"Is everybody having a good time?" Sonny Street raised his voice in an attempt to distract the audience from the argument.

When an old woman shushed him, the comedian looked to the producer for direction. Bert turned his hands palms up and shrugged.

I took my sample of buckle from the passing tray and enjoyed it along with the live entertainment.

"You signed an agreement. Your recipe must include at least one of our sponsor's products."

"You've got a lot of nerve, talking about agreements!"

Heather jabbed Elvira's shoulder. "You're in breach of contract. You don't deserve to win."

"I said you could use Scotch Girl flour if you wanted." Then she got a malignant gleam in her eye. "And who cares if I win? Big loss! It's my reputation I'm protecting."

A page, her head turned to follow the argument, tripped over my feet and righted herself using Auntie's shoulder for leverage.

"Sorry about that. Could I have your card please?"

I quickly marked my vote for the Lemon Blueberry Buckle, with extra points for entertainment value. She and the rest of the pages collected the voting cards and carried them to several women at a small table who worked with furious speed to tally the votes.

The announcer broke in to introduce the final segment. By the time the show began again, Heather's furious breathing had subsided into what could pass for excited panting. Elvira didn't seem fazed at all. She merely brushed her hands off with a kitchen towel.

"If we could have our first two guest join us, we can get down to business and present the prize!" Heather waved them onto the set as a page jogged up with a sealed envelope. The show's host opened it and pulled out a slip of paper.

"Our new Blue-Ribbon Queen is...Elvira Jenkins!"

When Donna Pederson gave Elvira a congratulatory hug, she held her shoulders and head so stiffly that I thought she would break on contact. The second contestant didn't seem to mind losing. She probably figured her chances were nil because she burned her cornbread. Instead, Betty slipped behind the counter and contented herself slicing Elvira's buckle into neat squares.

Heather Ozu held up a large, cardboard check and smiled for the cameras. She quickly said goodbye to the viewing audience. The minute the cameraman signaled that they were off the air, she shoved the check at Elvira and stalked off. The lights went up and Linda the Page, as I was starting to call her, announced that delicious treats awaited us in the next room.

"Exit through the door to your right."

"Let's go," Auntie said.

"I'm starved." I gathered up my purse and resisted pushing my way through a crowd of elderly women who tottered their way down the metal stairway.

"I mean home. I'm tired."

"That's because your blood sugar has dropped. We need food, and I'm not leaving here until I eat."

When I looked back to make sure she was handling the stairs all right, I noticed my aunt had left her untouched Lemon Blueberry Buckle on her chair.

"You didn't even try the buckle!" I waggled my finger in front of her face. "I hope you didn't vote, because it wouldn't have been fair."

We exited the room and followed the crowd down another short corridor into an enclosed area that was supposed to reflect Home Sweet Home. The decorator, probably a woman who lived out of a single-room bedsit and never cooked a meal beyond heating up a microwave dinner, had envisioned that every home baker must salivate over gingham and lace. Several couches and chairs covered in that fabric were arranged in the center of the room. Frilly curtains lined false windows painted onto the drywall, and several wooden kitchen tables placed around the room's edges overflowed with trays of bite-sized treats set out on gigantic paper doilies.

I grabbed a couple of bacon pinwheels—rolled puff pastry filled with bacon crumbles and parmesan cheese. To make certain I got the day's calcium intake, I added a few cheddar cheese sticks and handed two off to Auntie. She ate absently while her eyes roamed the room.

"You've eaten," she said. "Let's go."

"Is that Bourbon Bob?" I asked, pointing to a round man with a buzz cut. "The cook who put all my favorite ingredients together in the Gruyere-Covered-Bacon-and- Mushroom-Smothered Steak recipe? I want to propose marriage to him. Come on."

"I thought you never watched television," Auntie grumbled.

"I don't watch baking shows. Cooking shows aren't the same thing. They're all about education and household management. Practically like taking a college course. He's from the Grilling Channel. It must be a sister company."

"You don't grill."

"That doesn't mean I don't like to watch other people do it."

"I'm surprised. You didn't seem to want to be here tonight, yet here you are a big fan of the Baking Channel."

"Notice I said I like cooking and grilling. Not baking. Baking takes too long. A batch of brownies doesn't stand a chance against a juicy steak."

Auntie shook her head; her lips pressed together in a pained expression. "I never thought a niece of mine would be an anti-baker. You're a culinary snob, Sissy."

"You bet."

I held my plate in my mouth and grabbed two glasses of red wine from a passing page's tray and handed one to

Auntie. "Drink this," I said after I pulled the plate from my mouth. "You need to relax."

Bourbon Bob was surrounded by gaping, twittering women and most of the male members of the audience. I pushed my way through. When his warm eyes—the color of steak sauce—met mine, I sighed and said, "You're my hero."

His gaze went past me to Auntie's discontented face. "I can recognize a fellow cook anywhere. Know how? Because you're bored. You'd rather be home whipping up something on the stove. Am I right?"

That was part of Bourbon Bob's appeal. He called himself *a mere cook*, and he related to his audience because he enjoyed food and the accompanying social experience of serving something delicious to people he loved. His own family and friends were a regular part of the show. When they sat down to eat the finished product, they didn't offer savvy comments about the texture of the sauce or the flakiness of the fish. They ate like normal people and said things like Yum.

Auntie batted her eyelashes and gave him a coquettish smile.

"I can't say that I've ever seen your show, but I'm going to make a point of watching now."

"Next week is my special brunch episode." He put an arm around her shoulder and leaned his head in. "I'm making omelets on the grill in a cast iron skillet. Have you got a favorite filling?"

"I used goat cheese and leftover pot roast once, because it was all I had in the fridge. We'd had a party, or else I wouldn't have had such a fancy cheese hanging around. Turned out pretty good once I added some green onions."

He considered her suggestion. "Hmmm. You can find goat cheese at any grocery store these days, so it won't annoy my viewers." He broke into a grin. "I'll do it, with a few changes of my own, but I'll dedicate it to you. What's your name, honey?"

She handed him her business card and told him to consult her before he made any big career decisions. He raised his brows as he read the card and then tucked it into his shirt pocket. I may not have qualified as a fellow cook, but I still walked away with an autographed picture and a coupon for Real Men's charcoal briquettes.

"This isn't so bad." I snatched a miniature egg roll from a tray and took a bite. "In fact, it would have been perfect if we had just skipped the show."

On a table next to the partition wall, skewers of grilled shrimp called out to me. I munched on three—or four—and I only stopped chewing when raised voices came from the other side of the wall.

"That information is confidential," said a desperate voice.

The response came across in a hiss. "The truth is the truth, honey."

That was the end of the conversation, at least as far as I could hear.

"Excuse me." It was Linda the Page. She stared at Auntie as if she was the star of her own cooking show. "I couldn't help seeing the card you gave to Bourbon Bob. You read tarot cards?"

Ever the professional, Auntie gave her a coy smile. "I'm off duty right now, but for you, I'll do a sample reading. I just happen to have my cards with me."

Auntie dug her pack out of her purse and switched into Madame Guinevere mode, Word of mouth made her a popular woman over the next half hour, which left me free to roam the room, stopping to graze at every station I passed.

I skirted the clusters of women whenever baking techniques were the topic of discussion. The wisest woman in the room is the one who keeps her ignorance to herself and her mouth shut, right? The only danger point came when an audience member clutched my arm and said:

"What do you think? We need a tie breaker."

I recognized her as Lola from the line outside the studio. She pulled me toward a gang of women who had taken sides behind Bea and Jane. There was some kind of standoff taking place.

"Think about what?" I was certain that my thoughts and their thoughts didn't travel in the same circles.

"Butter or shortening?" asked Bea.

"Butter or shortening what?"

"Butter flavored shortening," said Jane. "Big difference. Which one makes flakier cookies? Or would you use a combination?"

The way they all stared at me with narrowed eyes, leaning forward, I could tell my answer was going to change the future of baking for women everywhere. I pointed at Lola, since she was to blame for getting me into this conversation.

"I agree with her."

Half the women seemed vindicated; the other half took on the appearance of vigilantes out to nab the killer of small kittens, so I fled.

I recognized a few audience members who had sat near us, and there were several minor celebrity chefs. Sonny Street worked the room, making jokes and shaking hands as if he were the star of the show. People certainly reacted to him as if he were. Blushing ladies; chuckling men. He was a hit.

"Thinks he's God's gift to women."

The woman who spoke was dressed in the most hideous assortment of mismatched clothes I'd ever seen. It was as if she had fallen into her closet covered in Velcro and thrown on whatever stuck to her. A pink-and-white pinstripe blouse was open to reveal a military green t-shirt, and the gypsy skirt in browns and blues did nothing for the black fabric scarf she used as a belt. Her bleached-blond hair formed a high pile on top of her head, and her tattooed eyeliner came straight out of the eighties. Other than that, her face was bare, so it surprised me when she introduced herself as the makeup artist.

"Fiona Flynn." She pointed a stubby finger at the comedian. "I keep telling that man not to use so much hairspray, but Sonny Street thinks he knows everything. He'll be lucky if it all doesn't snap off by the time he's fifty." She followed her prediction of doom with, "I am a professional. I know what I'm talking about."

My best friend trimmed my hair for me, and except for very rare occasions like dates, my makeup was limited to strawberry-flavored lip gloss. Even that was collecting fuzz on the bottom of my purse.

"Do you enjoy working with celebrities?" I said, hoping to disguise the fact that I didn't care.

"It's no different from working at a beauty parlor. That's where I got discovered. I did the hair and makeup for a few employees at the club. The owner liked my work so much, I got hired on the spot. Paid pretty well, too, but you know how it is. I have bigger dreams. My grandmother lives near here, so when I found out about the opening of Saguaro Studios, I moved in with her and was first in line with my resume."

"And here you are," I said.

The guests broke out in polite applause as the

remaining cast and crew of *Blue-Ribbon Babes* entered the room, followed by excited family members. The trio of children that had sat in the front row hung off Donna Pederson's arm until she directed them to the dessert table. I noticed that the tall man in the cowboy hat had ditched the birdcage and wondered where he could have stowed his large, feathered friend. It really irked me when people treated pets as an accessory that could be tossed aside when inconvenient. During my time as an authentic pet psychic, I'd listened to enough complaints from animals to know that their feelings could be hurt.

Pages plied the VIPs with fresh supplies. A tall, young man in a gray suit hovered around Heather Ozu. When Linda the Page offered her a drink, he intercepted and snatched two glasses, one for him and one for the host. Bert and Natalie were in conference over an ornamental vegetable arrangement shaped like a cactus. The rest drifted to the sides of the rooms where the yummies awaited.

After the initial rush to meet and greet, the three contestants were left, standing alone, Elvira as the confident bride and Donna and Betty hovering behind her, like bridesmaids waiting for someone to ask them to dance.

"I'll be a monkey's uncle." Fiona followed this surprising admission with a "Huh."

"Is someone's makeup out of place?" I joked.

"It couldn't be."

"You lost me. Who are we talking about?"

With a start, Fiona realized that she'd been speaking out loud. She didn't seem pleased at the thought. In fact, as far as the makeup artist was concerned, our bonding moment was over.

"Bye."

Before I had time to wonder if my deodorant failed me,

Auntie walked up wearing a satisfied smile. "I've handed out so many business cards my fingers are on fire. I think I've roped in a few paying clients. We should leave while I'm riding a high. All it takes is one negative response and the spell is broken. We can go now."

"Too late," I said through clenched teeth.

I'd been staring in the general direction of the contestants when Donna's gaze met mine. Mistaking me for an interested party, she nudged Betty. Together, they approached with hands held out in greeting and smiles firmly planted on their faces. Actually, Betty's smile seemed natural.

"I'm so glad that's over," she said. "Too much pressure. It's much more fun to cook for my family than a crowd of strangers."

"Are they here?" I motioned toward the three little girls, bunkered down in front of the brownies. "I assume they belong to you," I said to Donna, a logical assumption since children don't usually hang on strangers. "They're very cute."

Donna broke into a big smile that transformed her from serious, gluten-free baker to proud mom. "Thank you."

"My husband couldn't take off work. I had to leave the baby with my mother-in-law," Betty said with a touch of envy.

"I'm sure they watched you on television."

"Speaking of television," Donna said, "it does seem a teeny bit odd to include the votes of the viewing audience. I mean, how would they know which finished product should win? They can't taste anything over the television set."

"You didn't have to taste my cornbread to see it was burnt," Betty said. Her attention drifted to a woman who carelessly set an empty cup on the snack table. Betty bustled over and snatched it up, pausing to straighten out the underlying doily before she moved to the wastebasket.

"I think she's OCD," Donna whispered.

Elvira Jenkins had been watching us out of the corner of her eye and apparently decided we'd spent enough time with the riff-raff. It was time for royalty to move in. She stepped up behind Auntie and tapped her on the shoulder.

Auntie's expression didn't change as she beheld the new Blue-Ribbon Queen. Her face took on that immobility I'd seen her use to mask her excitement when tarot clients let slip an especially useful bit of personal information during a reading, such as *If only I could meet someone like Brad Pitt, but in a sexy job, like a fireman.*

"I need to use the facilities." With that declaration, Auntie swept off. Elvira's gaze followed her out of the room.

There was a shriek from across the room. One of Donna's daughters stood in a puddle of punch. Donna rushed to her aid, leaving me with the Baking Channel's best-in-show.

"I'm sure you've heard it already, but congratulations."

"Can't hear good news too often," Elvira said, eyeing me as if I were an exotic ingredient. I wiped my upper lip just in case I had a crumb mustache.

"How long have you been baking? Professionally, that is."

"All my life. It's by doing your best at things that you become good enough to win ribbons and titles. And by having integrity." She paused, giving me that kind of look that said somebody in the room wasn't up to her standards. "What did you say your name was, honey?"

"I didn't." Why did she want to know? Was that somebody me? Did she still keep in touch with people in Loon Lake and had she heard about the exposé? My ex-boyfriend

Jeff had exposed my cold reading methods to a buxom reporter. The story had been splashed all over the newspaper in an article about frauds. That same story had driven me out of Loon Lake.

"Frankie Chandler."

I waited for the fallout, but she only held out a hand to shake. On her index finger was a ring, and perched on the ring was a canary. At least I assumed it was a canary, because it looked just like Tweety Bird.

"Chandler," she repeated softly. "I seem to remember an Albert Chandler back in Loon Lake, years ago."

"That would be my father."

"Well, heavens to Betsy, isn't that a coincidence."

It could have been a coincidence, but it felt as if Elvira Jenkins deliberately sought me out. I wanted to know why, but before I could ask a few questions of my own, Linda the Page appeared at her side and respectfully addressed the Queen.

"The photographer would like to see you back on the set, Ma'am."

"Duty calls," Elvira said. With one last look, she charged out the door.

Linda remained behind.

"Your aunt is amazing! I only pulled one card from her pack. One card! And it was like she knew everything going on in my life."

Linda was in her early twenties. There are two things on the minds of women this age—men and career. The problems with both hadn't changed over the years. Instead of boyfriends who never called, these women had boyfriends who never texted. Nothing amazing about it, but I didn't want to burst her bubble.

"Really. How exciting."

"She's going to give me an entire reading when I'm not at work. I can't wait!"

"Is there anything left to drink?" A man stared pointedly at Linda's empty tray.

"Coming right up," she said, and she rushed off to reload.

Now that I was gastronomically satisfied, I suddenly felt guilty. In the rush to chauffeur Auntie to the premiere, I'd forgotten to feed my pets. When Auntie finally returned from the ladies' room, her face had an unhealthy flush and she was a tad breathless, but I put that down as too much excitement and too much wine. I suggested we leave.

"If I remember right, we go this way." I pointed to the doorway where we'd come in. A brief journey took us back to the set of *Blue-Ribbon Babes*. They'd brought down most of the lights, leaving the kitchen set in shadow. The only illumination came from battery-operated candles that marked the path out.

Halfway through the room, my footsteps slowed. I had goose bumps on my arms, and my air intake was coming in short, panting breaths. I scanned the shadows of the room expecting something nasty to jump out.

I stopped walking and sucked in a deep breath. I knew this feeling. I'd had it right before I saw a slideshow of deadly images projected by the golden retriever, Sandy. But I hadn't been able to read an animal's thoughts for over a month. A nice, quiet month.

"What's wrong?" Auntie asked.

My gaze scanned the room again, searching for the source of this feeling.

"Meow. Squa-a-awk."

The noise came from the kitchen set.

"Did you hear that?" I whispered.

"Hear what?" Auntie narrowed her eyes. "How many glasses of wine did you drink?"

I cocked my head and listened, but all I heard was a fluttering noise that reminded me of Tippi Hedren's last sane moment in *The Birds*. Then I remembered the cage that belonged to the tall man in the cowboy hat. Had he left the poor thing alone in the kitchen?

"Squa-a-awk! Meow!"

"It's that bird," I said, crossing to the set. The cage was tucked into the corner of the kitchen counter, over by a stainless-steel sink. I gave a nervous giggle. That's all it was. The bird was sending out waves of fear because he was afraid of the dark. Still, it was strange—and disappointing—that I'd felt them.

"That tall guy abandoned the poor thing. What a brat."

"What are you doing?" Auntie asked, looking back toward the reception room. "I don't think we're supposed to touch anything."

"Hey there, big fella," I said, holding my hand out. I'm not overly fond of birds. In fact, they scare me, but it raised my hackles to think that anyone would set a pet aside while they went and had a good time, as if it were an accessory. I knew only too well that pets had feelings, and this bird was definitely afraid. "Did someone leave you all by your lonesome?"

The bird fluttered its wings. "Meow!"

"Bird's got a screw loose. Thinks it's a cat." Auntie ran her hand over the island counter and clucked in disapproval. "You'd have thought the Baking Channel would have sprung for marble. It keeps your butter cool. You don't even need a cutting board."

The bird fluttered its wings. I stepped back, wary. "If you ask me, the whole set is pretty cheesy."

Auntie apparently decided that we weren't going to set off any alarms. Emboldened, she opened the refrigerator, reached for a box of butter and shook it. "Empty. Too bad." So was the carton of sour cream. "I thought we could take home the leftovers, so they wouldn't go to waste."

"I think those are just props to make the fridge look full. Just like that window in the wall makes it look like it's a real kitchen with a view of the backyard."

I turned, and pointing at said window, took a step forward. "But if you look closer, there isn't even any glass in the—"

My feet came in contact with a solid lump tucked behind the island, and I pitched forward. My hands stopped my fall before my face hit the floor.

"What in Hades is she doing down there?" Auntie shrieked.

With a knot of dread in my stomach, I turned my head. "Oh, jeez."

And that's how we discovered the body of Elvira Jenkins.

FOUR

"Hello, Frankie."

I looked up into the wary blue eyes of Detective Martin Bowers of the Wolf Creek police force. With his tall, slim physique; dark, wavy hair; and blue eyes that crinkled when he laughed—which wasn't often—Bowers could have been a billboard model for a golf resort, but only if that model had been on a bender the night before the assignment. He looked in desperate need of a weekend of uninterrupted sleep. The lines around his eyes spoke of long hours. He also needed a haircut. His dark hair curled at the collar of his brown sports jacket.

The last time we'd met had been in front of a burning building with an unconscious man and a panicked dog trapped inside. When I had telepathically tried to direct the dog to an escape route, I grabbed the hands of the two men next to me for support. Afterwards, I'd been able to read both of their minds, not something that's considered an asset by potential boyfriends. Detective Bowers was one of those men. The other belonged to Seamus McGuire, owner of Canine Camp, a doggie daycare.

I smiled weakly. "I didn't do it."

He didn't smile back, and the panic I'd held at bay so far broke loose.

"Tell me this is a mistake. Tell me this isn't happening again. Tell me I did not just land on the body of the Blue-Ribbon Queen." I lowered my voice. "Tell me I did not just throw up on a studio set."

He took a seat on the couch to my right. "Sorry, kiddo. It's real." He grimaced. "And you did."

"What's wrong with me?" I said with a laugh that was half sob. "Why does this keep happening to me? Normal people don't run into dead bodies every time they turn around."

He kept his voice cool. "Technically, it doesn't keep happening to you because you didn't discover the body of Margarita Morales." He was referring to last month's murder victim. He added a brief smile, as if that revelation would cheer me up. "Are you up to telling me about it?"

I blinked a few times and gathered my thoughts. The police had taken Auntie to another room to interview her, probably to keep us from influencing each other's story. I tried to be as concise as possible.

"We drove here."

"Who's we?"

"My aunt came with me. Or I came with her. She was the one with the invitation."

"Where is she now?" He looked around the empty room.

"I don't know. Somewhere. The police led her away."

He raised one brow.

"Not led her away as in you're under arrest, but as in we'd like to interview you, privately."

The other brow went up.

"My aunt was with me when I found the body," I snapped. "They wanted to talk to her, just like you want to talk to me." I let loose a snort of disgust. "Do you want to hear my story or not?"

He wore his blank cop-face, so I couldn't tell what he was thinking.

"Go ahead."

He kept his tone neutral, which I hate. I mean, *I* found the body. He should be eager to hear what I had to say.

"We saw the show. Afterwards, a page led us to this room for the reception. We ate. We drank. In order to leave, we had to go back past the set. That's when we found her."

"That's good for starters."

"What do you mean, starters? That's it!"

"How about some details?"

"We walked by the pretty set?" I was hyperventilating and might have been shrieking at this point.

His expression switched into one of complete sympathy. His eyes, the color of deep Caribbean waters, met mine in a direct stare that almost hypnotized. He lowered his voice to a soothing tone, as if he were auditioning to do voiceovers for a meditation tape.

"Bear with me. I realize this is very, very hard for you, and I really, really appreciate your help, but I'm trying to imagine the scene. I need you to help me see exactly what you saw, so I'm going to walk you through it again, very slowly. Don't be nervous. I'm right here."

I guffawed. "Does that technique actually work on nervous witnesses?"

His eyebrows shot up. "Yes. It does."

"Because it makes me want to punch you. Stop talking to me as if I were about to break out in a fit of the vapors." I noticed that my irritation with him left me calmer.

He dropped the act, sat back, crossed one leg over the other, and opened his notebook on his lap. "Thanks. It'll take less time if I don't have to hold your hand. Now, the actual kitchen set, including the island, were out of your way. You didn't have to pass through them to get out of the building. Why were you poking around?"

"I wasn't poking around. You make me sound like Gladys Kravitz."

"Who?"

I narrowed my eyes. "The nosy neighbor on the television show *Bewitched*. Did you grow up in a cave?"

"Let me rephrase the question. Why were you on the actual set? Did something catch your attention? Something you heard or saw? Or did you have an—er—intuition?"

I knew what it cost Bowers to acknowledge the mere possibility of psychic phenomenon, even though he'd experienced it firsthand. He was a dedicated pragmatist, just as I once was.

"There was a bird."

"Big white thing? I saw it. Elvira Jenkins' husband left it behind because he went to a poker party directly from here. She planned to drop by the reception and then catch a ride home with her daughter-in-law."

"I thought someone abandoned it."

"Did you know the victim?"

"Only from the show."

He flipped through his notebook. "But her bio says she was from Loon Lake. That's where you're from."

"How do you know that? I only told you I came from Wisconsin."

He had the grace to look away. I'd always suspected he'd done a background check on me when he investigated the death of Margarita Morales.

"She was a complete stranger."

"So, it's just a coincidence that you're both from Loon Lake, Wisconsin," he said, his eyes focused on me with what I called his interrogation face. No expression, but the hint of a frown behind the mask.

"Yes."

He looked around the room. Empty party trays and overflowing wastebaskets were the only sign a celebration had taken place. A patrol officer had taken the names of most of the audience members and let them go, but they instructed lucky Auntie and me to remain behind. The joys of being witnesses.

"How did you wind up here?" Bowers asked. "I mean, no offense, but *Blue-Ribbon Babes* doesn't seem like your kind of thing."

I'm not sure why I felt the need to defend my honor. I blame him. It was his condescending tone and the smirk.

"What's that supposed to mean? Not my kind of thing."

"Feminine, homey things, like cooking and—" He caught my expression. "Like cooking."

"I'm not suffering from some kind of kitchen deficiency. I can cook."

"You know what I mean. It's the kind of thing my sisters would be into."

Bowers had great respect for—and fear of—the seven older sisters who raised him after his mother's death. It was a good thing we'd never made it past a minor flirtation, because I'd never make it past the inquisition.

He frowned. "You weren't doing some hocus-pocus? Attempting to read the minds of the audience for the Baking Channel?"

He leaned back on the couch, unconsciously putting

more distance between us as he re-crossed his legs to face away from me and held up his notebook for protection.

"I don't read *people's* minds. Except that once, and that was by accident. I don't even read pets minds anymore. And it's not as if I had a choice. As Penny would say, it's a gift from God."

"Let's hope that's where it comes from," he mumbled.

My eyebrows shot up and my mouth dropped open. "Not that I consider it a fun gift, like chocolate or a massage, but what are you suggesting? That there's something Satanic about reading animals?"

Bowers refused to enter into a theological discussion. "Why are you here?"

"I told you. I came because my Aunt Gertrude received an invitation."

His brows shot up. "Gertrude Pitt?"

"How do you know her?" I asked, and then I sucked in my breath. "She's not in trouble, is she?"

"She's being interviewed by Detective Gutierrez."

I swallowed hard. My mouth puckered because my saliva had dried up. Juanita Gutierrez, nicknamed The Python, was a formidable, drop-dead beautiful cop. Her intensity level ran so high that she actually gave off an energy signal when she felt strong emotions, just like an animal. I said a small prayer for Auntie.

He leaned forward, his elbows on his knees. "Frankie, if she received an invitation, your aunt must have known someone from the show. The premiere was exclusive."

"She says not. I already asked."

"It would be much better if you told me now than if Gutierrez finds out later."

"Are you calling my aunt a liar? You've never even met

her. My aunt received her invitation because she's won a few blue ribbons herself."

"Fine. Take me over the evening again, but with a little more detail this time."

I groaned, and he said in a pleasant, no-nonsense voice, "Just start when you got here."

"Fine. But prepared to be bored out of your skull."

"Comes with the job."

When I related the evening to Bowers, I skipped Auntie's reaction to Elvira Jenkins—both when she saw her step on set and when she met her at the reception. She might come off sounding a little petty, and I didn't want him to think badly of her before he'd even met her. By the time I finished, Bowers' eyes were closed.

"Are you still awake?"

"You were right. That was painfully boring." He opened his eyes. "Heather Ozu mentioned the altercation between herself and the victim. It would have been pointless to hide it, since they televised it. Did you recognize the voices you heard on the other side of the wall while you were stuffing yourself with shrimp?"

"Obviously, the one who said, 'The truth is the truth' was Elvira."

"Why obviously?"

"That seemed to be her catchphrase. She'd just said it to Heather on the show."

"Which means anyone could have repeated the phrase in sarcasm. Did it actually sound like her?"

"That was my first impression."

"Do you have any idea who she was arguing with?"

"You mean talking to? I don't think it was an argument." In my family, a conversation required at least one swear word and possibly physical contact before it qualified as an argument. "I think it was a woman, but the person was hissing, so I'm not sure."

"What do you mean, hissing?"

"Whispering with emotion."

His lips pressed together in a thin line of disapproval. "Can you think of anything to add that might be helpful?"

"Like what, super cop?"

"I heard you were talking to the victim a short time before she met her death."

Met her death. It sounded like a polite social introduction.

"I was just starting to talk to her when Linda the Page came up and told Elvira the photographer wanted her on the set."

"He took publicity photos right after the show, and then he left. He was gone by the time Linda passed Elvira the message."

"So, who told Linda to find Elvira?"

"Good question."

He studied me for a minute, and it looked like he wasn't sure he wanted to ask the next question. "You seem to have a gift for pegging personalities. What impression did the dead woman make on you?"

"She was baking, and she was on TV. To put it nicely, she came across as a take-charge gal, but that means nothing. I'm sure I'd act differently if I had a camera right in front of my face and had to put on a show."

"Point taken. Did you notice anything unusual in the way people were acting? Did anyone do anything that seemed, well, odd?"

Auntie's behavior was a tad odd. I must have shown some reaction, because he jumped on it.

"What is it?"

I squirmed in my chair. "Everything was odd. I've never been at a live show before. The cameras. The warm-up comedian. The cue cards."

I was saved from further explanations when I felt a crackle of energy as if someone had touched my skin with a live battery. My body did a little jump.

"Son of a—"

Since I knew animal control officers had carted the bird away until the husband could come for it, that wasn't the source of my gooseflesh. The last time I felt this live wire voltage pass through my system without the presence of an animal, Detective Juanita Gutierrez was close by, which was bad news for me.

Detective Gutierrez didn't like me, but that wasn't my current concern. For someone who'd lost her ability to receive telepathic communications, I was getting a load of messages tonight. First, the bird broke through to share its fear, and now this crackly feeling had come to me uninvited.

Auntie swept into the room followed by Detective Gutierrez, who brought a buzzing to my ears that resembled the dangerous noise given off by power lines. Her expression didn't betray her thoughts. In fact, she and Bowers had mastered the same bland look. And they carried the same notebook. I wondered if they shouldn't offer them options at detective training school.

"Auntie!"

I rushed over and gave her a hug. Gutierrez looked from my aunt to me and said:

"You've got to be kidding. You seem to attend murders like other people go to Bunco parties."

"This is just horrible," Auntie said, wringing her hands together, though she had the wherewithal to pause and pull out a business card for Gutierrez. "You just call me if you have any more questions."

Gutierrez stared at the tarot card and then turned her gaze on me. "Another psychic in the family? Surprise, surprise."

"I'm not technically a psychic, dear," Auntie said. "Just a simple but talented card reader."

The detective didn't show signs of leaving, so Bowers thanked her and said he was wrapping things up and would be right with her. She took the hint and left, but she strolled out just to show that he wasn't her superior and she could leave when she felt like it.

"I have one more question to ask you," Bowers said, and after a glance at Auntie, added, "Privately."

"I need fresh air," Auntie said, waving a fan of business cards at her face. "I'm feeling kind of warm. I'll wait for you outside."

Alone again, Bowers tapped his notebook against his leg. "I'm sure I don't need to tell you this is an official investigation."

"I would hope so."

"And that means I don't want to hear about any side trips to suspects' homes or accidental meetings with the victim's family."

"I wouldn't dream of it." And I meant it when I said it.

"Good. I'm glad that's settled."

His gaze softened for a moment, and he looked as if wanted to say something. In the end, he pressed his lips together and motioned toward the exit, dismissing me.

As soon as I stepped into the cool night air, a light bulb flashed. I held up a hand and blinked. About a hundred feet from the door, the police had cordoned off an area with rope and left a patrol officer on guard. A small crowd of gawkers leaned over that rope, and the press shouted a flurry of questions.

Auntie stood directly in front of the rope. I held back a scream. Her partner in conversation was Paul Simpson, a champion of sleazy reporting who had tried to run a story about my embarrassing past in Wisconsin after I'd refused to give him an interview about the murder of Margarita Morales. I jogged up behind her and grabbed her by the shoulders.

"How many subscribers do you have?" Auntie asked.

"Don't talk to the bad man," I said. Before he could answer, I steered her away, noticing as we walked that she clutched her business cards in her right hand.

"Did you give Paul Simpson your contact information?" I shrieked. I looked at him and debated whether to go back and demand he give it back, but it seemed better to keep walking.

"It's kind of automatic with me."

"Give me those!" I snatched the cards away and jammed them into my purse.

On the drive home. I wondered about the points Bowers had brought up.

"You didn't know Elvira Jenkins before tonight, did you?"

"On my honor, the first time I heard the name Elvira Jenkins was when they introduced her. That pretty detective asked me that same question several times. I finally had to ask if she was having trouble understanding me. You know, old people aren't the only ones who need hearing aids, and both the old and young can be vain about wearing them."

"She must have loved that."

"I'm sure she understood I was only trying to be helpful."

"Still, out of all the bakers in the United States, I wonder how your name wound up on their invitation list."

"I already told you. I've won a lot of blue ribbons in my time."

"At state fairs?"

"Well, no, but the competition is just as fierce at the local level."

When I opened the front door to my house, Emily wound her body through my ankles, pretending for a moment that I really mattered. There wasn't much to cheer me as I entered my sparsely furnished living room. The furniture was shabby chic—with the emphases on shabby—most of it purchased at cheap furniture stores and garage sales except for a blue and white checkered couch donated by my parents that gave the room its only spot of color.

I hadn't gotten around to decorating the walls in the year-and-a-half I'd lived here. My idea of personalizing the space was to leave chocolate wrappers on the couch. I tossed my purse on the armchair and went in search of my ginger mutt. I found Chauncey sprawled on his tummy on the kitchen floor, his nose touching his food dish. As soon as the kibble hit their bowls, my pets scarfed down dinner as if they'd gone for weeks without food.

I returned to my theme. "But there are other women in Loon Lake who have won just as many ribbons, aren't there? Why didn't they get invitations? And why invite anyone from Wisconsin at all? It's not as if this were a huge, important premiere. And Wisconsin isn't exactly next door."

"Honey, I don't know about you, but I'm dead tired."

I stopped yapping long enough to take in my aunt's

condition. Pale and tired, she looked her age, which as my mother's older sister made her almost seventy. With complete selfishness, I hadn't thought about how seeing a dead body might affect my aged relative. She might have fainted. She might have suffered a heart attack.

"I am so thoughtless." I kissed her forehead. "Get some sleep and don't set the alarm."

She gratefully accepted my invitation and went to bed.

I made up my temporary bed on the couch, and once snuggled in, stared at the ceiling. We'd gone to an event where someone died. Not someone we loved or cared about. Not even someone we knew. Auntie and I could consider our involvement with the investigation finished. Bowers could rest easy. And with that incredibly naïve, ridiculous thought, I fell asleep.

FIVE

The following morning, I woke to the sounds of movement from the kitchen. I rolled off the couch, folded my blanket, and prepared to deal with Auntie's mental hangover from last night's tragedy. Would she be in shock? Need a shoulder to cry on? Maybe she'd want to hop on the next flight back to Wisconsin. I needn't have worried, or in the case of the last option, hoped.

Auntie sat at the kitchen table, sipping coffee. She jumped up on my entrance, but I motioned for her to stay seated and got my own cup.

"Were you able to sleep last night?" I used that wouldn't-break-an-eggshell tone reserved for those in a fragile state of mind.

"Out like a light the minute my head hit the pillow. Are you sure you don't want to share the bed? There's plenty of room for both of us."

My bed was a single. "I like the couch," I lied. "Do you want to talk about what happened?"

She shrugged her large shoulders. "Talk about what? The show was pretty good. I generated a lot of interest in my tarot business. It ended on a bad note, but there's nothing you or I can do about that. Sad, but there it is."

I stared with admiration. The older generation was tough. That's how they managed to face and even flourish against wars, inflation, and a presidential assassination. For the most part, without whining.

"What else did Detective Gutierrez ask you, besides if you knew the victim?"

"She took my name and asked for my address. I gave her yours, since this is where I'll be for the next few days."

"That's it? She didn't want to know if you'd seen anyone suspicious or what your own movements were?"

"She asked me a lot of questions about things that weren't any of my business, and I told her so. How would I know if anyone wanted to kill that poor contestant?" Auntie drank the last of her coffee and rinsed her cup in the kitchen sink. "That poor woman. I wonder how her family is taking it?"

"Not well, I imagine. Speaking of the poor woman, why did you run off the minute Elvira Jenkins tried to introduce herself? It was rude and completely out of character for you."

"When you get to be my age, you answer nature's call without dilly-dallying." She set the cup upside down on the drying rack. "We're going to stick to our plans for today?"

"You're sure you're up for it?"

"Absolutely."

I wondered if she was putting on a brave face for me and if she might prefer to ponder the inevitable end that we each must face, albeit, not through violence. After all, Elvira Jenkins was close to Auntie's own age. My sturdy relative assured me she did not need a time-out to contemplate mortality.

"Let me get dressed and we can get shaking."

Half an hour later, we were at the Prickly Pear Bistro, ready for breakfast. It was a sweet little restaurant located downtown Wolf Creek. The inside decor reflected the bright purples, pinks, yellows and oranges of the namesake cactus blooms. The owner of the bistro, Penny Newcombe, had been my best friend since grade school. If my ex-boyfriend Jeff was responsible for my flight from Wisconsin, Penny is the reason I wound up in Wolf Creek, Arizona. Preternaturally perky, Penny is my opposite. Aunt Gertrude adores her.

"Little Penny! Look how big you've grown!" Auntie enveloped her in a hug that left only the top of her blonde head visible under yards of gauzy green fabric from my aunt's voluminous dress. As she rocked Penny in her arms, the many bangle bracelets on Auntie's arms set off a cacophony similar to wind chimes in a monsoon.

"She's a grown woman, Auntie," I said, "and you saw her two years ago at the Hardin baby's baptism."

Several diners stared with open interest as I tried to free Penny from my aunt's smothering hug. She didn't seem to need my help. She broke out in a goofy crooked grin and snuggled in to enjoy the love. Admittedly, once you get past your need to breathe, Aunt Gertrude is a great hugger.

"What have you been up to? How have you been?" Penny asked.

Auntie pulled away and straightened her neckline. "This and that. Nothing too exciting."

My mouth dropped open. Murder was nothing?

"Oh, my gosh! Yesterday was the *Blue-Ribbon Babes* premiere! Was it exciting? Did you have fun? Did you meet any celebrities? I taped it, but I haven't watched it yet. I was working."

Here was the perfect opportunity to mention the murder. I was just about to launch into a detailed description of the night that included the bits I'd skipped over with Bowers when Auntie grabbed Penny by the shoulders and held her out for inspection.

"More importantly, what's going on with you? I sense... yes... someone has a special announcement. You have an aura of peace."

Penny cupped her hands over her mouth and blushed. I should mention that Penny believes Auntie is truly clairvoyant, which is why my aunt plays it up whenever she's around her. Penny—dear, sweet, naive girl—even thought my own talents at fake-reading pets were psychic phenomena long before I'd stumbled upon my ability. I'm afraid both misconceptions are my fault.

After Auntie ran into Penny's father at a showing of *The Apple Dumpling Gang Rides Again* at the Arcade Theater canoodling with a woman who wasn't his wife, she did a reading for Judy Newcombe and gave her enough hints that the suspicious wife looked for evidence of an affair. and finding it, threw the bum out. I never had the heart to embarrass Penny with the real story, so I let her believe in Auntie's powers. As for allowing her to believe in my own skills, pretending to read pets was a great way for a twelve-year-old to earn a dollar, and Penny had a lot of dollars.

"She's exactly right," Penny said, jumping up and down. "Kemper proposed!"

She held out her left hand. A delicate woven pattern of two bands of white gold met in a cluster of small diamonds with one larger rock in the center.

I'm oblivious to most jewelry, which explains why I hadn't noticed the brand-new engagement ring on Penny's left hand. It also explained Auntie's amazing aura reading. Like all elderly females, she has a built-in radar for weddings and babies.

"Gorgeous!" Auntie exclaimed.

I'm not proud of my initial reaction. In my mind, Penny suddenly became part of an inseparable twosome. No more girl's nights out. No more giggled confidences. Kemper, nice guy that he was, represented the end of my paltry social life.

"Isn't it wonderful?" Penny asked. Her shining eyes held such joy that it kicked those thoughts right out of my selfish noggin. I hugged my friend with genuine pleasure.

"You guys are the perfect couple."

She blushed with pleasure. "You're just saying that."

"Really. You're going to make a great wife and mother. You're kind, giving, and your upbeat attitude is going to carry you both through a wonderful life together."

She grabbed my hand and squealed. "We have to try on dresses!"

I shook my hand loose. "Dresses?"

"You're going to be my maid of honor," Penny said, poking me. "Kemper and I are signing up for Pre-Cana classes," she said, referring to the Catholic program that couples go through before marriage, "so that gives me time to sew the dresses. I want to get some ideas on current fashions."

"Right. Sure." Clothes shopping ranks up there with having something amputated on my list of things I'd like to avoid. I'd been to enough weddings to know that maids of honor were required to wear ridiculous mounds of taffeta in eyeball-searing colors.

"How about tomorrow?" She squeezed Auntie's hand. "I'd love your opinion, too. Oh! And now that you're here, you have to see U Behave, Frances' shop!"

Penny was one of three people who insisted on calling me Frances. The first was my mother, and the second was Seamus McGuire, owner of Canine Camp, but since he picked it up from Penny, I blame her.

Auntie raised an eyebrow at me. "You have an actual storefront?"

"Not really," I mumbled, but Penny dragged us both down a short hallway that led to Penny's office and the restrooms. The door right before the Women's room led to my shop. The Prickly Pear was situated on a corner. Its own entrance looked out over Main Street. I had my own front door off Maricopa Drive, but most of the time I cut through the restaurant's dining room to get to work, probably since I usually ate breakfast there. My shop space was where the bakery that formerly occupied the Prickly Pear sold their day-old goods. Seemed appropriate, somehow.

"Can you have an animal business at the back of a restaurant?" Auntie asked.

"It's not actually in the restaurant. I have my own separate entrance. I only make appointments here. I see the animals in their own home environment." I really didn't know the answer to Auntie's question, but until someone from the city came knocking, I wasn't going to worry about it.

Penny flipped on the light and Auntie stepped in, spread her arms wide, and said, "The vibrations in here are positively—" She peered around. "Positive." Even she, enthusiastically launching into another psychic spiel, came up short.

The room was as barren as the day I took over, though I had taken the time to clear out the spider webs and dust bunnies last month. The display counters stood empty, as did the chipped shelves, all of them desperately in need of a paint job. The barren walls resembled a prison cell, especially the far wall with the lightning-shaped crack that suggested seismic activity.

Auntie strolled over and tapped the wall with her finger. "You just need some spackle and that will clear this fracture right up."

It was more of a gap than a fracture, but I agreed for the sake of peace.

She scraped at the edges with her thumb. Drywall crumbled to the floor. "Yeah. Not too bad."

At the crack's center, she had exposed a circle of drywall, making the mark look like a strange pagan symbol. She strolled past the counter and tapped the glass.

"You should sell those collars with studs. Dogs look ridiculous in them, but the owners don't think so, and they're the ones with the cash."

"I don't want to be a store. Just a simple animal behaviorist."

She snorted. "That'll reel them in. You've got the display cases right here. It would be a mistake to waste them. If you don't like the collar idea, you could add treats, leashes, and all sorts of pet supplies."

I gritted my teeth and thanked her for the suggestion, but already I'd wadded it up and tossed it into a mental wastebasket. The hanging shelves were the next object to fall under her scrutiny. She grabbed the edge of one and pulled down hard. The hinges tore from the wall.

"Wouldn't put anything heavy on these," she pronounced as she rested the shelf against the wall. "Good thing I checked." Hands on hips, she surveyed the room. "I bet you could fix this place up without hiring professionals. There's plenty of self-help books at the library. How's the wiring?"

I flipped off the lights before she could electrocute us all. "Let's get breakfast."

"Is there anything your aunt doesn't know about?" Penny cooed.

"She doesn't think so."

The food was delicious as always. My Cornflake-crusted French Toast crunched with perfection, and Auntie raved about her Eggs Benedict. My attention wasn't completely absorbed by my food, which was unusual for me. All through breakfast, the eyes of various diners drifted to our table. I'm a regular at the Prickly Pear, and maybe they were curious about Auntie, which was kind of touching and kind of disconcerting. I didn't think I was worthy of all that attention.

Penny refused to let us pay, and then she walked me to my car. Auntie insisted on scheduling a hair appointment, and as I had to meet with a client, it worked out fine. Auntie could walk to the stylist at the end of the block, and Penny promised to amuse my aged relative if the hair appointment finished before I returned.

As we said our goodbyes, Seamus McGuire stepped out of Canine Camp, the doggie daycare two doors down. He wasn't alone. A tall brunette pecked him on the cheek and got into a smart-looking red hybrid. Seamus blushed. With his freckled skin, I could see it all the way from where I stood.

"Who's that?" I tried to keep my voice indifferent. Seamus had shown some interest in me before things had gone terribly wrong at the conclusion of a murder investigation. I'd hate to think I'd lost all chance of getting to know him better just because I terrified him out of his mind by being able to read it. His was the second hand I grabbed that night while trying to direct the dog out of the burning building.

"Remember how you caught Tyler Watts trying to poison your pets?" Penny shook her head in disapproval of Tyler. "Well that killed his reputation as a trainer. Seamus couldn't pick up all the new clients, so Bethany moved into town and took over. She's a very good trainer from what I've heard."

"This Bethany person just happened to move to Wolf Creek?" I asked, still casual.

"I think Seamus went to college with her." Penny seemed to sense her next words might not go over with a loud cheer. She mumbled, "He sort of called her and asked her to come."

"Oh. That's nice."

"Bethany is nice."

If Penny met Hitler, she'd probably notice that he had a way with words.

Auntie studied Seamus with interest. "Are you talking about that nice-looking young man?" She waved at him. "Hello-o-o! Over here!" She sounded like she was hailing a taxi.

Seamus came when called because ignoring us would be too obvious, though he kept looking back at Canine Camp as if debating whether to dash inside and lock the door. He kept his gaze fixed on Penny until I introduced him to my aunt. He managed to jump his eyes from Penny to Auntie without risking a stop on my face.

"How do you like Arizona?"

"It's a lot prettier than I imagined. You actually have flowers. I thought it would be all brown and dead."

"It is a beautiful place. It really is," Seamus said in a dreamy, satisfied way that made me think the source of his pleasure didn't come from the scenery. "There isn't any place I'd rather live than here, in Wolf Creek, Arizona."

It is a nauseating peccadillo of People in Love to see the world as a bright and shiny place. It's particularly tedious to listen to when they're not in love with you.

"You're not going to break into song, are you?" I asked.

He flushed. "There's plenty to see, Mrs. Pitt. Have you been to MIM yet? Bethany and I checked it out last weekend. It's cool." He was referring to the Musical Instruments Museum in Phoenix. They'd received great reviews in The Wolf Creek Gazette.

I didn't want to hear any more about Bethany, so I gave Auntie a kiss on the cheek.

"Gotta go. Be good."

If I'd been able to see the future, my instructions would have been more explicit.

SIX

I stared into the face of a tortoiseshell cat and tried to think of an explanation for why the animal would be crying by the backyard window every morning at five a.m.

"Have you noticed any other cats running loose in the neighborhood?"

Mr. Farley, the spectacled owner of Tabitha, popped his eyes open wide behind thick lenses, giving an impression of Mr. Magoo. "You're kidding, right?"

He had a point. Wolf Creek, with its coyotes, hawks, and occasional mountain lions, was not a safe place for a cat to wander freely. Those pet parents who thought kitty preferred to roam at large usually wound up posting pointless lost cat ads on mailboxes. Wiser residents would read them and hold a moment of silence, knowing the pet would never return.

"And you don't have new landscapers or anyone like that dropping by?"

"At five in the morning?"

Again, he had a point. I searched my memory banks for

other situations that left me itching to throw a shoe at a feline to shut her up, and it hit me.

"Is Tabitha fixed?"

He shifted his glasses and raised his chin, so he could look down his nose at me.

"It is the law."

"Have you had Tabitha checked out by a vet?"

"Of course I did. You think I'd call you before checking with a professional?"

My neck muscles cramped up and my temple throbbed. I hadn't a clue what to ask next. Tabitha lifted one hind leg to clean herself, and it crossed my mind that one little peek inside her furry skull might explain the whole situation. I reasoned this could be a test to see if I had regained the ability to control my conversations with animals. Well, as much as I ever could control them. What could it hurt if I tried it just this once?

A lot. That's what. No. I wasn't going there. Not after my experience with Sandy, the golden retriever who witnessed a murder. And then there was that moment afterwards when I was able to pick up Seamus' and Bowers' thoughts. What if I started reading Mr. Farley's mind, too? What if he turned out to be some kind of pervert? Or a serial killer? Or wore women's underwear? Yuck.

"Have you changed her food lately?"

"No."

"Her toys?"

"No."

"Taken away her catnip or given her catnip for the first time?" Withdrawals or a bad trip were possibilities. At least they could have been if she had been human, but I didn't see a difference between a catnip-deprived feline and a crack addict. My client didn't agree.

Mr. Farley stood. "No. I haven't." He adjusted his glasses. "I'm surprised. I heard great things about your insights into animals. I could have had this same discussion with the sales clerk at Pet World."

"Animal behavior is a bit of guesswork, since we can't actually read their minds."

"Like heck you can't!" He trotted to a credenza and brought back a newspaper. "That's not what this says." He held up the front page of The Wolf Creek Gazette.

They'd gotten hold of a picture of Auntie and me from a wedding six years ago. We both had our mouths open in laughter and looked mentally unhinged.

Is Psychic Team Ready to Botch Blue-Ribbon Murder?

In an amazing coincidence, Frances Chandler and Gertrude Pitt, both well known for plying the public with their psychic "abilities", were present at the premiere of the Baking Channel's latest sensation, Blue-Ribbon Babes. Ms. Chandler fancies she can communicate with animals, while Mrs. Pitt limits herself to flipping tarot cards for guidance.

Mrs. Pitt threw down the gauntlet for the murderer of contestant Elvira Jenkins, saying, "I will not rest until the killer receives justice!" She's in for many sleepless nights. Ms. Chandler wisely had no comment. Lucky for Wolf Creek, we have an excellent police department, who should be able to solve the crime in spite of this proposed interference.

The byline belonged to that evil reporter, Paul Simpson. The last time we'd met, I'd shoved a sample of dog food in his face when he threatened to expose me as a fraud, with the exposé from Loon Lake's own busty Lois Lane as proof. In my defense, it was homemade dog food with human grade ingredients, but it sounded as if Paul might be carrying a grudge.

"It says right here that you communicate with animals."

Mr. Farley obviously didn't have an ear for sarcasm.

"You can't believe everything you read in the paper. There's been a mistake, because I wasn't interviewed for this story, and I've nothing to do with the police."

He carefully folded the paper back up and tucked it under his arm. "So, what you've given me is all I'm going to get? I hope you don't expect me to pay for a few wild guesses."

I plastered on a smile, but my cheek twitched. "Of course not."

After leaving my non-paying client, I headed straight to the Prickly Pear. Penny explained that Auntie had gotten bored, so she had driven her back to my house.

"Did you tie her up and gag her before you left?"

Penny took one look at my dark expression and said, "What's the matter?"

"Can I use the phone in your office?"

It was going to take some calming down before I confronted Auntie, because really, who else could have given out the information? However, my current level of anger, somewhere between *I want you fired* and *I'd like to turn you into cat food* was perfect for Paul Simpson. Penny closed the door behind me to give me privacy, and soon I had *The Wolf Creek Gazette* on the line.

"Paul Simpson, please, and if he's on another line, disconnect it."

There was a pause. "Can I ask what this is regarding?" The receptionist didn't ask who I was; she asked what I wanted. *The Wolf Creek Gazette* probably had a black hole where they sent complaints about Paul Simpson, so I added, "I'm a source. I've got some dirt on Frankie Chandler for him."

"One moment please." Her voice now registered disgust, but I'd rather have her think I was a sleazy source and put me through than think I was one of the many normal human beings who thought Paul Simpson was a loser and send me to voicemail.

"Simpson here. What has that spacey broad done now? And it better be good, cause I'm not paying for the obvious."

His voice contained a whiney quality that grated on my ears.

"I see you're still fascinated by my psychic skills, Mr. Simpson." I began with a sweet tone because I didn't want to sink to his level. "But what you printed in this morning's paper was a lie. I could sue, you know."

"Is this really Frankie Chandler?" And then he laughed. "A lie, huh? I don't think so."

His confidence threw me. While I knew that a scenario with Paul Simpson groveling at my feet was pure fantasy, I would have settled for an apology. What I heard was the evil snicker of a devil's minion.

"Your aunt was a talker. Quite a pleasure, in fact. Usually I have to work to get a source to open up, but she just poured out the material. More than I could use, in fact, but there's always tomorrow, right?"

I knew I'd lose my edge if I showed any interest, but I had to ask. I did so through gritted teeth. "What kind of material?"

"Seemed to think the two of you were spiritual caped crusaders, using all your tricks in the pursuit of justice. I've got quotes to back me up, and they all start with 'Sissy and I'." He snickered.

"But you didn't check your facts," I reminded him. "I'm certain I didn't get a call from you to verify my part in the story."

"She represented you as a team. I spoke to a representative of the team. That's all I need to please my editor. And I did confirm that you and Sissy were the same person."

Paul Simpson probably didn't have an ounce of humanity in his stocky little body, but he wasn't hatched on a lonely beach like a baby turtle. He had a mother who probably liked him. He most likely reciprocated the sentiment, and judging from his age, his own mom must to be around Aunt Gertrude's age. I took the sympathy shot.

"I can't believe you would betray the confidences of an innocent, little old lady. For Pete's sake! She was in a fragile state of mind, having just seen a dead body. She wasn't responsible for what she was saying."

"Are you saying she's loony? 'Cause I could get some mileage out of that."

Maybe he was hatched, the repulsive reptile. I was tempted to sacrifice Auntie's reputation for the sake of killing any future stories on me, but I figured he'd somehow drag my name along for the ride.

"My next phone call is to my lawyer."

No such person existed, but it made a good exit line.

I didn't stop to explain to Penny as I headed out the door. I wouldn't put it past Paul Simpson to be dialing Auntie up right now, just to spite me.

At least one mystery was solved. Now I knew why everyone had stared at us throughout breakfast. They'd had their morning paper with coffee and a good laugh at my expense for dessert.

As I pulled into my driveway, I discovered that an unlisted phone number doesn't mean that people can't track you down. I counted six reporters in my front yard. Technically, it was four reporters and two photographers.

"Ms. Chandler!"

I held up my hands, and the people quieted, ready for a statement. "The story you read in the paper is completely untrue."

"Were you present at the murder?" asked an older reporter with a trilby hat.

"Of course not! I went to the premiere like dozens of other people and was just as surprised when the poor woman turned up dead."

A young, freckled photographer lowered his camera. "But didn't you and Madame Guinevere discover the body?"

That wasn't in the article. My face must have registered surprise, because he raised the camera and took a snap.

"Anything about the crime has to come from the police who, as I said, we are not working with. That's all I've got to say on the matter. And if you don't leave, I'll be calling those same police—the ones we're not working with—to complain."

As they moved to their vehicles, I pulled the photographer aside.

"Who told you I found the body?"

He jerked his head toward my house. "Your aunt."

"I suppose she's been free and easy with the interviews," I growled.

"Technically, she refused to open the door to strangers, so she shouted her responses through the keyhole."

I asked him nicely not to print what she'd told him. He laughed all the way to his car.

Inside my living room, Auntie reclined on the couch, with a women's magazine spread open on her lap. Face up on the coffee table lay The Wolf Creek Gazette.

"Where did that come from? I don't subscribe."

"Sharlene was nice enough to drop it off."

"Who's Sharlene?"

Auntie raised her brows. "Why, she's your next-door neighbor! Don't tell me you don't even know the names of your own neighbors."

Temporarily sidetracked, I asked, "When did you meet my neighbors?"

Auntie focused her gaze on her hands and played with a hangnail. "Around. It's not that difficult to meet people if you're friendly, like I am."

"What did Sharlene want?"

"She thought I might like to keep a copy of the paper, since we were in it. I made her pass it to me through the window because I didn't think you'd like those reporters in your house. They looked like they might rush me if I let her in."

"You shouldn't have talked to them, either."

"I was just being polite. Besides, no harm done." She poked the paper and gave me a coy smile. "Have you read it?"

"A client showed it to me. Have *you* read it? You sound like you're proud of it."

She brushed a hand over her hair. "I'll be honest. That wouldn't have been my choice of photograph."

The paper made a handy prop as I waved it in Auntie's face.

"When did you talk to Paul Simpson? You weren't alone the night of the murder long enough to talk to him."

"He called my cell phone last night."

"I didn't hear the phone ring."

"I keep it on vibrate. Do I need to announce every personal call I get?"

"Yes, but that's beside the point. You told Paul Simpson we were working with the police."

She blinked. "Of course I did. When that reporter called me, I couldn't believe my luck. It's a good business move, and seeing as how you haven't had as many clients as I have toes on one foot since I've been here, I would think you'd be pleased." She gave a martyred sigh. "I'm looking out for you, Sissy, not that I expect any thanks. Who else could get us exclusive coverage in such a short time? Maybe I should get an agent."

"Do you have any idea the kind of fallout we're going to see over this?"

"Hopefully a lot. I could use some clients."

"He's making fun of us!" I read it aloud with the proper inflections, so she couldn't miss the point.

"The only thing people will notice is that we offer psychic services. They'll look us up on the internet—you do have a web page, I hope."

"I'm working on it." I wasn't. "Besides, I'll have to rethink things now that I'm an animal behaviorist."

She threw her hands up and spoke to the ceiling. "The girl doesn't have a web page. Can you believe it? No wonder she can't make ends meet."

I grit my teeth and growled, but she only grinned.

"I was repeating what the young whippersnapper at the computer store said to me. Turned out she freelances, and she designed my site. I'll give her your phone number when I get back to Loon Lake."

She slapped her thighs and stood. "I'm going to start on dinner."

I made it my mission to beat her to the kitchen. Auntie is a marvelous cook, but I might not survive her haphazard methods, which usually left my kitchen in need of a decontamination crew. Oven fried chicken was on tonight's menu. I got moving.

"I can find my way around, Sissy. You just relax. Maybe a glass of wine will calm you down."

But I was already ten steps ahead of her. I flung open the cabinets and searched for a mixing bowl for the batter.

"Don't bother. I'll just use this."

She pulled down a cereal bowl.

"You'll want to beat raw eggs, and I'd prefer that you not do it in the same bowl I use for my Peanut Butter Oaties."

She cracked the first egg into my bowl. "We'll wash it, silly. You worry too much."

Turning to toss the eggshell into the sink, she left a trail of egg white on my linoleum. I grabbed a paper towel and held Chauncey's snout at bay with one hand while I cleaned up the mess with the other. My dog already figured out that Auntie cooking meant good things for his tummy.

"You want to grab the chicken from the icebox for me?"

She hadn't put a plate under the bagged carcass as I'd suggested, so while Auntie cut the bird into pieces—using my paper scissors—I waited for the water from the kitchen faucet to reach scalding hot, so I could clean the bloody juices off the refrigerator shelf.

Whatever tensions Auntie might have been harboring from the day, she released them in the rigors of rubbing down the chicken with olive oil, using vigorous strokes and pats that made me yearn for a massage. She beat the pulp out of boiled potatoes and garlic and viciously snapped the ends off the green beans. I set the table and killed time reading a dog training guide. When she finally plated the finished masterpiece, the doorbell rang.

Auntie set the chicken on the table, and I noticed she'd laid the food out on a decorative tray that normally hung on my kitchen wall. It was a pretty, mustard yellow tray with handles.

"You can't put food on that. It's only for decoration."

"Seems a waste not to use it."

"The tray isn't sealed. And there's lead in it."

"That's only children who need to worry about lead."

The doorbell rang again.

"You get started without me," I said. "I'll be right back."

I flung open the door and froze at the site of Detective Martin Bowers. His jaw muscles twitched, and his eyebrows joined together like Oscar the Grouch. He was still on duty, because he wore a blue sports jacket over a white shirt and beige slacks.

"Did you time it? We were just about to die of lead poisoning."

He grabbed my elbow and pulled me outside.

"Are you sure you're through with the pet psychic nonsense?"

I wrinkled my nose. "I suppose you're talking about that little article in the Gazette."

"That little front-page article. Yes."

I threw out my hands. "You got me. I contacted the sleaziest reporter I could find and helped him write an article making fun of me and my aunt."

"Good point." He ran this over in his mind, relaxed, smirked, and then let loose a chuckle. "It wasn't very flattering, was it?"

"Not at all."

"And that picture..."

"I saw it."

"The story made our department sound pretty good."

"I'm glad you liked it."

The wary expression came back. "There's usually a

grain of truth hidden in Simpson's stories. How exactly did he find out about your aunt?"

"He was waiting outside as we left Saguaro Studios, and when confronted by a sleazy, no-good reporter, my aunt's response was to pass him her contact information."

He tilted his head and looked into my eyes. "Auntie gave him the story?"

"A fine business move, she says."

"As long as it's not true. I don't want you to stick your nose into a police investigation. And please don't become one of those idiot women in books who says I'm being an unreasonable chauvinist because I don't want you to get people killed and destroy evidence. Besides, it would be better for your aunt if the two of you stayed under the radar right now."

He took a step toward the door, but I pulled it shut and barred the way.

"What's that supposed to mean? Better for your aunt. It sounds like a threat."

He wouldn't meet my eyes. "It's friendly advice. She is —a person of interest."

"A person of interest?" I repeated. "You mean a suspect?" I'd heard the pause and knew he'd changed his word choice mid-sentence. He wore his policeman's face, an almost bored look.

"If I'd meant suspect, I would have said suspect," he said.

"How could you possibly think she had anything to do with Elvira Jenkins' death? Auntie doesn't even live in Arizona."

My stomach growled, reminding me that dinner awaited. "This is just silly. My aunt is a—well not exactly sweet, but a little old lady who couldn't hurt a fly. We'll take your advice and stay out of the investigation. Problem solved. Thanks for coming." I reached for the doorknob.

"Not that simple. This is a professional call." When I didn't invite him in, he sighed and said, "I want to talk to her, but if you'd prefer, I could get Detective Gutierrez to come out."

I shuddered. "No. Gutierrez doesn't like me. You're the lesser of two evils."

He smiled. "That's good, because I was bluffing. She's been assigned to another case. A B&E." Naturally, he was pleased. Bowers and Gutierrez both had gigantic egos and an even bigger case of professional rivalry. As I understand it, murder trumps breaking and entering.

"Gutierrez already interviewed my aunt last night. What more could you have to ask her?" But even as I pointed out the obvious, another thought occurred to me. Bowers once made a comment about fraud regarding my pet psychic business. Had he gotten wind of Madame Guinevere's recent activities in my home?

"This isn't about those silly tarot cards, is it?"

He put on his neutral face, but his lips twitched as if he were holding back a grin. "You mean the ones she gave Gutierrez, the coroner, the EMT, and everyone within throwing distance? Sort of, but only as it relates to the death of Elvira Jenkins."

There were few ways to interpret that statement. Had Auntie predicted the woman's death with a lucky guess and the victim complained about my aunt's downer techniques to a friend? Before she died, of course. Did Bowers think the prediction was actually a threat? I couldn't really stop him from interviewing my aunt, but at least I could be present if he tried to grill her or trap her or use Guantanamo techniques on her to force a confession.

A flash of light temporarily blinded me, but after I blinked a few times, a freckled face came into focus, grinned at me, and then took off running.

"Hey!" I shouted, prepared to pursue. "That's one of those reporters."

Bowers blocked my way. "Just ignore them. There's not much you can do about it, and if you tick them off, they can do plenty of damage through innuendos." He did a quick scan for other lurking paparazzi. "But I suggest we get off the street."

The door swung open before I could grab the knob. Auntie caught sight of Bowers.

"Don't just stand there. Why don't you invite the nice-looking young man in? Would you like to join us for dinner?"

"He's busy working," I said. "He can only stay a minute."

"Thank you. I believe I will." Bowers pushed his way past me with a smirk. I heard a crinkle and noticed he carried a plastic bag in his hand.

"You look familiar," Auntie said, leading the way to the kitchen. She laid out another place setting and invited him to sit. She seemed flustered that my square table didn't demarcate a clear head of the table for the man in the room, but she made up for it by giving him an extra napkin.

"We met, briefly, last night at Saguaro Studios, but we didn't have a chance to talk. You were distressed. I'm Detective Martin Bowers."

Her only acknowledgement of his status in the investigation was to say that it was a sad business. Then she folded her hands and said grace. I was impressed that Bowers knew all the words. Probably drilled into him by his big sisters.

He looked appreciatively at the fried chicken, but then

he took a closer look at the serving tray. "There isn't any glaze on that."

"Nope." I gave him a sweet smile.

His eyes met mine, and as I watched, his facial expression work its way through puzzlement, realization, and horror. He'd finally made the lead poisoning connection.

"Is that—"

I nodded. "The cause of death. You still have time to make out a will, because it's a slow death."

We both poked and prodded at the chicken, filling up on the side dishes that came from safe, glass bowls, but it wasn't only fear of the grim reaper that kept him from enjoying Auntie's cooking. Guilt was written all over his face, and that's when I knew I wouldn't like the bag's contents.

"It's wonderful that Sissy has such nice, clean friends," Auntie chirped with Midwestern hospitality.

She'd repeated that same saying since my childhood. When I was younger, I assumed it meant my pals scrubbed behind their ears. As a teen with an active imagination and hormones, I thought perhaps it meant the guy friends didn't visit bug-infested brothels and the women friends didn't work there. Now I thought it meant that Bowers' fingernails passed inspection and that he hadn't drooled on his shirt once during dinner.

"How is your investigation going?"

That seemed to decide it for him. He pushed his plate away.

"So, are you from Loon Lake as well?"

She paused, then added a roll to her plate and picked up the butter knife. "As well as what?"

Bowers nodded at me. "As well as Frankie."

"You mean Sissy?"

JACQUELINE VICK

"Sissy?" Bowers cut short a snort when I gave him a dirty look.

"A lifelong resident," Auntie boasted, buttering her roll. "No better place on earth. We haven't been invaded by alleged progress. You can still walk to the cinema at night for a G-rated movie without worrying about a gang of hoodlums knocking you over the head."

"Sounds like a nice place. Elvira Jenkins, the victim, was originally from Loon Lake."

Auntie didn't miss a bite. "Isn't it a small world?"

"Elvira Jenkins is around your age."

Auntie set down her roll. "Just how old do you think I am?" she asked with a sweet smile.

Bowers recovered nicely, probably because he'd been raised by a zillion sisters who taught him how to maneuver dangerous female topics, like age. "Of course, you're probably younger than the victim, but it's still funny you hadn't run into each other before last night."

"Nice save," I whispered out of the corner of my mouth.

"Loon Lake isn't that small, Detective. There are plenty of people living there whom I've never had the pleasure of meeting."

"So, you didn't know the victim?"

"I saw her on the show last night, so you could say I knew who she was."

"You didn't know the victim before yesterday?" he clarified.

"I'd never met Elvira Jenkins before yesterday."

I looked at him, but his expression betrayed nothing. Why did he think Auntie was lying? Because I was certain that's why he kept rephrasing the same question. I took a closer look at Auntie. Her hands were clasped together under her chin, she wore a sweet simple smile, and her eyes never left his face. She was lying. No one stares that hard unless they're trying to prove they haven't got anything to hide. At least no one in our family.

"Didn't know her at all." He repeated.

"Nada. Elvira Jenkins and I have never crossed paths."

"Funny."

Bowers wasn't laughing when he said it, so funny wasn't a ha-ha good time reference. The way he stressed that one word told me something was on its way that I wasn't going to like. I braced myself.

He reached into his pocket and pulled out a crumpled card that I immediately recognized as one of Auntie's business cards.

"Don't tell me you're here for a reading," I said with a forced chuckle. The thought of Detective Martin Bowers facing off with my aunt, he of the stoic expression and Auntie with her iron will regaling him with messages from the alleged spirit world. The urge to giggle left me as I thought of what kind of cop revenge Bowers could plot against Auntie after he lost the battle of wills—because he would lose. My temples throbbed.

"By the time forensics finished with the body last night, you were already home," Bowers said to Auntie. "We pried this card out of the victim's cold, dead fingers."

Okay. Bowers didn't phrase it like that, but he might as well have based on the effect he produced. In me, that is. Auntie's expression didn't change, but I hyperventilated.

"We need a paper bag." Auntie made a move toward the kitchen cabinets, but Bowers put out a restraining hand.

"She'll be fine. I have a few questions for you about the victim." His tone didn't invite argument.

Auntie gave him a shrewd look and then sat back down. "What can I tell you?"

"You can tell me what you and the victim talked about, for starters."

"Last night? I talked to so many people." She put the fingers of one hand to her forehead. "Wait a minute. I think I introduced myself and give her one of my cards."

I snapped to attention. "When was this? I don't remember you and Elvira talking."

She brushed her fingers toward the crumpled card. "Obviously, I gave her a card." Her face brightened, as if all became clear. "That's right. She was having her fifteen minutes of fame, and it seemed too good of a business opportunity to pass up. You never know when someone's going to let your name slip, not that I think a Blue-Ribbon Queen is going to be interviewed on national television or anything, but she still might be asked to cut the ribbon for an opening. Maybe for a bakery." She tapped the card. "That's why she had this on her, poor woman. I'm so happy she didn't toss it in the garbage, as I suspect most of my prospects do."

Auntie was definitely dancing around the truth. How could she forget a conversation with the Blue-Ribbon Queen, let alone her last conversation with the recently murdered Blue-Ribbon Queen? Especially as she took such pains to be rude to her when the woman introduced herself. And if I could see what she was doing, there was no way Bowers missed it.

"The witness who saw the two of you talking—and you were standing on the set at the time, in case you've forgotten—well, she felt that the conversation was more...personal."

Oh, cripes. A witness! I would have given anything to know what Bowers was thinking. Suddenly, it occurred to me that maybe I could.

I stared hard at Bowers, and using an image I'd tried

before on Chauncey, I tried to imagine an information highway traveling between his head and mind.

Meanwhile, Auntie followed her line of reasoning. She actually tittered. "Two old ladies chatting about tarot cards and baking. I was excited about being there; Elvira was excited about her fifteen minutes of fame. We probably sounded excited, especially if your witness was a youngster. Was it a youngster?"

His expression revealed nothing to me, but Auntie must have seen something there that I missed, because she nodded and smiled.

"That's what it was. Youngsters always expect old ladies to be demure and quiet."

Those were not the expectations of anyone young that I knew. My imaginary highway wasn't getting anywhere, so I relaxed my shoulders and tried to place myself in Bowers' position. Literally. I'm a cop. I've come to the home of a charming woman to interview her houseguest. I'm remembering what a witness told me—

Bowers' elbow shot out and poked me in the side.

"Sorry about that," he murmured.

Auntie picked up her roll and pointed it at him. "Are you trying to get a sense of what the victim was like? Because if you're looking for information on the victim's personality, she reminded me of Vicky Perkins. A slip of a girl back when I was a younger woman. Vicky was as self-centered as God makes 'em. Always butting in where she wasn't wanted, almost to the point of being rude. No one could tell her a thing. The similarities are worth noting."

Bowers said, "The comparison is worth considering, but I'm surprised you were able to come up with such detailed insights on a woman you never met."

Auntie tugged on my arm. "But wasn't she kind of bossy

on the set? She just charged out and took over. That little host didn't stand a chance. Isn't that right, Sissy?"

They were both watching me, Auntie expectantly, and Bowers through narrowed eyes.

"Oh. She's right. Absolutely right," I said, happy to give Auntie my support. "Elvira Jenkins came across as a strong personality. Very strong."

Bowers looked from Auntie to me as if trying to size us up. Maybe he was wondering if we were lying. Maybe he was considering our familial relationship and the possibility that I might someday resemble my aunt and hang about the house wearing large, colorful dresses.

"You want to stick to your statement that you didn't know the victim?"

"I said I didn't know Elvira Jenkins."

He slid a book out of the bag and laid it on the table. "I was able to speak with Mr. Jenkins today and go through his late wife's effects. I found this."

He angled the book, so Auntie could read it. She took a hearty bite of bread and wiped the butter off her lip with the back of her hand. I shot up and moved around Bowers, so I could peer over his shoulder. I put one hand on his shoulder and leaned forward to get a better look. It was a high school yearbook from Our Lady of Perpetual Help High School, known throughout Loon Lake as "the girl's school." One page was marked, and Bowers flipped it open and pointed to a picture of a young girl with braces.

"I believe that's you?"

Auntie finished chewing. "I hated those braces. Tinsel teeth. That's what they called me."

He watched her face as he flipped the page, and I knew he was setting her up, ready to pounce on her response. I wanted to shout a warning. He shot a look up at me. His brows furrowed, and I realized I was pressing my nails into his shoulder. I released my hold, and he turned his attention back to the page.

"That's the victim."

A chubby girl with braids smirked at us from over the caption Elvira Doud.

I squeaked.

"Exactly," Bowers whispered out of the corner of his mouth without moving his gaze from Auntie.

Dabbing her lips with her napkin, Auntie said, "The victim's name was Jenkins, not Doud."

Bowers pulled the book back and looked at the name. Score one for Auntie. Then he pushed the book right in front of her and tapped the photo. "You're telling me you didn't recognize her?"

She merely sighed, as if she were dealing with an impatient child. "Did you see the body? Then you should know that fifty years make a bit of difference. Well, maybe not quite fifty." She smiled the way old women smile at handsome younger men. "Now why don't you finish your dinner? You've got to keep up your strength."

Whatever he was searching for, he finally gave up, but only for the moment. He complimented Auntie on dinner and wished her a nice visit. Though he smiled enough to show off a nice set of teeth, his eyes had that hooded look, as if he were already thinking about his next approach.

"I'll just show Detective Bowers out," I said. Auntie made a noncommittal noise and gathered up the dishes from the table.

Once in the living room, I didn't waste time.

"You don't really think Auntie had anything to do with the murder, do you?" I playfully punched his arm, probably harder than I meant to, because he flinched. I didn't really expect him to share his thoughts, and he didn't. When we reached the door, Bowers turned to me.

"I need a favor."

"A favor? You interrogate my aunt and then expect a favor?"

"It's a small favor."

"How small?"

When he didn't answer, I thought of the last time he asked me for a favor, and I think I blushed.

"Don't tell me you need a date, because I'm not up for it." When Bowers needed someone to hang on his arm at a fundraiser, I'd agreed, but only after I heard La Hacienda Chop House was catering. I desperately wanted to try their sautéed-onion-and-blue-cheese-smothered steak.

He took my hand in his, and we walked to his car. "It wasn't so bad, was it?"

Remembering my disappointment that night, I pulled my hand away. "They served fish. How can a chop house serve fish? You owe me a steak."

"That's all you remember from that night?" He raised his brows, a smirk on his lips. Those same lips had delivered a pretty good kiss that night. My face warmed at the thought.

"The only thing of importance," I said.

He unlocked the door and pulled out a humongous yellow object that he held by a handle at the top. "This is Petey."

"What's that?" I knew what it was, but I hoped I was mistaken.

"A birdcage. Petey lives inside."

"What am I supposed to do with a bird? I know nothing about birds. I don't think I even like birds."

"Mr. Jenkins is in a depression right now. He's not capable of looking after Petey. It's just for a day or two."

Reluctantly, I reached for the cage, but Bowers insisted on carrying it back to the house for me. I couldn't credit his insistence to gallantry; his tightened grip on my hand made me pretty sure he wanted to ensure the package was delivered.

He handed off the cage with mumbled thanks. Hoping that Petey had transformed into a little green parakeet, I lifted the cover. The huge feathered monstrosity from the *Blue-Ribbon Babes* premiere glared at me from two shiny black eyes and squawked. It couldn't form intelligible words, not having lips, but it definitely sounded like my cat Emily if she ran around screaming at a sharp, ear-splitting volume.

"Meow! Meow! M-e-o-w!"

The memory of the last time I'd heard that squawk gave me the chills. I dropped the cover, and the bird went silent.

"Is this a joke?"

"Nope."

It dawned on me there may be more to Bowers' move than a grab for free pet sitting. I could hardly bring myself to ask. "Did you bring Petey here so I could read him?"

He took a step back and swore. "No!" He shook himself off as if he'd been temporarily infected by cooties. "Just keep an eye on the bird until Mr. Jenkins feels up to taking him back."

"Bowers!" I grabbed his arm as he attempted to leave. He shoved his hands in his pockets, probably an offensive move to make certain I didn't get any ideas about tossing him the cage and slamming the door on him.

"You didn't say. How was Elvira Jenkins killed?"

"She was hit on the head with Betty Hernandez's cast

iron skillet. We found the weapon right under the counter where it belonged. No fingerprints, naturally."

Burnt cornbread. Bashed brains. That skillet had a lot to answer for.

A black-and-white blur shot through the living room. Emily stood under the cage, her hackles up and her mouth open as if she had just hit the jackpot. Bowers made his escape. I could still hear his laughter after I closed the door.

I left the birdcage on the coffee table and headed for a confrontation in the kitchen. As I cleared the last dishes from the table, I put together my approach. Antagonizing Auntie wouldn't get me far.

From the corner of my eye, I noticed Chauncey creeping past me, his cheeks bulging.

"Stay!"

He reluctantly complied, his front paws stepping side-to-side like one of those bears trapped in a tiny zoo cage.

"I told you not to give him the bones."

"Let him enjoy himself," Auntie said. "You worry too much."

I held out my hand. "Drop it."

He refused to give up his prey, so I wrapped one arm around his thick neck and pushed in on his cheeks behind his back molars. He clamped down harder. Snatching a leg bone from my plate, I waved it under his nose. Greed kicked in, and he dropped the first bone to claim the new prize. When I pulled them both away, he gave me a disgusted look and slunk away, defeated.

I tossed the bones into the wastebasket, plugged the sink, and turned on the water. "You didn't tell me you went to high school with Elvira Jenkins."

Auntie dumped the unscraped dishes and silverware into the sudsy water.

"You just threw knives in my water."

"They sink to the bottom," she said. "Just don't make any sudden grabs."

"Back to Elvira." I reached into the water, gently, pulled out a dish, and scrubbed.

"You heard what I told that pleasant officer. It's been a long time. I don't kid myself that I'm the same person I was back then. She wasn't either."

"You want to tell me you had no idea who she was when she walked out on that set?"

Rather than answer, Auntie started drying for me. "Remember when you were a little girl and used to have sleepovers at my house? And we'd bake cookies, and I'd tell you ghost stories?"

I smiled at the memory. "Those were good times."

"They were, but it's still not a good idea to live in the past." And with that cryptic advice, she kissed my cheek and left me to finish washing up. She only made it as far as the living room.

"Sissy!"

I dropped the dishrag and ran to join her. Emily was sprawled over the top of the bird cage, as if calling dibs on the contents.

"What is that?"

"Elvira Jenkins' bird, Petey."

Her eyebrows rose a fraction. "Couldn't B—I mean, doesn't she have a relative to care for the poor little critter?"

"Apparently not. Her husband is distraught, and I don't know if she has other family."

Her eyes misted up as if she were remembering the loss of her own spouse. "It's a kindness to help people out during hard times."

Obviously, the advice only applied to me, because she headed into the bedroom with Chauncey close on her heels.

Though I couldn't very well ask my aunt to sleep on the couch, I was starting to regret giving her my bed. Chauncey abandoned me in a heartbeat, which I expected, but even Emily, after a last longing look at the cage, scurried along to make certain she claimed a good sleeping spot.

I moved the birdcage to the center of the coffee table, cautiously lifted the cover, and stared into two beady eyes. Someone had murdered Elvira Jenkins. I could reach out my fingers and touch her pet, a pet that had been on the set the night she died. Since I'd already received an impression from Petey, I knew I might be able to take the smallest peek into his head and discover something about Elvira's murder, but I was determined to try any other available options first.

The bird could talk. Maybe his vocabulary extended beyond Meow.

"Petey." I snapped to get his attention. He clacked his beak shut as if to make certain I knew his favorite snack would be my fingers.

"Elvira," I said, slowly.

He turned his head sideways, giving me one eye, which was so coquettish that it made me laugh. "Meow."

Most people didn't refer to themselves by their Christian names when addressing their pets. They used a typical nickname. Maybe he didn't know his pet parent by Elvira.

"Mommy."

"Meow."

I curled my fingers, made a face, and growled. "Killer."

"Meow."

I recalled a time when I ran across a family from Mexico who needed directions to Phoenix. We crossed the language barrier through an impromptu game of charades. I retrieved a skillet from my kitchen. I didn't own cast iron, so I settled for aluminum. With an exaggerated stalking walk, I passed his cage and then swung the skillet at an imaginary head.

The bird let loose a squawk and flapped his wings. I'd gotten the message across to him, but it was clear he didn't have the words in his repertoire with which to answer me. I was going to have to go in and fish the information out manually.

After a steadying breath, I reluctantly imagined a large, solid door. This was my mental barrier against animal messages, which I hadn't opened since the end of the Margarita Morales investigation. It was a hokey idea, but it worked. Usually.

I allowed it to open, just a crack, just enough to let Petey's thoughts through, if he had any. Immediately, a steady hum throbbed in my ears. Animals give off energy signatures that often sound like various hums that changed in volume, pitch, and intensity, depending on the subject. The combination of energy signals from many animals comes together into a kind of white noise until I focus on a particular one. That buzzing sound used to be my constant companion until I learned how to block it out with a mental image of a door and an imaginary radio dial that allowed me to tune in or turn off the noise.

As I concentrated all my energy on Petey's little birdbrain, I caught sight of my reflection in his shiny metal food dish and lost my focus.

Bowers once mentioned I made faces when I concentrated. He was right. How embarrassing. What I saw in that reflection—scrunched-up eyes, wrinkled nose, a curled upper lip—was reason enough to give up psychic readings.

Refocusing on the door, I called out to Petey and waited

for some kind of response. I considered opening the door wider but dismissed that idea as foolish. Who knew what else might come barging through?

After a few minutes of heavy concentration, I gave up. Dumb, dumb, dumb. Opening that mental door was a good way to get involved in something that should fall to the police. Not to mention I might see something gross. And what would I tell Bowers? The bird says the murderer is Donna Pederson. Arrest her. That wasn't going to fly. I'd just wind up frustrated and paranoid and annoyed.

I reached for the cover, and the door image crept back into my head. It came to my attention in the same way that it might catch the eye if, while trapped in a decrepit mansion on a stormy night, the door handle to an empty room turned.

A light began to build around the doorway. As it grew brighter, I found it hard to breathe. I looked the bird in the eyes, imagined him behind that door, and invited him to tell me anything he knew about the murder. I threw in an image of dead Elvira just to make sure he understood.

Silence. The light dimmed.

My shoulders relaxed with relief. It wasn't going to work. Not surprising, as I'd never tried to read a bird before. They were supposed to have tiny brains. Maybe there wasn't a lot going on in his noggin. Or maybe Petey had nothing to say.

I reached for the cover, intending to put Petey to bed, when I felt a rustle in the air. A flutter really, like a bat, or a sparrow, or an enormous moth. Instinctively, I swatted the air around my head, just in case something had slipped past the screen door and intended to take up residence in my hair.

A train-like roar of "MEOW!" blasted through the room

and sent me flying back onto the couch. My head connected with the wall, and I saw stars. I clutched at the cushions and hung on for the next round, breathing hard, but nothing happened.

That was it. I'd made a connection only to find that Petey had an obsession about mimicking cats.

"I'm trying to sleep in here," Auntie yelled from my bedroom. "What are you doing? Rearranging furniture?"

I croaked out, "Sorry!"

The first thing I did when I caught my breath was to slam that stupid mental door shut. I'd never learn. Just a peek inside Petey's head. What was I, a moron?

Rising cautiously, just in case there were leftover vibes, I threw the cover over Petey's cage and set about making up the couch. Not that I was going to get much sleep. Not only did I have a dead woman's bird in my living room, but I was getting the impression that Auntie was holding something back.

What did my aunt have to hide? That very disturbing question kept me awake long past midnight.

SEVEN

At six a.m. the next morning, I woke to the incessant ring of my telephone. I rolled off the couch, smacked my knee on the coffee table, then lurched into the kitchen, almost tearing the phone off the wall when I answered.

Only one person would call me this early—a time-zone challenged woman from Wisconsin.

"Hello, Mother."

She didn't waste time with niceties. "Why are the police asking me about your aunt? What have you done to her?"

"I haven't done anything!" That sounded too much like my childhood mantra, so I assumed a grownup voice and asked, "Why do you ask?"

"A Detective Bowers called." She paused. "He was very polite." If Charles Manson had shown up at my parent's door, a swastika clearly carved in his forehead but uttering please and thank you, Mom would have given him the benefit of the doubt.

That was a dirty trick, calling my mother. I'd let Bowers

know what I thought of him next time I saw him, but for now, I needed to focus on damage control. What bits of information had he wheedled out of my sweet, unsuspecting mother with his manipulative manners and false charm?

"What did he want to know?"

"Nothing important, but that's not the point. He was the—" she lowered her voice to a whisper, "police."

Mother loves the police. She cries when anything in uniform passes during a parade—even the scouts—but her experiences so far have been limited to admiration from afar.

I repeated my question for the third time, taking the roundabout way.

"Martin Bowers is a friend of mine."

"Oh. I didn't know that. Martin is a nice name."

"So, what did the two of you chat about?"

She immediately responded. Chatting was something upstanding people did with neighbors and family. Chatting didn't have nefarious connotations.

"This and that. Nothing worthwhile that I can see. He wanted to know about the bust-up between your aunt and Elvira Doud, but that's old news."

"She married. She's Elvira Jenkins now."

"How nice."

Elvira. Auntie had known the victim well enough to have a bust-up, the little liar. Worse, Bowers knew she knew. The bright side, I supposed, was that I knew he knew she knew.

"Bust-up? There was a bust-up?"

"Everyone knows about that! The entire town had bets on who'd lose the first tooth. Those girls were sturdy country girls, and when you steal someone's boyfriend using their own Lemon Blueberry Buckle recipe, well, Elvira was just asking for it."

Lemon Blueberry Buckle. Elvira won the *Blue-Ribbon Babes* competition with a Lemon Blueberry Buckle recipe. Once I started breathing again, I repeated it back. The whole scenario sounded unbelievably stupid.

"Elvira Jenkins, I mean Doud, stole Auntie's Lemon Blueberry Buckle recipe and used it to steal her boyfriend? That sounds like a bad Debbie Reynolds' film."

"Debbie Reynolds didn't make a bad film. And then that nice man, Martin, asked me if your aunt kept in contact with Elvira over the years."

I noted that he was no longer the police.

"I debated over telling him about the letters," she continued, "but it's really not fair to hold things back from an officer of the law."

"Letters?" I whispered, clutching the counter for support.

"Oh, you know. Just nasty things that Gertie needed to get off her chest. Eighteen-year-old girls are so unstable, what with hormones." She whispered the last word. "Though it would have been better if she had burned them instead of mailing them. I don't know how many made it through after Elvira left Loon Lake. The post office forwarded them for a while, but then they started coming back, unopened. How long does a forwarding order last?"

"So, Aunt Gertrude drove Elvira out of Loon Lake with a campaign of harassment?"

"Don't be silly."

Silly? I thought it was a pretty practical conclusion.

"She left for love. She followed what's-his-name after he joined the Army, or Navy, or some branch of service. The boyfriend. They all called him by some nickname that didn't make sense to me. Of course, I never did get most jokes."

"Anything else?"

"I don't think so."

I gave her a minute to scan her memory banks.

"You never told me," she said. "Why did Martin call me in the first place?"

I'd been hoping that Mom had forgotten that little point. I wished I could lie to my mother, but it seemed cruel to keep her out of the picture, especially if Auntie was about to be hauled in for murder.

"Elvira may have died."

"Oh, dear."

"It might have been murder."

There was a pause. "Did Gertie do it?"

"Mother!"

"It's better to face these things. If you went to Mass once in a while—"

There was a rustle from the direction of my bedroom. "Auntie's awake. Do you want to speak to her?"

"Just tell her I'm setting the prayer chain in motion. I don't know what Father Jakius is going to say. I've still got him praying for you."

I heard my mother yell "Albert!" as she hung up the receiver, which coincided with Auntie's morning descent on my kitchen.

Why hadn't Bowers mentioned the murder to my mother? What reason had he given for his phone call? My mother was an innocent; she'd never question why a police officer would be calling her about someone she knew. Or at least she would be too polite to voice her question out loud.

Auntie shuffled into the room in her bathrobe and fuzzy pink slippers and rubbed the sleep from her eyes. Even though she resembled an oversized four-year-old, I decided it was time to have a grownup conversation.

"We need to talk," I said.

"Hmmm."

While Auntie set about making coffee, I pulled a chair out from the kitchen table, sat down, and crossed my arms.

"You forgot to mention to Bowers that you knew the victim. Knew her really, really well."

"Elvira? I told you. That was a long time ago."

"There is a big difference between I haven't seen the victim in years and Who??? You deliberately mislead the police." Lied to would have been a better word, but there are some things you can't say to your aunt, though that boundary of respect was crumbling fast.

I jumped up and paced the kitchen floor. "And what about the Lemon Blueberry Buckle? She won the Blue-Ribbon Baking competition with your recipe. You want to tell me that didn't make you mad enough to kill her?"

"Not my recipe, I can assure you. Did you see the face Heather Ozu made when she tried it? If Elvira had stuck to my recipe, that little host would have gone to Heaven."

"Instead, Elvira's the one who took a trip to the Pearly Gates."

"You're making a big deal out of nothing."

I put a hand on her shoulder and leaned my face close to hers. "Hate letters aren't nothing."

She shrugged my hand off. "Oh, those. A childish thing to do, but I was only seventeen at the time. Maybe eighteen."

"What did you say in them?"

"It's embarrassing. I'm sure I used a few naughty words. And I think I mentioned that I'd like to stab her eyes out. Or kill her. I can't remember which one."

I stared at my aunt in her voluminous, high-necked white nightgown, with her long, graying hair hanging down her back in a single braid. Her pink, fuzzy slippers. Except for the slippers, she could have stepped out of a wholesome television program, like *The Waltons*. Was this woman capable of carrying out her threats decades later? Was Mom right? Did Gertie do it?

She pointed at my kitchen clock. "Don't you have to get ready for Penny?"

I couldn't bring myself to ask Auntie if she had done away with her rival. Mother always told me that the state of ignorance, though not bliss, was still a pretty nice place to hang out in. In this instance, I agreed. And I was a coward. Instead, I showered and then picked out a nice top to go with my jeans. Today was dress shopping day. Though it might not be my idea of a good time, it was an important part of the wedding ritual.

When my friend arrived with a big goofy grin on her face, I invited her in with the girlish giggles and enthusiasm I felt the occasion warranted. Then I noticed the gigantic binder in her hand and considered changing into military khakis, because my dear friend had come prepared to divide and conquer.

Penny had armed herself with cutout pictures of dress styles and swatches of her favorite colors, all neatly laid out in an album. This was going to be a long day.

"Who's that?" She wiggled her fingers at Petey's cage, which still sat on my coffee table.

"Petey. I'm, er, pet sitting."

"What a cutie! You're a big cutie, Petey."

She made a few kissy noises. Petey rewarded her with a snap at her fingers. She took a step back and gave him her sternest look, which had all the severity of a miffed kitten. I wasn't fooled. Penny grew up on a farm where everyone—human or animal—was expected to earn its keep. Frugal by necessity, farmers couldn't afford pity for problem pets.

"I wonder if he would taste like chicken?" she wondered aloud.

"No eating the guest," I said. Then I asked Auntie, "What are you going to do while I'm gone?" It wasn't a pleasant request for information but a demand, like asking a criminal to check in with her parole officer. Penny gave me a surprised look that said I shouldn't talk to my elders in that tone, but Penny didn't know Aunt Gertrude like I did.

"Browse online with your computer. Maybe send some emails. Read a bit. What I usually do when I'm at home in Loon Lake."

"You're sure you don't want to come with us?" Penny had already made the offer several times.

I seconded the motion. "I could keep an eye on you that way."

"This should be girl time for the two of you. After all, once Penny is married, you'll hardly see anything of each other."

Auntie let that depressing thought hang in the air, and I made a silent vow to forget my worries and have a good time today. I didn't have to keep that promise for long. I'd just secured my seatbelt buckle when Penny poked my arm, hard.

"Ow, Miss Boneyfingers. That hurt!"

"When were you going to tell me about the murder?"

"You've known all this time?" First, I felt a wave of relief; then I felt guilty, because the relief came because I hoped the topic of murder would kill Penny's mood for dress shopping.

"It's all over the paper. And the television news." Her

blue eyes widened with excitement, and she clutched my arm. "Holy moly. Did you actually see the body?"

"I threw up right next to it." I said this with the same misplaced pride that one might have when announcing a celebrity sighting.

"That must have been awful." Her shoulders shook with a shiver. "Did you want to talk about it? Are you up for shopping?"

Here was my shot at getting out my commitment, but what kind of friend would I be if I accepted her offer?

"No," I said, with a forced smile. "This is your day. We'll talk about it after we try on dresses."

"Are you sure?"

I was dying to share my news but, convinced that my motives were selfish, I kept my mouth shut. Unfortunately, since murder was on my mind, all my efforts to produce that giggling, joyous atmosphere that follows bridal parties like a happy cloud fell flat.

At Patsy's Prima Donnas, the only Wolf Creek bridal shop, I was forced to squeeze into a floor-length spandex dress in ocean blue. The color reminded me of *Blue-Ribbon Babes* and murder. For a moment, I was lost in memories of Elvira Jenkins lying dead on a rubber kitchen mat. Then I caught a glimpse of my reflection in the three-way mirror and gasped in horror.

"I didn't know I had bulges." I turned side to side. "How did I get a bulge there?"

Penny handed me a billowy off-white jacket that covered up the sore spots, so I didn't go into apoplexy when she added the dress to her list of favorites.

The bride-to-be wasn't having as much luck.

Penny has an adorable figure, so the fault didn't lie with the model. Her first choice, an angular style designed by a local seamstress, made her look as if she could cut a sheet of paper with her elbows.

"Maybe it's too modern," she sighed, frowning over her reflection in the mirror.

A tight silk number with fitted lace sleeves that draped at the ends made her resemble an angelic Morticia from The Addams Family, and a gauzy white dress with a black bow made her look like a present. A black-and-white present for a funeral. Like Elvira Jenkins' funeral.

Determined to push away thoughts about death, I grabbed a gown of fluff and feathers from the nearest rack and told her to give it a shot. Her lack of enthusiasm was justified when she stepped out from behind the dressing room curtain.

"You'd better stay away from my house until I get rid of the cockatoo."

"Ha-ha. It may be a joke to you, but you're not the one everyone's going to be staring at," Penny said. Her shoulders drooped. "This was supposed to be fun."

I attempted to lighten the mood with a jolly laugh. "Everyone has bad hair days. You're having a bad dress day." I escorted her back behind the curtain. While she changed into her street clothes, I slid my stretchy blue dress onto the return rack. "A good dose of chocolate will fix everything. We'll grab a shake from the Ice Cream Palace and take it to the park."

I really hate shopping, and I wasn't above bribery. "I'm buying. And while we're there, you make a list of everything you're looking for in a dream dress."

Penny pulled open the curtain. "I already have a list, silly. It's in the front section of my binder."

I pointed to the deadly elbow dress. "And that style made it to the favorites?"

"I was experimenting. I thought I could surprise Kemper with something unexpected." She lowered her voice. "Maybe even shock him."

"If you come down the aisle looking like Big Bird's relative, he'll certainly be surprised."

After an eye-roll to show my humor wasn't appreciated, she trotted out to let the owner know we would be back.

It started to drizzle, so we skipped the park and opted for U Behave. One thousand calories later, we sat on the empty counter in my shop, feeling the burn of ice cream eaten at breakneck speed. At least I felt that way. Penny had gotten a small, fat-free yogurt, citing a wedding dress diet.

The ice cream almost took the edge off the depression that came from sitting in the vast wasteland of my store. Maybe Auntie was right. I should branch out and sell treats and leashes and those ridiculous cubic zirconia-studded collars on the side. And maybe I could think of satisfied clients and hang photos of their pets up on the walls. Okay. I had one satisfied client who was more like a friend. She had a shih tzu named Cake, who I might be able to disguise and pass off as several small breeds. Or would that be illegal, as in false advertising?

"Enough about my problem." Penny scraped up the last bite of yogurt. "Let's talk about yours."

Intending to give her a rough draft, I didn't stop until Penny had heard every grisly detail. She listened with full attention, hands folded neatly in her lap, and when I finished, she poked me in the ribs.

"I can't believe you waited this long to tell me! We're supposed to be best friends."

"It was your moment," I said, repeating Auntie's phrase. "I didn't want to spoil the wedding glow with news of a corpse. I thought I could hide it from you for a little while."

"Fat chance."

Penny slipped out of the room and returned with *The Wolf Creek Gazette*. Today's front-page photo was the one of Bowers and me taken on my front stoop last night along with the story of how we were working together on the investigation.

"He's still handsome as ever," Penny said with a grin, but my focus wasn't on him. My upper lip was drawn back and my eyes squinted shut against the camera's flashbulb, but Bowers looked perfectly handsome, as if he had posed for the shot.

"How can they turn this stuff around so fast?" I moaned. "Bowers is going to kill me. But it's not my fault. If he hadn't come by to question Auntie—"

Penny gasped. "Question your poor aunt? Why?" Penny put a hand to her mouth and half closed her eyes in thought. "You said Elvira Jenkins was from Loon Lake. I wonder if she had anything to do with the old Jenkins Farm out on Hart Road."

"There's an old Jenkins Farm?"

My family lived in town; Becky's family farm was on the rural outskirts, but still. I knew the Oberweis family raised goats and sheep. The Kruger's had a dairy farm, and I knew the old gentleman with the corn field. His name wasn't Jenkins. Loon Lake wasn't big enough to hide an entire farm from me.

"How did I not know this?"

"Everyone in Loon Lake calls it the Crawley's Place, but my grandfather was friends with old man Jenkins. We always thought of it as his property, even after he passed on."

I felt better. I knew the Crawley Place.

"The point is Bowers questioned her, and she

pretended she didn't know Elvira. Why would Auntie lie about it?"

"Older people forget things all the time. I have an uncle who calls me Whatsyerface."

"You mean my aunt forgot her entire youth? Give me a break. She fought with the victim over some man."

"How romantic," Penny cooed. "Poor thing. She must be so shaken up from losing a friend. You've got to look out for her."

"It would help if she told me the truth. First, Auntie says she doesn't know the woman, but it turns out she went to school with her. Small oversight due to an aging memory, right? Like maybe Elvira was the quiet kid in the back of the room who never talked, the one nobody remembers? And then I find out the two of them fought the fight of the century, which included Lemon Blueberry Buckle, serial hate letters, and betting between the townsfolk over who would win."

"Hate letters? Lemon Blueberry Buckle?" Penny gave a nervous giggle. "I'm sure you're exaggerating."

"Let's just say it was one of those days that Auntie wouldn't likely forget."

"The two of them made up a long time ago, I'm sure."

Penny sounded more hopeful than certain. She hates it when people hold grudges, or sulk. I tried to soften my response.

"Um, maybe they didn't get the chance, because Elvira moved away not long after. But you have to at least agree that Auntie would remember her sparring partner."

"It's been over fifty years," Penny reasoned. "While high school doesn't seem that long ago to us, maybe your aunt really did forget. She's been married and widowed since then and raised three boys. Anyway, the answer always lies with the victim, right?"

"I know zilch about Elvira Jenkins."

Penny licked the back of her spoon several times, which reminded me of Chauncey licking his empty food bowl, hoping for one last morsel. I handed her the remains of my shake.

"It's just a dribble. Not even a hundred calories worth."

She only hesitated two seconds before grabbing my cup.

"The thing that worries me is how quickly Bowers found the connection between Auntie and Elvira Jenkins and that he found it worth asking about. Then, like an idiot, she lied to him, which wasn't smart. It will only make him more interested than he already is."

Penny waggled her spoon at me. "Or she just forgot about Elvira. It may be that simple."

"Whatever her reason, Bowers is now focused on Auntie's connection to a murder victim. I don't like it."

"I'm sure he was just tying up loose ends."

"No." I shook my head. "It wasn't like that at all." I remembered the way he kept studying her and thought of the way a dog reacts when you wave a tennis ball in front of his face. His gaze locks onto it. You could dance a jig and holler his name over and over, but his attention would stay riveted on the toy. That's how Bowers looked. Like he had a new toy that he wanted to rip to pieces.

I clutched Penny's arm. "Bowers wants to rip my aunt to pieces!"

Penny cocked her head, a thoughtful expression on her face. "I'm sure you're wrong about that, but it is kind of nerve-wracking to know that the police are interested in your aunt. Because some of them—not Bowers, of course—might not give your aunt the benefit of the doubt."

"Gutierrez." The name shot out in a whisper of reverence and fear. "That woman doesn't like me. And she's the one who interviewed Auntie right after we found the body. They were in a different room, so I have no idea what my aunt might have said." I slammed my fist into my open palm. "She should have had an attorney! They might have tricked her into incriminating herself. How else would Bowers have found out about Auntie's previous relationship with Elvira?"

"I thought you said Bowers and Gutierrez were competing for the same promotion. Why would they help each other out?"

I tried to keep my voice steady. "What if they were willing to work together to solve the murder? What if they were ordered to? The news outlets have been making a huge deal out of the story."

"True. It's got something for everyone. Murder. Celebrities. Baking."

"What if there's pressure on the police to come up with a culprit? What if my aunt is the easiest target?"

Penny gasped. "Oh, my gosh. She could go to prison." She turned an unusually serious gaze on me. Unusual for the typically upbeat Penny, that is. "Frances, you can't let that happen."

I rubbed my temples to fight off a growing headache. "How can I help my aunt if she keeps lying to me?"

"Well, what do you know about Elvira Jenkins?"

"It's easier to list what I don't know. I don't know who benefits from her will; I don't even know if she had anything to leave. Maybe the house and bank accounts are in her husband's name."

"So, she had a husband? That's good information."

"I don't know if she had enemies, or if she was the best

loved woman in Fountain Hills, or in Loon Lake, if the crime is related to her past. The only thing I do know is that Auntie knows more than she's telling."

"Are you sure? It doesn't sound like there's anything left to hold back."

"Which makes it worse. What evil thoughts lurk in Auntie's brain? She lied about knowing the victim, and she lied about their fight." I snorted. "Did I mention the fight involved a Lemon Blueberry Buckle recipe? Doesn't that sound like a bad Debbie Reynolds film?"

"Debbie Reynolds didn't make a bad film."

No wonder Penny got along so well with my mother.

"What other little surprises could there be?"

Penny made loud sucking noises as she pulled the last bits of shake through the straw. "Your aunt is a sweetie. She wouldn't kill anyone. You need to forget about her and concentrate on the real suspects. For instance, the other contestants might have resented her winning the prize."

"Kill someone to be Blue-Ribbon Queen?"

Two thousand dollars wasn't anything to sneeze at, at least not for me, but would anyone permanently eliminate the competition for that amount? And though I hadn't heard of the show until Auntie invited me to the premiere, there might be bakers out there who considered an appearance on cable television a serious honor. I considered the mentality of someone who labored over recipes, trying to get just the right mix of spices and texture, all for a blue satin ribbon. It suggested a touch of insanity.

"And you said she fought with the host."

"But that's the kind of spontaneous thing that makes you whip out a gun and kill someone right then and there. By the time you lured someone to meet you and kept the appointment, you'd probably be back to your senses and just toss around a few insults." I snapped my fingers, certain I had a brilliant idea. "Now if one of the sponsors killed her because they thought they'd lose sales..."

Penny giggled. "Kind of a warning against anyone else who might downplay their products."

"Yeah. It's a stupid idea. The damage was done."

"But what if one of the sponsors pulled out of future shows? Wouldn't the producers be mad?"

"Back out within an hour of the show's airing? It *could* happen."

Penny hopped off the counter and dropped our empty containers in a plastic trash can. I didn't have any products, posters or paraphernalia in my shop, but I did have a trash can.

"Okay, smarty-pants. Think back to that night. I bet you can come up with at least three suspects." Penny put her elbow on the counter and rested her chin on her palm.

"There's always the husband. He was there for the taping. In books, they always suspect the husband. If she has a son or a daughter-in-law or vise-versa, they might not have gotten along with her, but they would be used to her. Why suddenly snap that night?"

"You'd be surprised at how trying a man's mother can be," Penny muttered. "Sometimes it seems that nothing's good enough for her little boy."

"Are you speaking from personal experience?"

Penny made a face. "Forget the family members, especially the husband. That would be too much if someone she loved killed her. I mean, think about it. You stand up before God and your family and promise to love each other forever, and then the very man you would trust with your life kills you?" She clenched and unclenched her hands. "The person you starved yourself for so you could look good in your wedding dress murders you? The person you eat pizza with every Friday night even though you hate pizza? The person you—"

"Penny, calm down. You've got sweat on your upper lip."

She gave a nervous giggle.

"Are you okay? That was quite a rant, and it sounded a teeny bit personal. Has Kemper done something stupid?"

"It's just the breach of trust. I can feel it more, now that we've made a commitment."

I put my arm around her shoulder. "I'm sure I can think of non-relative suspects. There's the host, Heather. She was awfully mad. Elvira just stomped onto the set and took over the show. I almost felt sorry for her. Maybe she snapped." I raised my index finger. "And maybe there was a representative of Scotch Girl Flour there that night, or a Cocolite rep. Or maybe Elvira threatened to get a page fired or something. She sounded kind of bossy."

"It's too bad Elvira didn't have a pet," Penny mused.

"Funny you should say that." I made a face. "Bowers left me the victim's bird. You've actually met Petey, the cockatoo. I've got to take care of him until the husband is able to take him back. Petey was on the scene when Elvira Jenkins was killed."

Penny's chin slid off her hand. "Oh my gosh! Who is the murderer?" Of my puzzled look, Penny demanded, "You asked the bird who killed her, didn't you?"

"The bird told me nothing. Anyway, I'm through with pet readings. Remember what happened last time?"

"Frances! You can't deny your natural gift. And it's your duty to ask the bird!"

Gift. That's how Penny saw being assaulted by messages ranging from *My bowl's empty* to *There's a murderer in the house!* Not to mention the headaches, the hallucinations, and having no quiet time of my own.

"I already tried," I muttered.

"And?"

"A dismal failure. The only thing I learned was that Petey has a thing about cats. Big surprise, coming from a bird. Besides. I was warned to stay away from the investigation."

On cue, Bowers strolled up to the front door. He was on duty because he was wearing a sports coat, but he must not have had any important interviews, because he also wore jeans. As I unlocked the door and let him in, Penny grinned at me from behind the counter and then skittered back into the Prickly Pear like a coward.

He glanced around my empty store and smirked. "I thought I'd wait until the crowds died down."

"Ha-ha." I put on my best angry face: eyes narrowed lips pursed in disapproval. Then I unpursed my lips. I didn't want expression lines. "Why are you calling my mother? That's below the belt."

"I'm investigating a crime. No one is off limits, not even mothers."

"And now you're here to hassle me about my aunt. I've got nothing to say."

He leaned against the counter. "Now that you bring her up, tell me how long ago she decided to come visit you."

The question took me by surprise. "Since I can't read her mind, I don't know when she decided, but she let me know three weeks ago."

He blanched when I mentioned mind reading. It crossed my mind that a little peek inside his head might let me know how seriously he considered Auntie a suspect.

Maybe last night hadn't worked because I was

distracted by the conversation between Bowers and Auntie. It was worth another shot.

I looked directly into his eyes and took a deep breath. The last time I had a peek, it was unintentional. Maybe this time I could control it. Seeing inside Bower's head might be exciting. Or disappointing. He was an attractive man. What if he thought I was one step below chopped liver? Or what if he only tolerated me because he wanted information for the case? I relaxed and tried to imagine the information highway between his thoughts and mine, hoping that something would come my way.

"Don't even think about it."

"About what?"

"You were making faces."

Drat! "One day, I'm going to learn to control my expressions, and then you'll never know."

"Sure, I would."

That surprised me. "How?"

He actually blushed. "Because it kind of...tickled."

I probably shouldn't have thrown my head back and laughed so hard that every filling showed. Bowers pressed his lips into a thin line of disapproval and narrowed his eyes.

"It would be an assault on an officer. I could arrest you."

The thought of Bowers and me and handcuffs brought up a response that no good—or even average but trying to be good—Catholic girl should have, and I pushed the image away.

"If you're looking at premeditation, you're out of your mind. My aunt didn't even know the woman lived here. They hadn't even spoken since—" I thought of Auntie's little missives. "For a long time."

"You mean since your aunt's letter campaign of hate against the victim. And don't tell me you don't know what

I'm talking about. Your mother said she was going to call you as soon as we hung up."

Deciding this conversation could only get ugly—for Auntie—I set my jaw and clammed up.

"You might want to ask yourself a question, Frankie," Bowers said as he opened the door to leave. "Why did Elvira Jenkins invite your aunt to Wolf Creek?"

"How do you know she did? The invitation was from the Baking Channel."

"Each invite had a numbered code on it. Your aunt's number was a three. That means the Baking Channel got her name from contestant number three, Elvira Jenkins."

"Oh."

"And then you have to ask, why did your Aunt Gertrude come?"

"That was two questions."

"But they were good ones," he said, and then he shut the door.

EIGHT

After Bowers left, I grabbed my purse and locked up U Behave. Stepping out onto Maricopa Drive, I planned to go directly home to check up on Auntie, but at the last minute, I walked around the corner onto Main Street and past the Prickly Pear. As I swung open the door to Canine Camp, a cacophony of barks and whines greeted me. A young woman stepped out of the office, and when she saw who it was, she took a startled step back.

Charlie is Seamus' wiz bookkeeper. She's an accounting student at the community college, and her mastery of figures belies her young age and trendy looks. I'd never seen her wear anything but black, and her dark hair currently sported purple streaks that matched the amethyst stud in her nose.

When I said I was there to talk to Seamus, she shot a worried look toward the dog pen. Seamus stood inside the exercise area, and Bethany clung to his side like a Siamese twin.

Okay, maybe she didn't actually cling, but she was standing pretty close to him, shoulder's squared and confident. The animals loved her vibe, and they wriggled and grinned and begged for pets and kisses, which she doled out from an endless supply as if she were a doggie love fairy. Her calm expression reflected the patience of a mother, and there wasn't any doubt that she was at the top of the food chain. I bet that Chauncey wouldn't merely roll over and grunt if she asked him to get off the couch.

Maybe Charlie thought we'd have a cat fight. Hardly. It's not as if Seamus and I had gone on more than one date. Possibly two. And they weren't really dates. I'd been fishing for information about Seamus' best friend, a murder suspect at the time, so dinner qualified as work, except for that one goodnight kiss. But it was a nice kiss.

Seamus waved, and Bethany looked at me with interest. As they waltzed over, I turned my attention to the forlorn, brown eyes of the Jack Russell terrier on the other side of the fence. The breed is usually pretty peppy, but this little guy seemed lethargic. I reached my fingers through the wire to encourage him to come closer.

"That's our newest addition."

Seamus scratched the dog's ears. He held out a ball, and the canine cocked his head, his short tail wriggling. Seamus tossed the ball, and the terrier took off like a shot, beating two beagles and a boxer to the prize.

"Poor thing misses mommy," I said as I stood.

With Bethany at a safe distance retrieving the ball, Seamus leaned close to the fence, panic in his green eyes. "You weren't, I mean, you didn't—" He waved his hands in the air and rolled his eyes in circles. I hoped that wasn't an accurate imitation of what I looked like when he'd seen me read the golden retriever last month.

"No. I didn't. It's common sense," I snapped.

Bethany wandered back to his side, and Seamus introduced us with a fumbling awkwardness that made me certain the two were a couple.

"Bethany, I'd like you to meet Frances. She's, uh, we know each other from, that is—"

I took pity on him. It would take a master storyteller to explain his peripheral involvement in the investigation of Margarita Morales' murder, including our two non-dates, and Seamus wasn't gifted with a raconteur's tongue.

"I'm Frankie, one of the local shopkeepers. I was hoping for some advice. I'm pet sitting a bird, and I have no idea what to feed it or how to take care of it." It occurred to me that buttering up Petey with a favorite treat might make him more talkative. "Are they fond of a particular snack?"

"Didn't the owner give you instructions?" Bethany asked.

Ahh. The owner. How to avoid mention of the murder. "It was an emergency situation."

"What kind of bird is it?"

The question annoyed me. It was a simple and logical query, and I would have loved to have leaned casually against the fence and spouted off genus and species and blah-blah-blah, but all I had to offer was my ignorance.

"It's big and white with a terrifyingly large beak. And it has long feathers on the top of its head. And it's noisy. I think it's a cockatoo."

"Yes. A cockatoo." Bethany nodded. "They eat seeds, nuts, grains, and it might enjoy a little fruit."

She picked up on my relief and laughed. "Nothing live or wriggly."

"Bethany worked at an avian rescue," Seamus announced. His chest swelled, and his eyes shone, as if she had single-handedly saved a species from extinction.

"How nice. Do I, um, have to take it for walks or, er, let it fly around?"

Bethany's dimpled smile froze. "I wouldn't. You have to be careful. They have the intelligence of a four-year-old, and they can be, um, destructive."

I assured her I would keep my guard up and thanked them for their help, and then I turned and walked out. Once I made it around the corner, I leaned my head against the stucco wall. Do I take it for walks? I guess, if I had really tried, I might have been able to look like a bigger idiot. As it was, I had come off like the sidekick in Young Frankenstein.

"The brain came from someone named Abby Normal."

Speaking of abnormal people, it was time to check in with Auntie.

I wasn't in the best mood when I arrived home, which was why the whispers and giggles of conversation that came from the kitchen were as welcome as a case of mange.

The hearty tones with a country flavor belonged to my aunt, but I didn't recognize the second voice. It was light and breathy and prone to fits of giggles. I dropped my purse and the bag of bird food I'd picked up on the coffee table, nudged Emily away from my ankles, stepped over Chauncey's prone body, and eased my way through the living room, curious and suspicious. My fears were confirmed with my aunt's next statement.

"Ooh. The World. You couldn't ask for a better card. Something good is coming your way."

There was a combination gasp and giggle before the other woman spoke. "My niece—"

"There's definitely a woman indicated. Yes, definitely a female influence. A b—"

"A baby!" The woman squealed and clapped. "You're right! She's due any day and I'm so excited. Will it be a girl or a boy?"

Lowering her voice, Auntie said, "In my profession, I really shouldn't say this, but—" She paused for effect. "Isn't it much more fun when it's a surprise?"

This was followed by more giggling. "You're right. Don't tell me!"

As if Auntie had any idea of the child's gender. I debated whether to interrupt the love fest or wait until the visitor left before I read the riot act to my aged relative for violating house rules. My aunt had donned her professional persona, Madame Guinevere, and was reading the tarot cards.

As annoyed as I was that Auntie had usurped my authority in my own home, I admired her technique. Ever the pro, she had managed to avoid specifics. The more general the exchange remained, the bigger the chance there was for a believable and exciting prediction. And by just letting slip a "b", she'd allowed the client, believing Auntie was about to say baby, to fill in the facts. If that hadn't produced results, Auntie would have put on a thoughtful expression, as if consulting with her spirit guides, and then tried another letter.

"All I can say," Auntie continued, "is that you can expect something wonderful, and soon. Be on the lookout." She picked up the World card and handed it to her client. "You can keep this as a reminder."

I crept toward the doorway to get a peek, but Chauncey, sniffing around the bag of bird food, knocked my purse onto the floor and yelped with surprise. I ducked back into the living room, and cover blown, called out, "I'm home!"

When I walked into the kitchen, all signs of a reading

were gone. The petite client had the white, soft, curly hair of a bichon frisé. She wore a pink linen shirt and matching Capri pants and looked to be a thoroughly nice woman. Auntie loomed large on the other side of the table. She had donned her purple Muumuu, the one she always wore for readings.

Auntie and the woman looked up, as innocent as Emily after she's destroyed a stuffed animal.

"This is Sharlene Walker, your neighbor."

We exchanged greetings. "What are you ladies up to?" I slipped a peek under the table and eyed the closed cupboard doors with suspicion. Those cards had to be here somewhere.

"Sharlene was just admiring your—" Auntie scanned the kitchen looking for something to compliment.

"Your cups," Sharlene piped in, holding up her yellow mug. Realizing she held a Quickie Lube giveaway, she added, "Too many people agonize over the perfect pattern. It's refreshing to see a casual approach."

Auntie nodded approval and raised her Economy Mart mug. "And I'm proud that you support your local businesses."

"Er, thanks."

After an awkward silence, Sharlene rose, thanked Auntie for her hospitality, and said she needed to get home to make dinner for her son.

"He drops by once a week just to make sure I'm fine."

Once she left, Auntie was quick to criticize. "Acts like he's doing her a favor. He only lives a couple of miles away, and maybe if someone paid more attention to the woman who gave birth to him, he might notice a thing or two." She frowned. "That woman is in trouble."

"Did you do another reading? I told you—"

"I don't need the cards to tell me when someone's got problems."

"Problems? A pregnant niece is a problem?"

Auntie tsked. "If you only pay attention to people, Sissy, you can see a lot. We should have a party and invite all your neighbors. It would be fun, and you could get to know them."

"I don't want to know them. I'm not a people person."

"That's because you won't make an effort."

She let the subject drop, and I poured out food for my pets and then grabbed a handful of the nuts and seed I'd picked up on the way home. Cautiously lifting the cover just a hair, I fumbled with the door and threw the food into the dish, but I wasn't fast enough.

"Meow! Meow! Squawk!"

Emily growled a response but didn't look up from her dinner bowl.

As I dropped the cover back down, Auntie commented that the poor thing needed some sunlight. "There's vitamin C and D in sunlight. Or something that's good for you. And it must be so boring to look at the inside of a cage all day, especially since you keep throwing the cover over the poor thing."

"Tell you what. You let him out when I'm not here, but make sure you lock Emily in my bedroom first. I don't want to return Elvira's pet in pieces."

I remembered Bethany's warning, but dismissed it. How destructive could a four-year-old be?

"And make sure the doors are closed, because I don't think he'd come back if he got outside."

Meatloaf and green beans were on the menu tonight. Auntie had decided that my mustard yellow tray was a favorite serving dish, but I slipped a few paper towels under the main course and felt the odds of surviving lead poisoning turn in my favor.

"Did anyone else stop by while I was gone?"

"No. Were you expecting someone?"

"Not Bowers? Or Detective Gutierrez?"

"No one."

I pushed my meatloaf around with my fork. "So, did you remember anything else about Elvira that you should tell the police?" I peered up through my lashes.

Auntie chewed, a thoughtful expression on her face. Then she swallowed and said, "Not a thing." She sprinkled her green beans with pepper. "How did today go?"

I studied her for a moment. Her gaze was steady, her mouth relaxed, and she wasn't fidgeting. It didn't look like she was lying to me.

"Everything went fine."

While we ate, I updated Auntie on the hunt for Penny's wedding dress. She cooed and clucked in all the right places, and I was just about to forgive her for bringing murder into my home when she said:

"There's a wake of sorts tonight."

"A wake? Tonight?"

"The Baking Channel thought it would be nice to have a little get together in Elvira's memory, and they invited everyone from the premiere. It will give me the opportunity to follow up on some of those business cards I handed out."

"You plan to use a woman's memorial to network." I could feel my lips and eyes scrunch in disapproval. If Auntie stayed much longer, I was going to need Botox to get rid of the expression lines.

"Don't be naïve. I bet half the business that gets accomplished in this country takes place at funerals and weddings. People see folks they want to catch up with, there's usually alcohol to loosen up tongues, and they're feeling generous about life, especially at funerals."

I resigned myself to another trip to Saguaro Studios.

"So," I said casually. "Mom wanted me to ask. You didn't kill Elvira Jenkins, right?"

I would have felt better if she'd burst into protests and bluster. Instead, Auntie stared off into space and said, "Your mother always was a smart one."

I dropped my fork. "What's that supposed to mean?"

"She gets right to the point. And of course you told her I was with you all night and couldn't possibly have done it."

I remembered her stalking off when Elvira stopped by to chat. How long was she gone? I couldn't remember.

"Of course you didn't do it," I said, and I wished I felt the conviction of my words.

NINE

The Baking Channel employees had the good taste to swap out the reception room's 1950s kitchen decor for a somber color scheme. The gingham chair where I had sat waiting for Bowers had been replaced by a black leather armchair, and the couches were covered with black cotton cloth that tied together behind each piece of furniture in a gigantic, somber bow. On one wall, a large publicity shot of Elvira smiled down upon the room.

The pages, who made rounds with trays of beverages and hors d'oeuvres, wore black pants and white shirts. Heather Ozu had toned down the Florida orange look with a burgundy shirt-dress and matching four-inch heels. Her expression changed from boredom to sympathy whenever anyone approached her. The same young man who clung to her side at the premiere was back on duty, listening attentively when he wasn't rushing to keep her drink filled.

Donna Pederson, she of the gluten-free cookies, approached us as if she were the hostess of the event. "Would you like something to drink?" She wiggled her fingers and called, "Yoo-hoo!", and Linda the Page brought over a selection of lemonade or coffee.

"Where are your kids?" I asked Donna.

"There's a babysitting service at our hotel. I didn't think they'd enjoy this."

"Probably not."

"The Baking Channel is putting us up until the police say we can go home, which is lucky. I'd never be able to afford it myself."

"How long is that?" I asked, my gaze darting to my own houseguest.

Donna shrugged. "Until they say otherwise, which is inconvenient, but what are you going to do?" As Donna's mud-brown eyes opened wide in her best can-you-believe-this-is-happening expression, she couldn't keep her thin lips from curving up in pleasurable excitement. "I still can't believe it. A murder took place only a few yards from all of us while we celebrated the show's phenomenal success. A tragedy."

Auntie inadvertently hit on the source when she raised her lemonade and gave a toast.

"Here's to the Blue-Ribbon Queen."

Donna clutched my arm. "But that's just it. She can't be the queen anymore, can she?" Her eyes searched out Heather Ozu. "This isn't the right time to broach the subject, but shouldn't the Baking Channel appoint a new queen? And soon?"

I objected. "That might not be sensitive. Elvira hasn't even been buried yet."

"But it is! And it's smart business. Just think of the public's point of view. Every time they think of *Blue-Ribbon Babes*, they'll be reminded that the queen is a corpse! That's just depressing. The company nee-s to consider the repercussions that a dead queen, especially a murdered queen, will have on Jane Q. Public's perception of their company and the show. In this day and age, the American people need heroes. Live heroes!"

I wouldn't categorize the winner of a baking contest as a hero, but Donna had obviously given the subject serious thought. She might have a point, but her enthusiasm made me wonder, once again, if it would be worth murder to claim the title of Blue-Ribbon Queen and a $2,000 check. If she were the killer, there must be more to her motive.

"You're a nutritionist, right? I suppose if you had the title for your gluten-free baking it would help spread the word on healthy eating."

"You'll have to find another way to say your baked goods are flourless, because gluten free doesn't sound that tasty," Auntie said, with her usual tact.

"Technically, there are flours without gluten, but you're exactly right about people's perception being wrong, wrong, wrong." She jabbed a finger at Auntie and stepped forward so suddenly that my aunt took a stumbling step back. "Do you have any idea how many products have wheat in them? It's everywhere you look, and it's as insidious as carbon monoxide."

"Too bad you can't invent a gluten detector," Auntie said. "You might sleep better at night."

A fanatical light in her eyes, Donna launched into her stump speech for gluten-free goods.

"My dream is to open a bakery that people with celiac disease can be proud to call their own. For too long, they've been banished to small sections of the grocery store. For too long, they've been forced to bring little baggies of food to family celebrations. I want to free them from that unfair burden. I want them to come out into the fresh air and shop like normal people. I mean, just buying a birthday cake can be murder!"

Donna covered her mouth. "I didn't mean that."

She might not have meant to say it out loud, but the idea of murdering someone to get your dream bakery up and running was an even better motive for murder than a silly baking title. And having been a contestant on the show, she would know exactly where Betty's cast iron skillet would be placed after her cornbread segment, giving her a ready weapon.

"Why don't you let me see if your shop will be a success?" Auntie held up her tarot cards and told Donna to choose one.

"I don't believe in that nonsense. You make your own future through planning and hard work."

And murder? I wondered.

"A peek now might save you time later if the whole venture's going to flop."

Auntie doesn't appreciate criticism, and I knew Madame Guinevere was planning a particularly ominous combination of cards, should Donna relent, but the gluten-free baker missed the threat as she waved at Fiona Flynn and beckoned her to join our group.

"This is my new best friend," Donna said with a laugh. "She made me look so good the other night."

"It wasn't hard," Fiona said with a practiced diplomacy that would have gotten her a seat on the UN. If beauty perfection hovered so close to Fiona's fingertips, I did wonder why she couldn't spare some of that magic for herself. She currently wore a gypsy blouse in forest green, a jean skirt, and combat boots. Her bleached hair stuck out in a ponytail at the side of her head, like Chrissy from *Three's Company*.

"Do you work on all the Baking Channel shows?" Auntie asked.

"All of them." She blew her bangs out of her eyes. "Every—last—flipping, one."

I studied her—shoulders slumped, mouth strained around the edges from the effort of making it look as if it was a joke.

"You don't sound happy about it."

"I'm burning out. Let's face it. There's only one look the producers want for these shows, and it's pretty tame. I miss going crazy with colors, like zebra stripes or a bleached flower in the part of electric blue hair."

Her former clientele must have been circus performers.

"I don't think that would fly here," I agreed, "although Heather has those bleached bangs."

Fiona stuck her nose in the air. "Ms. Ozu goes to her own personal stylist. That's fine with me, because I've got bigger things in mind."

She couldn't keep the grin off her face, though she kept her voice cool and collected. "I'm going to open my own shop in Tucson. It's a college town. Young people are more experimental with their looks. I should fit right in."

With her bleached, dry locks, Fiona didn't strike me as having her fingertips on the pulse of Arizona's youth, but then how would I know? I hadn't qualified as a youth for many years.

"Can you afford to take the risk?" Donna asked. "It costs a lot to own your own place. Trust me. I've done all the homework, and the startup alone can drain your bank account."

"My grandmother left me some money."

"Your granny's dead?" Auntie clucked with sympathy. "I'm so sorry."

"That's okay," she said, averting her eyes. "She was old."

Her lack of sympathy startled me into blurting out, "Was this the same grandmother who generously took you into her home, so you could pursue a job at Saguaro Studios?"

She raised her chin to challenge my disapproving gaze. "Yeah. Her."

"Huh. That was sudden."

Something wasn't right. A few nights ago, Granny had been the key to Fiona's new life in Arizona, and today her death hardly made a blip on Fiona's emotional radar. I continued to stare.

"I'm sorry for your loss."

"Thanks." She was the first to blink, which meant I had the upper hand, and I took advantage of my position to work in a question about the night of the premiere.

"I meant to ask you. At the reception, you saw someone you knew. Who was it?"

Her face flushed a mottled red. "I was mistaken. I thought it was my former boss, but it wasn't."

She excused herself. Actually, she just turned and walked away. As I watched her leave, I spotted Linda the Page as she wandered the room with a tray of cookies, and I made a beeline across the room.

"Can I talk to you for a minute?"

"As long as we keep moving," Linda said. "We're short-staffed tonight."

I walked alongside her as she offered her tray to the guests we passed.

"You came up to Elvira and told her that she was wanted by the photographer."

"That's right."

"Who told you?"

"Jeremy." Off my puzzled look, she pointed out the young man who looked as if he were about to genuflect to the Baking Channel's star. "He's Heather Ozu's assistant, which means butt-kisser and slave. I wouldn't have his job for the world."

"Who told him?"

"I was offering drinks to the VIPs. Heather, Natasha, Jeremy—although he only thinks he's a VIP. There were family members. I just can't remember. But I'm sure if Jeremy was involved, then the order must have come from Heather Ozu."

Her face scrunched up. "Of course, if I'd known she was going to be murdered..."

"How could you know?" I snatched the last cookie from her tray. "Don't worry about it."

"Do you think the family blames me?"

She pushed her long hair behind her ear and blinked to hold back the tears. No kid should have to carry that kind of worry around.

"They don't. I'm certain." I gave her shoulders a quick squeeze. "You didn't do anything wrong. A determined murderer would have found another way to get Elvira onto the set."

That cheered her up. Now if only I could figure out a way to bring up the subject of murder to Jeremy.

I wandered back over to Donna and Auntie, because they were positioned a few feet away from where Heather Ozu held court with the show's director with Jeremy looking on and admiring, Natasha Young, and the producer, Bert Hamilton. I considered my approach. Should I rush in and intimidate them into answering me? Play dumb so they wouldn't suspect my crafty questions? Josh the truth out of them? Auntie solved my problem. She swept over and inserted herself into the conversation.

She held out her cards to Natasha. "Pick one."

Natasha was a nice person and a good sport, because she played along and picked a card. I listened closely. It's actually a pleasure to see Auntie at work. She's a pro at reading people. Heather and Bert looked on with amused expressions, and Donna and I both edged forward, which meant even the gluten-free baker was susceptible to the thrill of psychic phenomena.

"The Ace of Pentacles." Auntie shuffled it back into the deck.

If I were reading the cards for Natasha, I would take into consideration how focused and professional Natasha's behavior was on the set. I'd assume that she was looking forward to an upward career trajectory, and that *Blue-Ribbon Babes* wouldn't mark the high point on her reel.

"That's a good career card," Auntie said. "It represents new opportunities."

"Which could be good or bad," Natasha said. "Bad if it means the end of this show."

"Heaven forbid," Bert said, putting his hand to his heart for dramatic effect.

"This show is not going to end anytime soon," Heather said. "If anything, our ratings are going to skyrocket because of the extra drama."

Auntie leaned closer to Natasha. "But good if that means a new opportunity for you." She looked her up and down, trying to pick up clues. I followed her gaze and noted that Natasha wore a necklace of colorful paper beads, just like the ones they sold for charity. The director was a kind woman. Charms shaped like countries dangled from a silver bracelet. A stylistic choice? Or did Natasha dream of travel?

"Maybe this job was holding you back from your real purpose."

Natasha's gave Auntie a keen glance and murmured, "Now I wonder what makes you say that."

"I don't make these things up. The cards know. You just need a pro to interpret them for you. This is just a free sample. My usual readings are much more in depth. Pick another one and I'll fill in the details because I like you."

Natasha complied.

"There's more?" Heather rolled her eyes.

"Two of Wands." Auntie gave a brief nod. "You don't let things happen by chance. You've got goals. I see continuing education in your future as well as travel. Perhaps a job helping people."

Auntie hit home. Natasha's eyes opened wide, and then she grinned.

"That is so amazing! How about you Bert? Don't you want to find out what the future holds?"

"Why not?" He gamely pulled the Emperor card. "Does that mean I'll be in charge of the station someday?" He swept his arm to take in the room. "King of my castle? Where's my crown?"

He was making light of Auntie's prediction, but there's always truth to humor. I would focus on his desire to be at the top of his profession, if I were reading him.

"It definitely indicates a position of authority, and you'll have the respect of your peers."

His embarrassed laughter showed she scored another one.

"Heather?"

Auntie held out the cards. Heather opened her mouth

to say something but stopped. Her gaze went from the cards to Auntie's face, which was free of any expression.

"I'm sure Ms. Ozu doesn't need a fortune teller to guide her already stellar career path," Jeremy said, a condescending smirk on his lips.

When Heather's fingers dove into the middle of the pack, he changed his tune from apprehension to approbation. "Of course, it's all in fun."

He peered over her shoulders and looked at her choice. The Four of Cups, and it was upside down.

"Hmmm." Auntie held up the pack. "Want to pick another one?"

Heather held Auntie's gaze. "What's it mean? Not that I buy into magic."

My aunt gave a little sigh. "You may have missed an opportunity."

"What opportunity?"

Auntie pretended to give it some thought. "Maybe it's one you haven't heard of yet, like my little idea. It could save your show."

"The show doesn't need saving," Heather snapped, but her protest stopped there. Like any savvy businesswoman, she knew to listen to every idea, no matter how impracticable or foolish, and then discard the nonsense. Her eyes remained narrowed, and she spoke with the tone of a queen commanding the peon to share her side of the story. "Tell me what's on your mind.

"I'm well known for my talents with tarot, and I thought, well, wouldn't it be interesting if I read the cards for each guest on the show? Then you could follow up later to see if I was right. Short-term predictions, of course, and completely baking-related."

Well done, Auntie.

Heather sized up my aunt, probably evaluating her ability to draw revenue. "You're working with the police on the murder." She included me in this statement.

Jeremy gave a start, but since Heather didn't seem nervous, he held his place like an anxious hound on a lead.

"You're helping them?" Donna demanded. "How? Are you a professional?"

"We both are," Auntie answered without missing a beat.

"Interesting idea," Bert said, but he sounded amused. "We'd definitely have to get you a new publicity photo," he said to both Auntie and me, and then he tempered his laughter with a gallant bow of his head. "The picture in the Gazette doesn't do either of you justice."

Heather touched my aunt's arm in a business-friendly manner. "Why don't you stop by sometime and we can discuss it?"

"Probably won't happen. My aunt has to get back to Wisconsin," I said, hoping to crush Auntie's aspirations to be a public embarrassment.

"I at least have to stay for the funeral and pay my respects."

That was hard to argue, and it gave me another idea.

"You know," I said, "it was awfully nice of you to have this memorial. You must have gotten to know Elvira pretty well over the course of putting together the premiere episode."

Bert was the first to respond. "I don't think I'd say I knew her. I was there for the interviews, of course. She had a big personality, and it came across on camera when we tested her. Didn't you think so?" He directed his question at Natasha.

"Definitely," Natasha said. "We didn't really talk about anything personal, though. It was all about hitting her mark and finding the best angle to shoot her from. As for the memorial? I don't like social events, but tonight is different. A woman died on the set, and we all have to put on a united front."

"It's the right thing to do," Bert added. "The compassionate thing to do.

Natasha stuck out her chin. "I don't know that I'd take it that far. It's not as if we're doing it for Elvira." She motioned around the room. "How many people are here because they really cared about the woman? Heck, I wouldn't have recognized her on the street." She shook her head, looking a bit depressed. "Technically, this is another publicity event."

"I bet you got to know her pretty well," I said to Heather, "and even you, Donna."

Heather sipped from a bottled water. "I don't meet the guests until the show. It adds spontaneity, although with the way Elvira behaved, it would have been nice to have had a warning."

"She didn't behave well," I said with sympathy. "I would have been so angry if a contestant, lucky enough to be a guest on my show, said nasty things about the sponsors I depended on. How did Cocolite take it?"

"I understand their stock went up," Bert offered. "The buying public has the response instincts of a teenage girl. You say it's not good for them, and they've got to have it."

"That's a relief," I said, disappointed over another dead motive.

"We never really got a chance to chat," Donna said. "Before the show, I was pretty nervous, and then afterward, we took all these publicity shots. It was grueling, and I thought it would never end. By the time we finished, my girls were starving. I just had time to drop in at the reception for a quick hello before I took them back to the hotel for pizza."

Heather added, "I barely had a chance to snack on something before you discovered the body and the evening came to an end."

She made it sound as if the celebration of the year screeched to a halt because of my inconsiderate blunder.

I gave Jeremy my most innocent smile. "I heard the photographer asked you to find Elvira. You're the one who sent her to her death. Not intentionally, of course."

"Photog—Elvir—" All the color drained from Jeremy's face. He took a long drink from his water bottle, probably to gather his thoughts, because as soon as he drained the last drops, he said, "I didn't talk to the photographer."

"Then who told you to get Elvira?"

His glance moved from face to face, searching for the right answer. "I don't know. It just came up."

"But who brought it up?"

"I don't know. Someone."

It was tough on Jeremy, because if he named one of the three faces staring at him, he'd be fingering a boss, or at least management. I questioned them one at a time, starting with the nicest person in the room.

"Natasha?"

"I remember knowing that Elvira was wanted on the set by the photographer, but I can't tell you who told me."

"I remember hearing about it, too," Bert said.

"Do you remember who told you?"

He turned to Natasha. "Was it you?"

"Maybe," she said. "Now that I think about it, I heard it from Heather."

"If so," Heather said, "I was just repeating what I'd heard."

The killer had been clever. What do people do when they hear a bit of news? Repeat it. And gossip is very hard to trace back to the source.

Someone caught Heather's eye, and she excused herself, but not before Auntie pressed a business card on her, Natasha, and Bert. Jeremy bumped my arm as he skittered after his boss, and coffee splashed down the front of my blouse.

"Figures. It's dry clean." I dabbed at my front until my napkin was soggy. "I guess I should be happy it's not red wine."

"Try soda water."

The advice came from our friend from the premiere, Jane, and she looked as neatly pressed as ever, in a powder-blue cotton dress. She was followed by her neighbor Bea. The duo had become a trio, because the group now included Lola, who still wore enough jangling jewelry to arm an art fair. I thanked her, told Auntie I'd be right back, and headed for the exit that she said led to the restrooms.

I ran into another maze of temporary flats and wondered which direction to take. I headed left. The hallway took another left, and I could see where the passageway ended up ahead. There was an open door, and I stepped through and stared. I was back on the *Blue-Ribbon Babes* set. Yellow tape surrounded the kitchen, but everything else had been removed. The cameras were probably in use somewhere else, and the bleachers had been folded back up flat against the wall.

Anyone could have left the reception, killed Elvira, and then come back in, unnoticed. Should be simple to figure out, right? Why not start with everyone who used the facilities that night, since they could have followed the same route I just used? I imagined myself running through the reception, shocking people by asking, "Did you use the potty the night Elvira died?" Almost sounded like a 70s song title. I held back a giggle.

Rather than retrace my steps through the maze, I crossed the room and took the original route back to the reception room. An event of some excitement was taking place directly inside the door. People crowded around, and in the center of the pileup, I could see a white head of hair that stood taller than the rest—the cowboy who caught Auntie's eye during the taping. Next to him were a man in his thirties, the woman with the bright ginger hair, Mayor Haskins and his wife, Toni.

I'd hit it off with Toni when we'd met at a fundraiser for her husband last month. A quiet, friendly woman who abhorred the spotlight, she stood on the periphery of the crowd, so I made my way around and joined her.

"Frankie!" She brightened at the site of a familiar face. "Were you part of the studio audience, or did you know Elvira personally?"

"An audience member," I said, nodding to where Mayor Haskins was fending off the fans. "I don't remember seeing the two of you here that night."

"We weren't. We only came to the reception for Elvira's sake. Can you believe someone asked Mike for an autograph? It's highly inappropriate. I realize this isn't a wake, but shouldn't the focus be on the family and Elvira herself? We were afraid his appearance might detract from the solemnity of the occasion, but when they asked us to come, Mike thought we should, out of respect. Elvira volunteered on his campaign."

"Really?"

"She did a lot of volunteer work in the community—fundraisers and charity events. She dedicated a lot of time to prolife and anti-pornography causes. A really energetic woman. She'll be missed." Toni glanced at the smiling faces that surrounded us, chatting and laughing as if they were at a cocktail party. "Maybe not by anyone here, but definitely by those she helped."

"I wonder if she made any enemies." I wondered out loud.

"Unfortunately, I can't pick out just one. Elvira had been involved in protests for years, long before I knew her. People can get pretty riled up for their cause, so there probably were protestors from the opposing side who didn't like her."

"I'm only here because my aunt had tickets to the show. I didn't know the lady at all."

"It's such a shame. This tragedy comes at a time when the family was already in mourning." Toni motioned toward the woman with the red hair and lowered her voice. "That's Catherine, Elvira's daughter-in-law. She just suffered a miscarriage. Her second or third. It's so sad. She and her husband, Tim, desperately want a family."

I must have been staring, because Catherine's gaze met mine, and she wandered over and joined us.

"Catherine," Toni said, "I'd like you to meet Frankie Chandler, a friend of ours."

"I'm so sorry for your loss," I said.

"It's still too hard to believe," she said. "Elvira just wasn't the type to get murdered, if that doesn't sound too crazy."

Toni quickly said, "I know exactly what you mean. She had a strong personality. It's hard to believe anyone could get the better of her."

That reminded me of my aunt's sentiment when she heard I'd been involved in a murder. *We're not that sort.*

What kind of person did you have to be to wind up a murder victim? I decided that you'd simply have to make someone dislike you enough to want to eliminate you.

Up close, Catherine oozed Sex Appeal. Her thick, red curls broke free in spots from a classy French braid. Her chosen nail polish—a feminine, soft rose—made her long, slender fingers appear more delicate, and her skin, even though it was the pale coloring that so often goes with red hair, had a healthy, natural glow. The two-piece black suit accentuated her curves even though her white, lace blouse came with a high neck. It was an expensive suit, tailored to fit, and I wondered what profession would provide the perfect environment for the competent, feminine look.

I sucked in my breath as it occurred to me that she was dressed for Love Your Face success. Jennifer Peters, the woman who murdered her maid and almost killed me in my own home, was a Love Your Face rep. She had the same professional-yet-feminine look.

"What is it you do?" I blurted out.

Catherine blushed. "I haven't worked outside the home in many years, since before Tim and I moved here. We've been trying to start a family," her voice caught, and she took a steadying breath. "So I haven't taken on work. I'm grateful I don't have to."

"Grateful for what?" The man who'd been standing by the cowboy joined us, and by the way he wrapped his arm around Catherine's shoulder in a protective gesture, I assumed he was Elvira Jenkins' son, and I took a closer look.

A large man with the sturdy physique of a boxer, he wore his brown hair cropped short, and his dark hazel eyes, though surrounded by laugh lines, reflected the sadness of a basset hound.

"My husband, Tim," Catherine said. "I was just saying

how nice it is that, even in this economy, I can afford to stay home."

He rubbed her back, and his smile strained around the edges. "Why shouldn't you? Being a wife and—and a homemaker is a full-time job."

I thought he might have been about to say wife and mother, and I felt a twinge of sadness for him.

"What did you do before you got married?" I asked.

"Public relations." Catherine gave a wry grin to Toni. "Pretty similar to politics, actually."

Tim winked at her. "A lot of your clients were politicos, weren't they?"

Catherine shot him a warning look.

"Sounds exciting. Was that in Arizona?"

"Out east. And it wasn't all that exciting." She shot another look at Tim, and it sounded like a dig. "But I was good at it."

"The best," Tim said, and he kissed her cheek.

Her cheeks flushed. However, Catherine's blush wasn't a pinkish flush of pleasure and embarrassment that Regency romance readers would recognize with a sigh. This was the scarlet that accompanied unpleasant thoughts.

"My business was very successful until—" She took a quavering breath. "Then I met Tim and, well, things changed."

We suffered through an awkward silence, something I'm incapable of enduring.

"It sounds like your mother had a lot of energy." I said to Tim. A lame choice of words, but I thought it might move us back to safer topics.

Catherine answered for her husband. "That she had. It was always Elvira's way or the highway, but she always kept everybody's best intentions at heart."

I'd known people like that, and though I wouldn't want any of them to get killed, I wouldn't mind if they mysteriously evaporated.

"Why don't you come to our house this Thursday night?" The offer came from Toni. "Catherine and Tim will be there. It's a thank you to everyone who helped with Mike's campaign."

While she jotted the details on the back of a grocery receipt she found in her purse, the man with the white hair joined us. Catherine introduced him as Stan Jenkins, her father-in-law. I repeated my condolences.

"It's a shock," he said. His voice was surprisingly high and gentle for such a big man. Almost hoarse. Maybe he'd been crying over this touching tribute, but it didn't look like it. Eyes clear. Not shaky. Definitely recovered enough to take back his bird. I broached the subject in a roundabout way.

"You probably miss Petey."

His brows shot up. "I forgot all about that bird. Petey was Elvira's baby."

I cleared my throat. "He probably misses home. He's been squawking and talking nonstop."

"Talking?" Toni asked.

"Well, just a word here and there. Mostly about Emily, my cat. Meow, Meow, Meow!" I plastered on a grin to make sure Stan didn't think I was complaining. "Did you want him back yet?"

"You know, it would be a blessing if you could handle him for a few more days while I get my bearings. I don't feel anyone, including an animal, should have to depend on me right now."

His eyes moistened up, and I felt like a jerk for bringing

it up. "No problem. You just let me know when you're ready."

I dug through my purse to find a business card. "I've got my number right here."

A hand reached around me and held out a tarot card. "This has my cell phone number."

Stan took a step back, and his expression suggested the need for a shot of whiskey. "Gertie?"

Auntie broke into a huge grin. "Hello, Bull."

TEN

"You're going to have to talk to me sometime."

I swerved to avoid a jackrabbit and continued to drive in silence.

"It was such a surprise, seeing Bull after all these years." Auntie gurgled out a girlish giggle and reached up to pat her bun. "He said I hadn't changed a bit. I couldn't believe he even recognized me. I'm sure I've put on a little weight and there's gray in my hair. I never imagined in all my days that I would run into Bull Jenkins again."

"You knew perfectly well he would be there tonight. I saw you giving him the eye at the *Blue-Ribbon Babes* taping."

"I thought he looked vaguely familiar, but I couldn't place him."

"You knew he was Elvira's husband."

"How could I? I haven't seen her for years."

"Come on! Jenkins? A coincidence?"

"There are lots of Jenkins in the world."

"And you just happened to go to the mat over this particular one?"

"A long time ago, Sissy. How could I know they'd still be together? Once Bull left town to join the army, I never heard from him again. Elvira left not long after, and though I'm sure her intent was to harass him into marrying her, I had no idea how it all turned out."

"You're unbelievable. Admit it. As soon as you saw Elvira Jenkins walk out on that stage, you knew who she was, and you knew she married your old sweetheart. You probably knew it all along! That's why you flew all the way to Arizona to attend the taping of some lousy baking show premiere!"

She pressed her lips together, and a flush ran up her cheeks. "Sissy Chandler, you hold your tongue. How dare you call me a liar?"

I turned into the driveway and slammed the brakes so hard that we both lurched forward.

I turned sideways in my seat and looked directly into her pale blue eyes. Mother considered it possible that her sister had done away with her rival. Who would know Auntie better than her own sister?

"Tell me right now. When you disappeared to go to the washroom, were you really paving the way to become the next Mrs. Stan Jenkins?"

Auntie fussed with her seatbelt, but in her agitation, she couldn't unclip it. "I don't have to sit here and listen to this."

"Yes, you do, because you made a public spectacle of yourself tonight, and it's only a matter of time before Bowers discovers you lied to him about, well, about everything!"

"That nice young man? He couldn't think anything of the kind. I'm sure he recognizes an innocent person when he sees one."

"My mother—your own sister—thought you were capable of killing Elvira."

"That's because my little sister has always had a lot of faith in me."

I dropped back against the seat. "You're taking it as a compliment?"

She jerked at the buckle again, muttering, "Of course I'm capable. That doesn't mean I did anything about it."

Watching Auntie struggle with her seatbelt, the idea of her having the finesse to kill a person seemed stupid, and I felt the urge to laugh. This woman couldn't even get out of the car, and here I was accusing her of having the stealth to murder a woman not fifty yards away from an entire room of revelers. And she couldn't keep a secret if her life depended on it. If she murdered Elvira Jenkins, she would have burst into the room, breathless, and shouted, "I haven't seen Elvira Jenkins. Why do you ask?"

"It's push, not pull." I reached over and undid the clasp. "Somebody knocked Elvira on the head with a cast iron skillet, and it must have been someone from the reception or someone who worked on the show. Who else would know the skillet was under the counter with the rest of the leftover baking stuff?"

"Well, it wasn't me."

"Fine. We'll go with that assumption. For now," I added to let her know that I was still ticked off at her for lying to me. "I took a wrong turn when I went to the washroom and that hallway leads right back to the set. Anyone could have left the reception and returned without raising suspicions."

I said black, so naturally Auntie said white.

"Not necessarily. There's an entire studio. Someone could have entered the building the same way we did. Or someone might have already been in the building working on another show. All they had to do was lure her back there and kabong! After all, Elvira lived around here. Unless she changed from when I knew her, she must have had enemies."

"When you put it like that, it makes her murder impossible to solve." I opened the car door.

"Well, starting tomorrow, I'm going to get a move on solving it. I don't want that reporter fella to think I'm a liar."

"Why not? Paul Simpson is a big fat liar himself."

"I have my reputation to protect."

That sounded too much like what Elvira Jenkins said on the set of *Blue-Ribbon Babes*.

"What about the police?" I said. "The fact that you never told Bowers about your little love triangle means that he has good reason to haul you away for obstructing his investigation. That doesn't bother you?"

"Don't be silly. He never asked me if I knew Bull Jenkins or if I ever dated him."

"But you didn't offer the information, either."

Auntie shook her head. "Sissy, if we had to read every policeman's mind to figure out what information he wanted, well, we'd have to be psychic, for real."

That was one topic I wanted to stay away from. Instead, I tried to show her how ridiculous the idea of Gertrude the Investigator sounded.

"What did you have in mind? Have you made out a list of suspects? Are you going to drop by their houses and demand they spill all?"

"As for suspects, I say we start with people we know. There's Heather Ozu, Donna Pederson, Natasha and Bert. Betty seemed too nice to kill anyone, but I suppose we should keep her on the list. That's good for starters."

"None of them seemed as if they knew Elvira well

enough to want to kill her. And what if they refuse to talk to you?"

"I'll hint that I know something, and I'll take it to the police if they don't talk."

"That would be a bad idea. If you stumble onto the killer, you'll give him or her a reason to shut you up. And what about the family? You've conveniently left them out."

"Bull wouldn't hurt a fly, and I can't believe his son or daughter-in-law would either."

"You better come clean with Bowers and tell him about Bull."

"If he asks, I will."

I kind of hoped he wouldn't ask.

ELEVEN

Bright and early the next morning, Auntie shook my shoulders. "Wakey, wakey!"

She pulled open the front room drapes, and I threw my arm across my face to ward off the sunlight.

"What time is it?"

"Saguaro Studios opens at eight. We need to get the jump on Heather before she forgets her promise to talk to me about my tarot card reading idea."

I rolled on my side and buried my face in the couch cushion. "The minions get there at eight. Celebrities like Heather probably wander in at ten or so. One of the perks." I opened my mouth to yawn and choked on a dog hair.

"Not our Heather. That woman looks ambitious, and you don't get places by sleeping in."

She nagged me into the shower, but because I had to take Chauncey for his morning walk, and because I demanded breakfast before left, we weren't on the road until 8:30.

This time, we didn't have a handy invite, so the security guard—according to his nametag, Howard—wasn't about to let us on the lot. Auntie leaned over me and put on her best aw-shucks grin.

"Howard!" Auntie called out to him as if they were best buddies. "Heather Ozu will be so upset if I don't show up. You've heard about that awful murder business?"

"That's why I'm not letting anybody on this lot who isn't on the list." He jabbed his clipboard to make his point.

"Well, I'm a consultant she's, er, consulting with to save the show. Here's my card."

She handed him a Queen of Hearts tarot/business card, and after studying it both front and back, he looked at her with newfound respect.

"You're that woman from the paper? The one who's working with the police?" When his gaze landed on me, he raised a bushy brow. "What about her?"

"She's my sidekick. She tries to help out when she can."

I folded my arms and muttered, "I'll give you a sidekick right in the—"

"You'll vouch for her?" Howard asked.

I couldn't imagine why a homemade business card and a critical article in The Wolf Creek Gazette would raise my aunt in Howard's esteem, but I went with it and gave him a toothy smile as I endured his inspection.

A young woman exited the car behind us and wandered up. "What's the holdup, Howard?"

It was Linda. I almost didn't recognize her out of her page uniform. When she saw Auntie, she gushed about how great her Skype appointment had been.

"Skype appointment?" I asked, but Linda had already rushed to the passenger window and leaned in to hug Auntie.

"It was just like being in the room with you! And you

remember the problem I had with you-know-who? Your solution worked like magic."

"When did you have time for an appointment?" I asked Auntie.

"Not everybody needs eight hours of sleep, lazybones. Some of us are night owls." She winked at Linda.

Linda's approval gave Howard all the validation he needed to let us through, but I got out of my car and escorted her back to her hatchback.

"Detective Bowers said that you saw my Aunt Gertrude and Elvira Jenkins arguing the night of the murder." It was a lucky guess. Linda had left me to retrieve another tray of drinks shortly before Elvira Jenkins was killed.

Her eyes opened wide. "I had to tell him what I saw."

"Of course you did. Do you remember the time?"

"I was going back to get another tray of drinks. You remember. I was with you when that guy said he was thirsty. I remember looking at the clock because I hoped my shift was almost over, but it was only going on seven o'clock."

"Did you overhear any part of their discussion?"

"It sounds stupid, but I thought I heard them say buckle and bull. I was going to ask if they needed anything, but they sounded pretty angry, so I just kept moving." She glanced toward my car. "I hope I didn't get your aunt into trouble."

"She is capable of that all on her own."

Howard let us pass after giving us directions to Heather's private office. I followed his instructions and curved around the lot between stages two and three until I came upon a row of modular buildings.

We climbed the small metal staircase to the last one in

the row and knocked. When no one answered, Auntie pushed her way inside.

A small reception area took up the first room. It was sparsely decorated with cheap, metal furniture. The doorway to the next trailer was closed. Auntie knocked, and when no one answered, she threw open the door.

The office had plush carpeting, a real wooden desk, and on the walls were pictures of Heather Ozu posed with various celebrities and politicians, including Mayor Haskins.

"Are you thinking what I'm thinking?" Auntie said.

"Only if you're thinking we should wait in the reception area until Heather gets back."

"I suppose it wouldn't hurt to go inside," she said, ignoring me. "After all, we came here to look for her, and she just happened to be out."

Auntie went through the door.

"That's trespassing," I called after her, my feet planted in place.

"Don't be silly. No one was at the reception desk to tell us not to go inside, and it's only natural to wait for her. While we're at it, we can do some snooping."

I opened the door to the outside and glanced both ways. There were a few people in the distance, but they weren't headed in this direction.

Inside Heather's office, Auntie flipped through the papers on Heather's desk.

"Stop it." I shooed her away and tried to put them back in order before someone walked in. I hadn't intended to invade Heather's privacy, but the big red PAST DUE stamps were hard to miss.

"Someone's not paying her bills," Auntie observed from over my shoulder.

"None of our business." I patted the edges and put them in a stack. It looked too neat, so I mussed them for a natural look.

Auntie yanked open the top side drawer and said, "Oh, my. Just like Grandpa."

There was a racing form for Turf Paradise racetrack dated the last week of April. Horse betting. Several names were circled in red. I jotted them down on a sticky note, shoved it in my purse and closed the drawer. I'd check later to see if they had won their races.

"We've gotta get out of here," I said. "I think Heather Ozu would be seriously miffed to find us here."

"She is."

Heather wore black skinny jeans and a sparkly red t-shirt. She had a hand on one hip and her expression could have cleared the room—if only she would move out of the doorway and let us escape.

"Heather! I was just about to leave you a note. We were in the area and Auntie insisted on talking to you about the idea she—er—pitched to you last night." I thought pitched was the right term.

"We didn't see your assistant," Auntie offered.

At the mention of Jeremy, Heather let out a delicate snort and moved to her desk. I slipped out of her way.

"That's because I fired his butt. Can you believe he stole from petty cash?"

She dropped into her chair, and her gaze roved over her desk.

"You're ambitious," she said to Auntie. "I like that. Too many people wait by their phones, hoping I'll call them. Like I don't have anything better to do." She opened her middle drawer and swept the papers off the desktop. "But

I'd prefer to save the talking until I see if the murder works to our advantage."

"There are advantages to murder?" I couldn't keep the shock out of my voice.

"We're replaying the episode as a tribute. People will respond one of two ways. Either they won't care, or they'll tune in like ghouls. If the latter happens, we're sure to get an order for twelve episodes. Maybe more."

"Maybe you could have a murder a month, just to keep ratings up." That was Auntie's suggestion.

"I wish. As for you," she pointed a long orange fingernail at Auntie, "I want to see how much publicity your investigation gets. Then we'll talk."

Auntie had a gleam in her eye, and I didn't think Bowers would let me off lightly if another interview appeared in The Wolf Creek Gazette.

"The police don't like to advertise their movements," I said.

Heather shrugged. "Makes no difference to me, but a story in the paper—several stories—might make a difference to you. Appearing in the paper would raise your profile with the public, which would make you worth having on the show. No profile, no deal."

"We'll call you," I said, backing out of the room. "Thanks for your time.

I shuffled Auntie out of there before the two of them could launch a publicity campaign, but once outside on the metal staircase, my aunt did an about-face. "Wait here. I forgot something." Not eager to face Heather again, I waited.

There were more people walking about the lot now. A woman in ratty jeans and a faded t-shirt walked toward me, her face buried in a newspaper. She turned into the trailer next to us. I really didn't want anyone to recognize me from the awful photo that Paul Simpson used in his article, and I debated whether to get moving and leave my aunt behind. Finally, I heard a peel of laughter. Auntie trundled out, chuckling.

"Bonding with your new boss?" I asked.

"I forgot to ask her if she murdered Elvira Jenkins."

I closed my eyes and took a deep breath with the wild hope that, when I opened them, I'd wake up back in bed surrounded by loved ones, just like Dorothy in the Wizard of Oz. It didn't work. Auntie was still here, and we were still outside of Heather Ozu's trailer.

"Please, please tell me you're joking."

"You heard what she said. The lady wants an active investigation, and I didn't want to waste a lot of time being coy. Direct is best. She thought I was a hoot. Said she liked my style and I should use that approach when I read clients for her show. Notice she said when, not if. I think she likes me."

"Must be your stellar personality."

We passed stage three on our way back to the parking lot. The huge rolling door stood open, and employees bustled around like worker ants. Auntie and I wandered in, unchecked.

I hoped to bump into Natasha or Bert, but when I saw the set, I wondered if I had wandered into the wrong stage.

The partitions that formed the winding hallways had been removed, giving me a clear view of a cavernous room, with the *Blue-Ribbon Babes* set front and center, though if I'd been asked to swear that it was the same set, I would have had to pass.

On the count of three, a construction crew lifted a new

white countertop and set it into place. A few people with paint brushes put the finishing touches of soft pink on the walls. The ficus tree had been replaced by a pink, flowering shrub that showed through the window frame.

The place looked like an advertisement for feminine hygiene products. The only hint of blue came from a circle of blue ribbons painted around the border of the fake window.

The stands were still folded back, and directly above them, a light shown from an office window. Natasha Young gazed down on the activity. I waved, but she didn't see me. Or she ignored me.

"Come on."

Auntie followed me up a staircase that led to a small square room crammed with equipment. Natasha stood in front of a row of monitors, and she was speaking with someone though her headset. She turned on our entrance and removed it.

"We were just visiting Heather and thought we'd say hi, but I wasn't sure we were in the right place. It looks so different. Pretty."

"I'm changing everything. New colors. New props. New camera angles. I want to separate the look of the series as much as possible from the premiere episode. Sponsors are worried. We've got to keep them happy or there won't be any show."

"Wiping all traces of Elvira's murder away. I can't believe the police allowed it."

"They didn't talk to me about it, but I got the okay from the studio attorneys."

I looked at the spread of monitors embedded in the console behind her. "Why so many?"

She glanced over her shoulder at them. "Each one

represents a different camera. I get them positioned exactly where I want them ahead of time and study the angles until I can see them clearly in my head. Then I can direct from down on the floor. A lot of directors stay up in the booth, but I like to be right where the action is happening. I can experience what the studio audience is experiencing and pick up their vibe. Then I amp things up or calm them down, depending on the angle I choose. Chatty Cathy time? I shoot head on. Difficult details? I shoot from overhead. Trying to get things moving, or at least looking like they're moving? Then I go to the camera on the side."

"Do you just decide spur of the moment?"

"Sometimes. But I always study the recipes ahead of time, so I know which bits are going to need extra attention and close ups."

"That's pretty cool," I said. "I didn't realize how much thought went into it. I thought you just set up the cameras and let it go."

As long as we were here, I wanted to find out more about Natasha, but I wasn't about to use Auntie's direct approach. "So, was my aunt's reading right? Are you moving on to greater things? Hollywood?"

Natasha made a face. "Been there, done that. Too many ambitious wackos, too much butt kissing, and too much stress."

Her expression suddenly altered; I could see the fear in her eyes. Her breathing quickened, and her hands twitched. It was the reaction single people have when a toddler enters their home, filled with breakable antiques. I looked to where her gaze was fixed. Auntie had discovered a camera hooked up to a single monitor. She held it in front of her face and watched the results on screen. Right now, she had her eyes crossed and her tongue out.

"That looks expensive." I said. "Put it down."

She reluctantly complied.

"Natasha, you sound so creative and talented that I can't imagine why you're not directing your own series by now." I crossed to the window and pointed to the set. "This show can't be that exciting for you. Nothing changes. It's just bakers in front of an oven week after week."

"True. But the people in these small studios tend to be nicer. No one's cutting your throat to get your job. I'm still doing what I love. What more could I ask for?"

"Something overseas?" I said, remembering how Auntie mentioned travel in the director's impromptu reading.

"There is something I'd like to do," Natasha said, breaking into a grin. "There's a charity called God's Little Helpers that's looking for filmmakers to put together footage of projects going on in poor countries." She ticked the examples off on her fingers. "Digging wells, building schools, employing women so they can support their families after all the men have been killed off in wars. That kind of thing. The finished product would be a resume reel." She spread her hands in an open gesture, like the spokesman in a commercial when they arrive at the big finish. "When people see concrete examples of the great things that are being accomplished, they're more likely to contribute money. And those folks need money."

"Oh, honey," Auntie said. "You just lit up like a firefly. That's your real passion. That's where you should be."

"When my contract is up at the end of the season, that's where I will be, if the position is still open."

A crackly voice came over her headset, and Natasha said, "I have to take this." It was said nicely, but it was a dismissal, so we worked our way back downstairs and outside.

As we walked to the car, I stated what I thought was obvious. "That gives her a motive for murder."

"You can't be talking about that sweet young woman who wants to dedicate her life to helping charities."

"And she might miss her golden opportunity unless *Blue-Ribbon Babes* gets canceled. She can't be certain that God's Little Helpers will still be looking for filmmakers after the show's first season ends."

"Sissy Chandler, you are the most cynical person I've ever met."

"Murder will do that to a person."

I couldn't really blame the murders. Cynicism had been my close friend for a long time, and if my career and dating prospects didn't improve soon, the two of us would grow unhappily old together.

"Where are we headed next?"

"I've got to drop you off."

"Why?"

"I've got an appointment."

"Take me with you."

I rubbed my temples to ease the throbbing.

"Another headache?" Auntie tsked. "Maybe you should relax and let me do the talking."

"That's not a good idea. Aren't you the one that said overkill is the quickest route to failure in our business?" I still included myself in the psychic biz because that's how Auntie saw me.

"Tell them I'm your teacher and I'm evaluating your performance. No, that makes you sound like a newbie. Oh. I know. Tell them I'm an official from our union. Everybody's got a union. They'll be impressed."

"I don't think it's a good idea."

"Come on, now. I want to see you at work. I promise I won't say a word. Just watch."

She promised three times more before I finally gave in. Shows you what a sucker I am.

TWELVE

Harold and Janice Butler were very nice people. They owned a nice home in Cave Creek, had nice, pleasant personalities and nice smiles on their nice but plain faces. That's why it surprised me that their pet of choice would be a chow.

Chows are smart. Chows are loyal. Chows aren't particularly nice, and they tend to take to one person only. Let's say they resent the rest. I wondered which of these nice people Teddy considered his best friend and which one he considered his competition.

Those thoughts were completely irrelevant to the Butler's particular problem, but my mind was distracted by the zero possibility that I could figure out Teddy's troubles using guesswork. Teddy was depressed.

Join the crowd. I was depressed, and my head ached. Auntie and I were making little headway on finding out who killed Elvira, and until the police let her go home to Wisconsin, Auntie would be sharing my home. Teddy didn't have an Aunt Gertrude. Teddy hadn't stumbled over a dead body. What could he have to be depressed about?

"How long has the poor thing been this way?" Auntie asked. I'd introduced her as my apprentice who was along to observe, as in not talk. I shot her a look.

"Oh." Auntie put her hand over her mouth. "Was there something different you wanted to ask?" To Janice she said, "I really shouldn't butt in, but I get so excited about helping animals."

They all looked to me for the important question from the professional.

I cleared my throat. "When did you first notice his depression?"

"He was happy-go-lucky up until a few weeks ago. So social, and he loved his food. Sometimes he'd nudge me if I was late with his lunch. And he looked forward to playtime. He even brought me his ball when he was bored and stared at me until I gave in and played fetch. Such a sweetie."

No need to tell Janice that her dog's cute behaviors were bullying tactics that showed he thought she was the family pet.

"When my grandchildren get pushy, I give them a time out just to let them know I'm not a doormat," Auntie said, showing the insight that made her such a good tarot card reader.

"What changed?" I asked, before Janice could absorb the insult.

"Nothing, really. His feeding schedule stayed the same. In fact, we showed him extra attention, but none of it brought back our sweet little Teddy bear."

There were certainly enough toys lying around to amuse him. Probably too many. Just like humans, too many choices could overwhelm a dog and make him crazy.

"You could try cutting back on the number of toys available. Just give him one at a time and put it away when you're done."

Janice recoiled from me with a huge gasp. "But he'd get bored!" She turned to her husband for support.

Harold, a tall, thin man, crossed his gangly arms over his chest. "I don't want to be handing out toys and putting them away every other minute. It's easier to just leave them out." His Adam's apple bobbed up and down as he spoke. "It's never been a problem before."

I made a desperate shot in the dark. "Does Teddy have a crate? Some animals find their crate a secure retreat, kind of like when you slip into another room to get some peace and quiet."

Auntie raised her hand. "Been there, done that. I used to send you kids out to look for broken glass for craft projects."

"My point is," I said, wrestling the conversation back, "if you took the crate away, he might get nervous."

"A crate?" Harold drew back in shock. "That's just cruel."

Janet shook her head over and over. "No. No. No. No crate. We'd never do that to poor Teddy."

Auntie nodded agreement. "We used to let Peaches out the back door in the morning and let her run free. She'd visit the neighborhood dogs and say hello. Had her own routine. Of course, sometimes she'd eat poop and come home smelling like a sewer, but I just wouldn't let her kiss my face for a few days."

Their smiles slipped, and I thought they might fall off altogether unless I came up with a solution they felt good about.

Teddy's warm brown eyes moved from face to face. I had to find a common-sense solution, just like I'd done for years as a charlatan pet psychic. It shouldn't be that difficult. The answer usually rested with the pet parents. Janice radiated the eager energy of a mom about to go on a baking spree, and Harold seemed the type of benign man who would shy away from any controversy.

"You know," Auntie said, reaching into her purse. "I find that animals are so sensitive to their owners. Perhaps the solution lies with one of you."

I shot her a quick look, surprised that our thoughts followed the same path. I shouldn't have been, really. When I was a kid and she was teaching me how to cold read, we almost always came up with the same conclusions. When had I stopped looking up to her and started thinking of her as an annoyance? My cheeks grew warm with shame, and I resolved to be more patient with her while she remained in Arizona.

Auntie pulled out her deck of tarot cards. "If you want a reading..."

The back of my neck tingled as if someone were watching us. I jerked my head round to look over my shoulder. Nothing. When I turned back, Teddy jumped up, his tail wagging furiously. He did a doggie bow, shook his head and snorted. He was greeting someone. Or something.

"Well, look at that!" Auntie reluctantly put her cards away. "Maybe he just had indigestion. It always makes me lethargic."

Light panting tickled my ear, as if I had picked up and hugged up a toy poodle, except the breath was cold. I rubbed my ear against my scrunched-up shoulder.

A flash of light swished through the room, and suddenly a long-haired silver pup with pricked-up ears swirled in circles around Teddy's feet, yapping in ecstasy.

I jumped out of my seat.

There was something off-kilter about his bark. It sounded hoarse and dry, and it was followed by the kind of echo that comes with cheap microphones. His fur shimmered with a brightness that couldn't be explained by excellent brushing techniques.

"Um, I thought you only had one dog."

Harold stared, and Janice twittered nervously. "We do. Teddy." She nodded her head at the chow as he rubbed his back into the carpet. The silky terrier stood over him, panting.

"What about the little guy?"

Janice grabbed Harold's hand. "Little guy?"

Auntie leaned over and stage-whispered. "Maybe your headaches are because you need glasses, Sissy."

Harold coughed. "We had a Yorkie, but he died."

"Not a Yorkie. A silky," I whispered, not exactly splitting hairs, but when you're staring at a dog no one else can see, you like to be clear about these things.

"Yorkie. Silky. Who cares?" Harold said. "He looked like a Yorkie."

Janice's nice lady face was replaced by flaring nostrils and pinched lips. "If you'd cared, maybe you wouldn't have let Bonzo out without his leash and maybe he'd be alive today."

"Good grief. You act like I pushed him in front of the car!"

All the air was sucked out of the room as if someone were operating a cosmic vacuum sealer. At least, I assume that's why I couldn't get any when I inhaled. Wheezing hard, I crouched on the floor to get a better look at—I couldn't say it. I couldn't even think it. A doggie ghost?

Bonzo looked over his shoulder at me and yipped. Then

he trundled over and licked my hand. It tickled, and I'm sure he meant well, but I snatched my hand away and rubbed off the drool on my pants. Except there wasn't any. My hand was dry.

How in the name of everything that walks on four legs could I be communicating with a dead dog? It was bad enough that live animals used to barge through my imaginary mental door at will, but dead animals?

"Ms. Chandler," Janice said, this time in a crisp, no-nonsense tone. She watched me closely, and I realized I was still on my hands and knees. "What does Bonzo have to do with anything?"

I got up and tried to formulate my answer without any of the harsh language I was tempted to use. It amazed me how even kind, loving, nice people could be so dense. "Bonzo and Teddy were friends, right?"

"They got along fine," Harold said. "I used to throw the tennis ball around the backyard for both of them." He added this last bit on a triumphant note, as if it proved he deserved pet parent of the year.

"Bonzo is friends with Teddy," I repeated in a slow patient voice I've heard people use with children. "Bonzo dies. Teddy gets depressed."

It took a minute, but they finally said, in unison, "Oh."

"You might want to get Teddy another friend. You can't replace Bonzo, but the three of them—I mean the two of them can play together." I couldn't bring myself to tell them that their dead pet was in the room. "The depression should go away."

Getting another pet is a big step, and I appreciated it when Janice said they would think about it.

As I walked to my car, I looked over my shoulder at

their formerly nice faces, now marred by the uncertainty that comes after a pet psychic actually communicates with their animal. People want it, at least they say they do, but the experience is nothing like a smooth magic trick from a polished performer. And that was when I read live animals. I didn't want to think about what dead pets might have to say to me.

At least I had my fifty bucks.

"That was genius," Auntie said, her eyes wide with wonder. "You think outside the box. I never would have come up with the idea of a dead pet. Did you see him in one of their family photos? I must have missed it."

In the car, I clutched the steering wheel and stared without seeing. A dead pet had invaded my skull. I shuddered, and if it had been possible to take out my brain and run it under soapy water, I'd be scrubbing away right now.

I'm a pragmatist. While everyone thinks vampires are sexy, I realize that characters who snuggle with them are snuggling with a cold, lifeless corpse. There wasn't anything cute and snuggly about a dead pet, either.

My breathing stopped. Last month, I'd been able to read Bowers and Seamus. What if Elvira tried to contact me from the grave?

"We should get some lunch, Sissy. You're kind of pale."

Putting my car in drive, I vowed to put a lock on that stupid, flimsy mental door. Bonzo slipped right through without even knocking first, and there was no way I was taking the chance that Elvira might pay me a visit.

We hit a drive-through, and then I dropped Auntie off and went to the drugstore for more aspirin. Now that pet messages were popping up again without my issuing an invitation, I would have to work harder at keeping the communication lines closed. I'd have to be prepared for the headaches, and I didn't want Auntie insisting I go see a doctor.

Funny thing was, ever since Bonzo made his appearance, my headache had disappeared.

THIRTEEN

"I'm home!"

I paused inside the door. Silence. No screeches. No Meows. No barks. Not a good sign.

A man's chuckle came from the kitchen, and in that room, I found Auntie and Bull, seated kitty-corner at my kitchen table. Bull looked up and smiled, his eyes crinkling at the corners in deep lines. It was a genuine smile, without a hint of embarrassment over the fact that he was holding Auntie's hand. In fact, he lifted it and gave it a squeeze.

"I was just telling Gertie here how nice it is to be able to talk about things with someone who understands. Someone who remembers the old times."

"Does she remember the old times?" I asked. "I'm surprised. She seems to have suffered from memory loss lately, especially when she's talking to Detective Bowers."

Off his concerned look, Auntie said, "Don't fret. It's not dementia. Just old age skittering up and taking a bite every once in a while." Nice man that Bull was, he didn't even detect the malicious undertones when she added, in my direction, "We're none of us as young as we used to be. Is it too late to hope for little grand nieces and nephews? I've heard once you hit your forties, your eggs dry up and wither away."

"Good thing I'm not forty. Besides, that's hardly the topic for mixed company." I slid into the free chair next to Bull, put my chin on my fist, leaned in, and gave him a smile that dripped with sympathy. "You must miss your wife dreadfully." I glared at Auntie. "Remember her?

Bull let go of Auntie's hand to rub his brow. "Vera was one hell of a woman."

"Vera's short for Elvira," Auntie said to me, with a vicious gleam in her eyes. "Sissy's a little slow sometimes. Not so good at thinking, but she tries her best. I think that's why she sticks to animals. They have low expectations."

It was then I noticed that Petey rested quietly in his uncovered cage, Chauncey lay out flat in front of the sink, and Emily stretched in front of the kitchen window. A picture of harmony.

"Did you drug the animals?"

"They respond to the personality of the person they're with. Me, I'm calm as a summer day."

From the way she batted her lashes—was that eye shadow on her lids?—Auntie was applying seduction 101 to a man who'd only been widowed a few days ago. It made me mad, not to mention disgusted and creeped out. I'd heard of old ladies who swooped in on available old men with post-funeral dinners, already angling to become the next wife.

"You are kind of lethargic," I said, leaning forward to pat her hand. "Not like that bundle of energy, Vera."

Bull chuckled and nodded. "Lots of us talk about what we'd like to do or how we'd like to help out, but Vera did something about it. She had the energy of ten farm hands." He placed his elbows on the table and leaned in, like an old cowboy telling a favorite story. "And she had values, something you don't see much of these days. Kids today have the attention span of a flea. Just look at the way she dug in there on the mayor's campaign. Putting in extra hours and never complaining, and all because she admired the man and believed in what he stood for."

"She sounds like a wonderful woman," I said. "It's hard to imagine that anyone would want to kill such a generous, kind, loving woman."

Bull barked out a laugh and shook his head. "Oh, she had a temper on her, but it was always justified." The smile left his face, and he narrowed his eyes. "And you hit the nail on the head, little lady. Who would want her dead?"

"I thought you might be able to tell us."

"I can't think of anyone, no matter how hard I try." He scratched his chin. "Honestly, she rubbed some people the wrong way, but that's not the kind of thing you kill someone over."

"No one owed her money?"

"Never a lender nor a borrower be. That was her motto."

"Did she know anyone's secrets?"

"She wasn't that kind of lady." He folded his hands on the table. "I don't want you to take this the wrong way, but Elvira didn't care about people enough to suss out their secrets. Other people's business was their business."

Not caring about people could be a good thing or a bad thing. Maybe if she paid more attention to people, she could have avoided the flat side of a cast iron skillet.

"She didn't have any worries?"

"She had no reason to. We had plenty of money. My wife was doing what she loved. And Vera was as healthy as a horse. Just ask Doc Zimmerman. Vera's been her patient for twenty-seven years, and the doc says that if all her patients were as healthy as my wife, she'd be out of a job."

"Yoo-hoo!"

Sharlene Walker fluttered in. She wore pink again—a twinset and matching Capri pants—which complemented her short snowy-white hair.

Bull stood when she entered the room.

"I thought I heard people in here," she said, her crystal blue eyes sparkling as if she'd struck gold as they took in the tall cowboy in the chair. She held out her hand and batted her eyelashes. "I'm Sharlene."

He took her small hand in both of his large ones. "Stan. Pleased to meet you."

"Can I help you?" Auntie asked, not sounding helpful at all.

Sharlene jumped at the sound of Auntie's voice and let out an embarrassed giggle. "I was hoping you had some extra business cards, Gertrude. My friends were so excited when I told them about the reading you gave me. They're just dying to set up appointments."

"Reading?" Bull asked.

"Tarot cards," I said.

It appeared Bull was too polite to gag or laugh or say something smart, but his silence spoke volumes.

Torn between romance and business, Auntie went into the bedroom to retrieve her cards.

"Won't you sit down?" I pushed out a chair.

"If I'm not interrupting," she said, even as she took her place at the table.

"Gertie and I are old friends," Bull said, only taking his seat after Sharlene was settled.

"How nice!"

He folded his hands on the table. "I just lost my wife, you see."

Sharlene reached out her hand and rubbed his arm. "You poor man. That's so awful."

"She was murdered, if you can believe it." He nodded, his brows raised, showing his own surprise over the situation his late wife found herself in.

Sharlene gasped. "Oh, my word!"

"What's going on in there?" Auntie swept back into the room with her cards and set them in front of Sharlene.

With her hand on her heart, my neighbor said, "I just can't believe how violent this world has become. Whatever happened to good manners?"

Auntie stared at her as if Sharlene's IQ were a couple of points below comatose, but Bull said, "Good point, Ma'am."

"I guess it is pretty rude to kill someone," I said. "I hadn't really thought about it that way before."

As if to show that if anyone in the room had manners, it was Auntie, she said, "Would you like some coffee, Sharlene? And how about a refill for you, Bull?"

"I'd like some," I said with a sweet smile, but Auntie conveniently ran out of coffee before she could accommodate me.

"Some people call me Bull, 'cause I used to imitate Andy Devine."

Sharlene clasped her hands. "I love Roy Rogers' films. So romantic."

I put on another pot of coffee. "We were just trying to figure out who could have killed Bull—er—Stan's wife."

Sharlene shuddered. "Such a horrible topic."

"And not appropriate in a lady's presence." Bull rapped on the table as if the matter were settled.

"I think it's better to face tragedies head on," Auntie

said. "That's the practical way of dealing with life. No use hiding your head in the sand."

"Vera was like that," Bull said. "Look where it got her." He stood. "I've got some paperwork to go over with our attorney that I shouldn't put off any longer. It's been a real pleasure to meet you, ma'am." He gave a slight bow in Sharlene's direction. "Thanks for everything, Gertie."

Sharlene hopped up and thanked Auntie, saying that she only dropped in for a minute, and then she rushed to catch up with Bull, leaving Auntie's business cards behind on the table.

FOURTEEN

After our guests left, I washed up the coffee cups while Auntie caught the tail end of her favorite soap opera. I dried my hands on the dish towel and joined her just in time to catch a Macy's commercial.

"I wonder how I'd look in pink," Auntie said.

"You mean pink as in cute-as-a-button Sharlene Walker pink?" I put my arm around her shoulder and squeezed. "You're fine just the way you are."

"Maybe we should go to the mall, so I can pick out some Arizona wear."

"Why? You're going home in a few days."

"Detective Bowers might not like that. He is investigating a murder, and I was a witness."

I steadied myself. "He didn't actually say you had to stay here, did he?"

"I believe it's protocol, and better safe than sorry."

We wound up at Macy's in the Fashion Mall in Scottsdale. Auntie was camped out in the women's department dressing room while I slumped in a chair next to somebody's husband who had the good sense to bring along a tablet.

"What do you think?"

The summons was for me. The guy didn't even glance up from his game of solitaire.

Auntie sashayed out in a cotton tunic of cerulean blue with the outline of a howling coyote stitched on in white thread. The pants were white clam diggers, and on her wide feet she wore her new leather sandals. I noticed she still wore her nylons.

"You look very southwestern," I said, and she giggled with delight. "But not very pink."

She gave a vague wave. "Pink isn't everyone's color. I decided it's best to stick with what looks best on me."

"A wise choice."

After we paid for her purchases, which included three additional tops and pairs of pants in the same style but different colors, we went in search of jewelry.

"You can't have too many pairs of silver earrings, I always say."

I kept myself from remarking that I owned zero pairs of silver earrings, because the man behind the jewelry counter caught my eye.

"Jeremy?"

Heather Ozu's former assistant-slash-slave turned wide eyes on us and almost ducked under the counter in embarrassment.

"What a nice surprise!" Auntie exclaimed. "We heard you left Saguaro Studios. Show business is no place for a nice young man."

Jeremy snorted. "It wasn't really show business. At least, I hope to heck that's not what it's like in Hollywood."

"They are professionals in California." Auntie nodded. "Speaking of professionals, now that you're in the jewelry business, what do you think about these on me?" She held up a pair of small silver earrings, and Jeremy plucked them out of her hand and rummaged through his stock.

"Not the right shape for your face." I think that was a nice way of saying big faces need big earrings, because he selected a pair of large loops and slid them across the counter.

"Heather Ozu said something interesting about you." I'd thought it over and decided that, if I was going to choose between them, Jeremy seemed more likely to tell the truth than Heather, now that he was through kissing her fanny and didn't have anything to lose. "She said she fired you because you stole from petty cash, but of course we didn't believe it for a minute."

"She said what?"

A woman in her fifties at the other end of the counter looked up. She wore a nametag, so she was either another employee or the manager. Probably the manager from the way Jeremy lowered his voice.

"She has a lot of nerve! First of all, I quit! And I busted my butt for her. Assistant!" He snorted. "Babysitter is more like it. I picked up her specialty coffee every morning because Heather Ozu couldn't possibly drink regular out of the pot like the rest of us. I picked up her dry cleaning and cleaned her cat's litter box, because Heather Ozu couldn't possibly do her own errands or get her manicured nails anywhere near a box of poop. Like she's so busy! And the worst part was having to listen to her whine about her terrible, overpaid life."

He launched into a high-pitched imitation. "My boyfriend didn't get me a Valentine. My mother spanked me when I was two. You don't know what it's like being a woman in this big, bad, world."

He picked through a tray of silver earrings and slapped

a few pairs on the counter. "As if she had it so tough. I work two jobs to pay my way through college. I didn't get a scholarship because my great-grandfather came from Japan, and her parents are millionaires. Mine run a tire store." He threw up his hands. "She doesn't even like sushi, for cryin' out loud!"

"You poor thing," Auntie soothed. "People are so hoity-toity sometimes."

He stared at her as if he'd been alone on an island and rescue had finally come.

"Thank you! Yes. You've hit it on the head. Hoity-toity. That describes it perfectly. They think they're better than thou!"

He picked out a matching bracelet and slid it on Auntie's wrist. "Stole from her. That's such crap. I forgot to enter a receipt for something she bought, so it didn't balance. I dare her to fire me for that!"

"I hope you haven't killed your connections in the industry," Auntie said. "I could read your cards for you and put your mind at ease." She rummaged through her purse.

"Don't bother. I'm not even a film major. I'm working on my master's in business, and I thought working for a studio might be fun."

"What finally pushed you over the edge?"

"I hadn't been paid in three weeks! I may still live with my mother while I finish school, but I've got bills to pay. Mother charges rent, and her late charge is ten percent."

Now I knew where he got his business acumen.

"So, Heather employed you directly?"

"No. I'm technically an employee of *Blue-Ribbon Babes*. I only started work for her a few months ago, when the Baking Channel got serious about putting the show on the air."

"So why blame Heather for your paycheck problems?"

"Because Heather Ozu is one of the show's producers. She has control over the money."

No wonder she was interested in the success of the show. As the talent, she could walk away and get another job somewhere else, but as a producer, she stood to lose big time.

"They can't be doing that bad, honey," Auntie piped up. "They were handing out a $2,000 check."

Jeremy threw her a sly grin. "They said they were going to hand out a prize, but all the winner actually got was a big, cardboard check. There wasn't money in the account to cover the real check. In fact, Heather explained that to the guests before the show. The other two thought the publicity would be a good enough prize, but Elvira Jenkins wasn't having any of that. She threatened to go public unless they made good on it if she won."

"And she did win," I said, considering. "I assumed that Heather hinted Elvira's buckle wasn't that good in revenge for the negative comments Elvira made about the sponsors, but maybe Heather couldn't afford to let her mouthiest contestant win."

Jeremy laughed. "I had to hand it to the old lady. Of course, she used Scotch Girl flour when she sent in her recipe. It was part of the rules, but she refused to play along, once she found out the winner would get swindled."

He picked up Auntie's rejections and put them away and then rang up her selections.

Auntie said, "You wouldn't happen to know who killed Elvira Jenkins, would you?"

He handed her the bag. "I know it wasn't me."

On our way to the car, I said, "The police could learn

from you. Did you do it? No. Thank you very much. Do you really think people are going to answer honestly?"

"Of course not. I watch their faces. After thirty years of reading cards, I would hope I could tell when someone is lying to me."

She had a point. Auntie was good at cold readings. Maybe the best.

"Who do you think is lying? Jeremy or Heather?"

"If I had to lay down money, I'd put it on Heather. She's a real go-getter, the kind that does whatever it takes to come out ahead."

"Agreed. So, if Elvira Jenkins was going to raise a stink over her lost winnings, I assume that Heather would want to shut her up. There must be something illegal about offering a prize and then failing to pay up. It might not have meant jail time, but it would have tarnished the reputation of the show. Sounds like it was a bad idea to mess with Elvira Jenkins."

"She always did have a rigid sense of right and wrong, when it suited her." Auntie turned to me. "I suppose your mother mentioned that she stole my Lemon Blueberry Buckle recipe. I let her try it before I made it for Bull. I wanted it to be perfect. She suggested I use almond extract instead of vanilla extract. The next thing I knew, she'd made it for him and insisted the recipe was hers because of the almond extract. The nerve. If I'd known she was sweet on Bull, I never would have let her in on my big surprise."

My jaw dropped. Auntie was finally coming clean about her dust up with Elvira Jenkins. I should have appreciated her honesty, but sarcasm got there first.

"Odd how you can suddenly remember every detail."

Auntie pulled her cards out of her purse and shuffled

them. "Just came back to me. Memories are funny that way."

"Funny. Hmmm. I prefer the word convenient. Or inconvenient, since your refusal to tell the truth up front has probably put you at the top of Bowers' suspect list."

Auntie snorted so hard she coughed. "As if anyone could consider me a suspect. We were rivals for love when we were teenage girls. If I didn't kill her back then, she'd hardly be worth my while decades later."

I wondered if there were other facts that had suddenly come back to Auntie. "Do you still insist you didn't know Elvira and Bull were married?"

She crossed her heart with her thumb. "On my honor."

"Then why did you accept Elvira's invitation to the premiere? You couldn't stand the woman. Or were you hoping to meet up with Bull again?"

"How was I supposed to know it came from her?" She pulled the postcard out of her purse and waved it at me. I snatched it away and studied it.

"You're right. There's no mention of Elvira Jenkins on this." I handed it back. "So, you actually came all the way to Arizona to go to the premiere taping of a show that you'd never heard of before?"

"And to see you. I wanted to find out how you were getting along. I thought you'd be using your talents, and then I get all the way here and you're an animal behaviorist." She stressed the title with a waggle of her head and a snooty accent. "Things are kind of tough in Loon Lake. Truth be told, I thought I might pick up some tips from you."

"You wanted to learn from me?"

"You can teach an old dog new tricks, you know."

I blinked to keep back the tears. All my life I'd admired

my aunt's ability to make people believe she held the answer to their problems in a deck of cards. If clients took two seconds to think about it logically, Auntie would have been a pauper, but she made the most of her loud personality and her knowledge of human nature and she turned it into a career that put two boys through college. She was a strong person, someone I looked up to, and now she was looking up to me.

"I'm honored that you think I'm that good." I hugged her tight. "You're not so bad yourself."

"I'm glad you think so, because that makes telling you about the séance a lot easier."

Keeping my grip on her shoulders, I stepped back and said, "Séance?"

"Seven o'clock tomorrow night. Appetizers will be served. It would make a nice follow-up newspaper story if we solved the crime in our own home. I mean your home. I thought we could get all the suspects together in one room and make them sweat. And everybody loves a séance."

"You haven't developed a, um, a gift for talking to spirits, have you?" Stranger things happened, as I well knew, but the idea of dead people floating around my living room didn't make me any happier than had the appearance of Bonzo at my reading.

Auntie threw back her head and enjoyed a belly laugh. "Heavens, no! Who ever heard of such a silly thing! Once you're dead, you're dead."

Unless you're Bonzo the dog.

"Who's invited?"

She counted off on her fingers. "There's Bull, his son, Tim, Catherine, Heather Ozu, and Sonny Street. I had to talk Donna Pederson into coming, but Betty was game. I asked Penny, because she adds credibility."

"You mean she believes you can do it, she's enthusiastic, and it might rub off on the others."

"And, of course, Detective Bowers."

I gasped. "You asked Bowers? And he said yes?"

"He seemed delighted."

"Of course he was." Why wouldn't a cop be pleased to be invited to a suspect's home? It would make his job a lot easier if he could catch Auntie in yet another lie.

"Now, I've told everyone they're invited because they cared about Elvira, though that's not necessarily true. Some of them didn't really know her. But I bet the murderer shows up just to keep an eye on things."

"If you expect him or her to confess, won't having Bowers there put a damper on things?"

"I thought he would make them nervous, and I know I tend to blurt things out when I'm nervous," she said.

Not so far, you haven't. I thought it, but I didn't say it out loud.

FIFTEEN

The next morning, Penny showed up on my doorstep.

"Why aren't you at the Prickly Pear?" I asked, stepping aside so she could come in. "Is something wrong?"

"I left Ann in charge, so I could run some errands."

"If you've come by to bow out of the séance, Auntie's in the shower." I headed for the kitchen. "We can have coffee while you wait."

She put a hand on my arm to stop me. "I wouldn't dream of canceling. Your aunt promised it would be exciting."

"Exciting." I squished my face up in a pained expression, wondering how Auntie planned to manipulate the audience. A CD of weird sound effects? Was she going to dress in a black, ragged dress and a turban? Would there be a crystal ball? I shuddered.

"I actually have a favor to ask." She raised her eyebrows and gave me a toothy smile, the one people give you when they're about to ask you to do something they know you'd rather not do.

That's how I found myself in a very unlikely place—St.

Mel's Catholic Church. I didn't even know there was a St. Mel. His name sounded too casual, like a nickname, but Penny insisted Mel was simply Mel.

"It's stupid to put all this worry into where we're getting married. We both live in Wolf Creek, and we attend St. Mel's. We should just get married there. I'm going to talk to Monsignor Robert, and I want moral support."

"Shouldn't Kemper be with you?" It wasn't that I was criticizing him; he just seemed a more suitable choice.

"He should, but he has a client meeting he couldn't get out of. Besides, this is just a preliminary meeting to set up our pre-Cana classes."

St. Mel's sat on top of a hill, a brown stone rectangle with a slim bell tower at one end. We parked the car in an empty lot and passed through an arched entry that led to a small patio surrounded by flowering shrubs. The front glass doors swung into a carpeted vestibule where a colorful poster announced the upcoming parish summer festival.

Turning left, Penny headed down a long hallway. At the end stood a door, but from its position, I couldn't think what waited behind it.

"It's the rectory," Penny explained.

In answer to her knock, a small man in clerical garb answered the door. His fine, white hair drifted across the top of his head in waves that didn't quite cover in spots.

"Right on time, my dear." Monsignor Robert expressed his approval with an Irish lilt, but when his gaze landed on me, he frowned. "And who have we got here?"

Penny introduced me, and the priest advised her that the meeting wouldn't be open to spectators. No offense. He motioned toward the entrance to the main worship area and invited me to wander while I waited.

I paused next to the holy water font, dipped my fingers

and made the sign of the cross. Bowers was wrong. I didn't burst into flames—not then, nor when I dropped a kneeler and took my place in a pew. I should have taken a picture and sent it to my mother.

The air inside was cool, and as I stared at the crucifix over the altar, I thought this might be a good time to put in a few prayers for Auntie.

"I know I haven't kept in contact," I began. How long had it been since I'd been to Mass? How long had it been since I'd been in a church? In a chapel? There'd been baptisms and weddings, but those were social events to me. I cleared my throat.

"The thing is, I'm not asking for anything for myself. Just keep an eye on my aunt, okay? She's in a spot of trouble, and it might take divine intervention to keep her out of jail. Um, thanks."

I felt a peace I hadn't experienced since childhood, but then I looked away, embarrassed and guilty. My journey away from the religion of my childhood was less a decisive move and more of a meandering drift. It had nothing to do with the Catholic Church, per se. I'd just gotten...busy. Other things seemed more important, but I couldn't put my finger on what those things were now.

And then there was Jeff. I'd known my decision to move in with him was not in line with the Church's teachings, and it seemed easier on my conscience to just ignore their rules and make my own. Unfortunately, they'd been right.

Bowers' words came back to me. His uncertainty about my psychic abilities. His suggestion that they might not be a gift from God. Well, what did that make them? It wasn't as if I'd consorted with witches and sought out ways to read pet's minds. The ability showed up, uninvited.

My mind slipped back to childhood Bible studies and a

passage that warned against fortune-tellers. I couldn't tell fortunes. But were there other psychic phenomena on the list that I was supposed to stay away from?

I shuddered. What if my involvement with psychic phenomenon had been responsible for my recent bad luck? What if I'd invited something creepy into my life? I had another thought that made my stomach flip. If I'd never communicated with animals, would Margarita Morales and Elvira Jenkins be alive today?

I'd never questioned where my ability came from. Should I have given it more thought, as in any?

My head spun to look back when I heard a click and I caught sight of a door closing. It was one of two booths. Confessionals. A light shone from above one to indicate the priest was in for business.

On impulse, I grabbed my purse and entered the side for the penitent. The two halves of the booth were divided by a screen, and though my side was in darkness, a small light shone in the priest. I could see a form moving inside.

I didn't wait for him to speak.

"I have a question about—about right and wrong. Not stuff like fighting with family or stealing, or anything black-and-white like that. I was just wondering—"

"Yeah?"

The priest already sounded bored, so I cut my question short.

"Well, if a person were to have psychic abilities, couldn't that come from God?"

Nothing could have prepared me for the vitriolic response.

"Heathen! Pagan! Messin' with the dark forces of Satan. I've a mind to dunk you in the 'tismal font."

I felt the words like a slap in the face. I grabbed my

purse off the floor, shoved the door open, and stumbled into the arms of a young man.

"Careful!"

It was a priest with sandy brown hair and a freckled nose. He set me back on my feet and patted my shoulder just as the second door creaked open and a twisted old man hobbled out. He was dressed in the uniform of a janitor, and he cackled when he saw my shocked expression.

"Jones," the priest said, his young voice filled with stern authority.

Jones pointed a crooked finger my way. "She did all the talking. Couldn't shut her up if I'd tried!" He turned a wounded expression on me. "I was just dustin' and mindin' my own business."

"Really." The priest sounded skeptical.

Jones gave a harrumph and wandered away. The priest pulled out a set of keys. "I've got to start locking this door," he said, and he suited actions to words.

The priest held out his hand. "Father Damien."

I gave a nervous chuckle. "Like The Omen?"

He joined in, laughing. "I prefer to think of Father Damien of Molokai." He looked at his keys. "I jumped the gun. Were you here for Reconciliation?"

"No. Not at all. I just had a question, but let's forget it. It was a stupid question."

"I love stupid questions." He motioned toward the pew. "Why don't we sit?"

His friendly manner made it easy to talk to him. Before I knew it, I'd poured out the whole story, from Margarita Morales and Sandy the Golden Retriever to Elvira Jenkins and Petey the Cockatoo. He didn't laugh. He didn't pull out a crucifix or douse me with holy water. He just sat, still and pensive, until his face creased into a smile.

"Well, we don't know exactly how St. Francis communicated with animals, do we?"

"No," I said, encouraged. "We don't. But Francis was a saint, and, well, I'm not. Should I worry?"

"The question to ask yourself, no matter what you're doing is, does it lead me closer to Jesus, or away from Him?"

I'd been hoping to get away with free advice and no strings attached. "Um, I don't really think about it."

"That would be a good first step, don't you think?"

"Sure," I said, with no intention to follow through. "Thanks." I moved to leave on a good note, but Father Damian took hold of my arm.

"Not so fast."

I sunk back down in the pew.

"About this tarot card business."

I brushed that aside with a wave of my hand. "That's all my aunt. I don't have anything to do with it."

"Can I assume she hasn't chatted with her parish priest?"

"I believe my mother has reserved permanent spots for both of us on the prayer chain. But Auntie just messes with it. She doesn't actually believe in it." It occurred to me that scamming people was probably on the *thou shalt not* list.

He turned to face me, and his brown eyes lost some of their humor. "Divination is not a healthy practice."

"Divination. Isn't that where you try to find water with a stick?"

He nodded slowly as if trying to give the little one a gold star for trying. "Dowsing is a form of divination, but I'm talking about fortune telling. Most of the time, it's a sham, but it's also an invitation, one you don't want accepted. Pass that on to your aunt, will you?"

"Yes, Father."

I started to rise. "Just to be clear, I'm not possessed or doing anything, well, evil."

"I think you're referring to Deuteronomy." He ticked off on his fingers. "Are you burning your children as offerings to other gods?"

"Nope."

"Telling fortunes?"

"Nope."

"Engaging in necromancy or communing with the dead?"

"That's a big no." I remembered Bonzo. "Do dogs count? And does it make a difference if I didn't start the conversation?"

Father Damien rubbed his hand over his mouth. "That's a good question." His brow wrinkled with uncertainty. "A really good question. I'll have to ask the monsignor." He shook his head as if to clear it. "The point is that you either rely on God for guidance or you rely on other forces, and if it's not from God, it's from the enemy. It's all part of that not having other gods before *the* God. And from a practical standpoint, why would you want to rely on a tip from the Father of Lies?"

"Good point."

"You're sure you don't want to receive Reconciliation?" He grinned. "Free sacramental grace." The smile left. "It sounds like you could use some."

Penny waved to me from the door.

"Another time," I said, and I made my escape.

"What were you talking to Father Damien about? You looked so serious."

"Necromancy," I said.

"Frances! Isn't that where you have sex with dead people?"

"No. You just chat."

"And are you...?"

"Definitely not. Not with people, at least." I mumbled the last part under my breath.

Penny looked over her shoulder to where Father Damien still sat. "He didn't put the kibosh on the séance, did he?"

"N-o-o-o-o." I hadn't brought it up.

"It's probably fine because it's for a good cause, right? To find Elvira's killer."

"I'm sure you're right," I said, though I believed if I had asked Father Damien, the answer would have been a big no.

I pushed open the front door and met with a wave of heat. "Everything okey-dokey between you and the monsignor?"

"Our first appointment is next Monday." She grabbed my hand. "It's really happening. I mean, I'm talking to the priest and looking for dresses and meeting wedding planners, which reminds me. I have one coming to my house tomorrow. Would you be there, please, please, please?"

"Sure," I promised. "What are friends for?"

"You can always rely on friends." Penny stopped walking and blurted out, "By the way, Kemper isn't coming to the séance." She rolled her eyes. "He says he's not *into it*, whatever that means." She clenched her hands. "You would think he would come just for me, but no."

"Penny," I said, squeezing her shoulder. "It's not that big of a deal."

She stared at me, and then she burst out laughing. "I think I'm starting to freak out."

"Ice cream," I said, falling back on our favorite prescription medicine.

"Make mine a double."

SIXTEEN

I spent the rest of the day shining windows, scrubbing floors, and giving the house a general airing out. I'm not that particular when it's just me, or even a relative, but I wanted strangers to refer to me as *house proud*. It sounded better than slob. Not that I wanted anyone in my house, but it was too late to cancel now.

The last time I invited a group of people to hang out in my home was a fourth-grade slumber party. This time Auntie did the inviting. Short of calling them back and uninviting them, which would give rise to Auntie's wrath, I was stuck.

The business cards that Auntie left out for Sharlene were still on the kitchen table, and as I wiped it down, I stuck them in the back pocket of my jeans.

I hadn't said anything to Auntie about my talk with Father Damien. I figured this event was already planned, it was in the name of a good cause, and there was no way in Heaven or Hell that Auntie would successfully contact the dead. Still, the thought of passing out invitations to evil spirits kept flitting into my head.

I left the cooking to Auntie. She whipped up a hot Mexican dip appetizer with chips, mini baked spinach quiches, and bacon-wrapped water chestnuts with barbeque sauce. I took over cutting veggies and mixing dip for the veggie tray, and I cheated on the deli tray with pre-sliced meats and cheeses.

"What's to drink?" I asked.

"Same thing I always serve. Plenty of hot coffee." She motioned toward the refrigerator. "I don't think that ginger ale you bought me has gone flat yet."

It was going to take something stronger than flat ginger ale and coffee to help me make it through the evening. I made a quick trip to the liquor store for bottled water, cold beer, wine—both red and white—and then I added margarita mix and a bottle of tequila in case the evening went sour and I needed extra bucking up. As a last-minute purchase, I got a new bottle of ginger ale for Auntie.

When I returned home, I left the bags in the car and trotted over to my neighbor's house. I wasn't interested in hosting a neighborhood block party, but maybe Auntie was right. If I ever found a homicidal maniac waiting inside my home, as I had last month, it would be nice to have names to attach to my shrieks for help.

Sharlene Walker opened the door and immediately invited me in.

"I can't stay. We're having a few people over tonight. I just wanted to drop off my aunt's business cards. You left them behind the other day."

She took them and then insisted I come in. "Oh, just for a minute. I know when I've had relatives in the house, a break was always welcome."

I couldn't argue with that, so I followed her into the living room. The curtains were open, which made the room light and airy. Sharlene had a distinctly feminine taste, with soft palettes and frills. A magazine lay face down and open on a pretty floral loveseat with a ruffled skirt. From behind the couch, a professional photograph of a younger Sharlene and a burly, pleasant-looking man looked down on the occupants of the room, which included a small, curly-haired mutt.

"That's Mimi." Sharlene switched to baby talk. "Wook who's here, Sweetums. Maybe the nice lady will scratch your ears if you ask nicely."

I obliged. The dog looked up at me with the saddest eyes, but I didn't take it seriously, because I think it's a trick animals use to get treats. Sharlene moved the magazine and invited me to sit next to her.

"So, is it a party?" Sharlene leaned forward, a bright smile on her face, as if my answer really mattered.

"Not really. It's more of a, well, it's something to do with the murder."

She shuddered and covered her heart, which seemed to be a habit with her. "Gives me the shivers just thinking about it. I can't imagine how horrible it was for you to find a body." She took a sip from a glass that was sitting on the end table. "Actually, I do. I found my late husband one morning last June." She turned her head to smile up at the photograph.

"I thought I'd let him sleep in because it was the weekend. He always worked so hard during the week. When he hadn't gotten up by ten o'clock, which was very unusual for him, I thought I'd give him a shake. You know how it is. Sleep too long and you're awake for hours the next night." She turned one hand palms up. "He never got up again."

"How awful."

"That's life."

She took another sip.

"I've still got Ricky, my son, so it's not like I'm alone." She moved the dog to her lap and gave it a snuggle. "And my little Mimi. I don't know what I'd do without her."

She went on to tell me about the great accomplishments that took up all of Ricky's free time and made it difficult for him to fit in visits to his mother's house. I half-listened, nodding when appropriate and adding noises of appreciation.

This went on for some time, and I slipped a peek at my watch. It was a quarter after five. At least I thought that was what it read, because the watch face began to blur. I blinked a few times without success. My focus remained foggy. Maybe Auntie was right, and I needed glasses. At least that's what I thought before my insides filled with an aching sorrow and a sense of helplessness so strong that I rubbed the center of my chest. An urge to keen rose in the back of my throat, and only by clamping my jaws tight was I able to avoid a full wail. Still, a low whine escaped, which I covered by clearing my throat several times.

Sharlene paused. "Do you need a drink of water?"

Afraid to open my mouth, I nodded. She trotted off to the kitchen, leaving Mimi on the couch. The dog stared at me with a penetrating look that gave me a shiver. Was Mimi the source of this awful, empty feeling? Was she sad? Sick? Did she still miss her "daddy"? Not my problem.

Sharlene returned with my water. I drank it down and stood.

"Why don't you come over tonight?" The words were out before the idea formed a solid thought in my head.

Sharlene cocked her head. "Me? But what about your murder?"

"It's actually a séance that Auntie's giving for the suspects."

She rubbed her arms. At least she didn't put her hand over her heart again. "That sounds creepy."

"Don't worry. Auntie can't really channel spirits. She's putting on a show, and if I can say so without making her sound egotistical, Auntie loves a big audience."

"Are you sure I won't be in the way?" She reached out and patted Mimi on the head, and contact with the dog seemed to decide it for her. "No. I couldn't. I hate to leave my sweetie all alone."

"Bring her along. The more the merrier."

She flashed a sweet smile. "I'll come."

The dog's brown eyes met mine, and she lifted her brows. I was certain the achy feeling I'd just experienced came from Mimi, so I narrowed my eyes and gave her a look that said she better not pull anything like that tonight.

It had become apparent from the frolicking ghost of poor, dead Bonzo and now this depressed pooch on the floor that no matter how hard I tried to block out images, no matter how strong a mental barrier I used, animals with something urgent to say were going to force their way into my head. It might be time to consider a lobotomy.

I wondered how Chauncey would react to his new playmate, but as I swung open the door to my house, bags in hand, it appeared there were bigger, more urgent problems. Auntie stood on the couch and waved her hands at me in warning. Chauncey, safely beside her, barked nonstop, and Emily joined in the noise, hissing from atop the bookcase.

"What's wrong?"

Auntie whispered, "Don't move."

I lowered my bags to the floor, searching for the source of danger. They were all staring down around my ankles.

"Is there a rattlesnake in the house?" I whispered. A low, drawn out sound like the squeal of worn out brakes came from behind me.

"What the flipping—"

Coming at me in an awkward, loping run, hooked beak open and ready to chomp down, was Petey the Cockatoo. I ran.

I dodged left, and the bird followed like a seasoned linebacker. When he followed me right, I turned tail and put the coffee table between me and the angry bird, but Petey came around the corner, head lowered and looking for blood.

We circled the coffee table three times before I thought to grab one of the paper grocery bags as a way to capture my pursuer. On the next pass, I dumped the contents safely on the couch, while Chauncey barked, and Auntie shouted.

"He's gaining on you!"

I turned to face my assailant.

Petey skid to a halt, fluffed his wings, and squawked. In a crouch, I crept forward, and once close enough, I dropped the bag over his head. He fought like a trooper, but I held firm until I got him to the open door of his cage and dumped him inside.

Auntie held out her hand. "Help me down. I thought he could use some exercise, and he was fine at first. Really. But then he got this horrible gleam in his eye and went for me."

A small trickle of blood ran down her ankle. I retrieved a damp cloth and some adhesive bandages from the medicine cabinet and patched her up.

"I wonder if birds carry diseases," I wondered aloud. "Maybe you should have this looked at."

"It's a scratch." She turned her ankle and considered my

work. "I don't suppose you have any of those clear bandages? They'd look better with my new sandals."

"I'm not going back to the store. Besides, your Madame Guinevere muumuu is so long, no one will see."

I still needed to change, which meant borrowing my own bedroom. As I rummaged through the closet, Auntie talked to me through the closed door.

"I've been thinking. The tarot card business isn't paying like it used to. Maybe I should move on to other things."

"Really?" Knowing that I wouldn't have to repeat my talk with Father Damien took a load off my shoulders. "I think that's a sound decision."

"I've been toying with the idea of broadening my skill set."

"What skill set?"

I didn't hear what came next; I had a sweater wrapped around my head as I struggled into it. Then I tried on a pair of pants, looked into the full-length mirror on the back of my door, and realizing I wasn't going to lose ten pounds in the next half hour, took them off again. I didn't even bother to hang them back up. They were headed for Goodwill.

"Sissy? Are you listening to me?"

"Sure," I lied. "Sounds like a great idea."

"Thank you, honey. I guess I just needed to hear that from someone objective."

By the time Penny showed up, I had on a peacock-blue sweater and black jeans. Auntie wore a dark purple Muumuu with a shiny gold pattern around the sleeves and a dazzling large crystal necklace around her neck. Her hair was in the usual bun, but she had tied it together with a purple flower. She looked as if she might break into a hula dance.

"I am so excited," Penny said, rushing into Auntie's arms for a big hug.

"Where's your young man? I want to meet him."

"He couldn't come." Penny looked at the floor. "Nothing to do with you or the séance. I think he was just put off by the whole murder business."

"Could be," Auntie said. "But at least he let you come."

Penny flushed. "Let me? Oh, we don't *let* each other do things. We're a couple, but we're independent and perfectly capable of having our own interests. For instance, he may like powder-blue for the groomsmen tuxedos, and I might like deep gray, but that doesn't mean we don't love each other!"

She chased the outburst with some hysterical laughter.

The doorbell rang again. Auntie took her by the arm and moved her out of the way while I opened the door. The happy trio—Lola, Bea, and Jane—beamed at me.

"Welcome," I said, stepping aside.

"Planning a wedding is a bucketful of stress," Auntie said to Penny. "Why, I remember my mother-in-law insisted on wearing white. That was back in the days when people had the good manners to avoid competing with the bride. Said it was her signature color." She snorted. "Black would have been more like it. That woman had a temper like the devil."

"Mother-in-laws?" Bea threw up her hands. "I called mine the *chupacabra* for the first year we were married. Then I find out she's just intimidated by my tamales." She jabbed her chest with her thumb. "I should go pro, mine are so good."

"Mine was a saint," Jane said, her lips twitching.

"We have to keep an eye on Doris," Lola said. "Clark's mother is fond of betting on the horses."

"What did you all do about your wedding problems?" Penny asked.

Auntie smiled. "You'll learn to choose your battles. There was no way that three-hundred-pound horse-faced woman was going to give me any competition by wearing a white dress to my wedding." She winked. "I was a looker back then."

Bea shrugged. "I lied. I asked for her tamale recipe, saying that her little boy was pining for them."

"Mine was a saint," Jane repeated.

"Choose my battles," Penny repeated thoughtfully, several times, as if memorizing a new mantra, and the women clucked around her like she was an orphaned chick and led her into the kitchen.

I took a last look around and found my place presentable except for the large dog stretched out on the couch.

"Off." I pointed at the floor.

Chauncey stretched with a groan and stared at me.

"If you don't move your fanny, I'm taking you back to the pound." I pointed at the bedroom.

He put his front feet on the floor, stretched out his back legs one at a time to show he wasn't in a hurry to do my bidding, and then trotted off to the hallway. When I reached out for Emily, she made a break for the top of the bookcase. The doorbell rang, and I left her to run free.

Elvira Jenkins' bereaved family members stood on the doorstep. Bull stepped in with a warm "Howdy" and went in search of Auntie.

"Calling my mother back from the dead seems a little sick," Tim said. He was dressed in a dark suit, something one might wear to a funeral, and his gaze darted around the room as if he expected to see a big picture of Elvira surrounded by candles and incense. "I don't like the idea. Not that I believe it's going to work, but it lacks respect."

Happy to declare myself free of any culpability, I spread out my hands and shrugged. "I've got nothing to do with it."

Catherine, contrasting her husband's somber look with a soft peach silk suit and a soothing smile, took her husband's arm and led him into my home. "I've never been to a séance. It sounds... interesting." The bright smile she offered strained a bit at the edges, but she seemed determined to make the best of the evening.

"I promise you that my aunt thinks she's helping, and she has the best intentions. At least there will be good food. And I bought alcohol to make the evening go down better."

I mentioned a decent brand of beer. That mollified Tim, while Catherine preferred white wine. While I retrieved the beverages, Donna Pederson arrived, and soon I'd slipped into the role of hostess. Just because I didn't like to entertain didn't mean I wasn't familiar with the protocol. Mother had wrangled me into helping her at family functions. I cooed convincingly over arriving guests as if I was happy to see them and urged people to fill up their plates from the buffet set out on my kitchen table.

Auntie wandered the room, warming up her audience. While speaking with Sonny Street, she suddenly grabbed his hand and turned it palm up.

"Let's see what your career line says."

He looked around, embarrassed, to see if anyone was listening. No one was, except me. I moved over and asked Auntie, in my most cheerful voice, what she thought she was doing.

"Reading his palm, of course."

"Why?"

"I told you. I'm expanding my resume. Now be quiet. I'm still new at this, and I need to focus."

"See anything good?" Sonny had moved as far away from Auntie as he could without leaving his hand behind. It made me think of those lizards that can detach from their tails to escape from predators.

"There it is!" Auntie poked at one of his lines. "You've got a big payoff coming up soon."

Suddenly Sonny wasn't so worried about what people thought about him having his palm read. He stepped closer and looked over his hand with interest.

Auntie, still too professional to speak in certainties, qualified her statement.

"A big job. Or maybe it's a job at a big venue. Whatever it is, something big is coming your way."

"Hey. Maybe I'll get a job at Cesar's Palace. That's always been my dream."

"Could be."

She grabbed Catherine Jenkins' hand next.

"Sorry, but I only know how to do career lines." Auntie squinted. "Ooh! I see something exotic for you."

Catherine sputtered with laughter. "Only if Wolf Creek is exotic."

"Maybe I got the wrong line. Let me try again."

"Shouldn't you get moving on the séance?" I asked, prying Catherine's hand from Auntie's grip.

Sharlene Walker arrived just then, holding Mimi. She scanned the room. "You're sure it's alright that I'm here?"

"Of course. Chauncey is locked up in the bedroom, so I could either put Mimi in there or outside."

"Can't she stay with me?" She clutched the little dog closer.

"I wouldn't want anyone to step on her." Never having owned a small dog, I assumed this was a major concern.

"She's very good at dodging feet." Sharlene kissed the dog's nose. "Aren't you, Sweetums?"

I motioned her inside. "Why not? Bring her in."

Bull raised a hand in greeting, and she moved to join him. Auntie watched her cross the room and came over to me.

"Did you invite her?"

I hadn't thought about Sharlene in terms of competition for Bull's attention. "I thought she might like it. Shouldn't I have?"

Auntie kissed my cheek. "You're a good girl, Sissy."

I wasn't expecting that, but I was happy to cross one worry off my list. Now I just had to make it through the séance. You'd never have known that anything as unusual as communicating with the dead was on the agenda. Everyone was chatting and mixing as if they had been invited to a simple, normal cocktail party. I barely heard the light rap on the front door over the noise of conversation.

Detective Martin Bowers looked down at me, and I wasn't surprised by his scowl.

"Not my idea."

"Auntie?"

"You got it."

He yanked me outside and pulled the door shut.

"If we keep meeting out here, I'll have to set up chairs on the driveway, so we can be more comfortable."

"Frankie, what is your aunt trying to prove? That she's not a suspect? Because an attempt to locate the murderer using voodoo will not count in her favor. We have all sorts of convicted criminals in prison who offered to help us with our case before we nabbed them for the crime."

"Not the same situation at all. Those people probably wanted to follow the investigation to find out how much you knew. Auntie doesn't really give two pins about what the police are doing. She's just having her version of fun. And you're not required to say a thing tonight. You've been invited to observe the suspects in close quarters."

"How thoughtful. And your aunt is going to magically pull the murderer out of a hat at the end of the night? Because we police require proof, not hocus-pocus guesswork."

His words were delivered in an even tone, but the glance he darted toward the house reflected his discomfort. The idea of dark rooms and moaning old women communing with the dead obviously did not appeal to him.

"First off," I said, "this could be amusing. Auntie's never tried a séance. She hasn't a clue what she's doing."

"That could be dangerous," he said. I remembered Father Damien's words with a start.

"Dangerous?" A weak, nervous laugh escaped my lips.

"I know you think the occult is a big joke, but I've seen the effects on kids who've dabbled, and there's nothing funny about it. They get involved in some pretty serious stuff."

I crossed my arms. "Really? So, you're telling me the secret to gang member success is to hold a séance? Instead of whipping out a gun, they pull out a deck of tarot cards? I think you might be exaggerating just a teeny bit."

"It's not the gang members who get involved in that crap. It's usually kids from well-to-do families with too much time on their hands and not enough guidance from mommy and daddy. And they don't play with cards. They torture and kill innocent animals. And it usually starts out with something as simple as a Ouija board."

The quiet, even tone he used to pass on this shocking information frightened me more than if he had shouted in my face.

"Okay, but this is just a silly old woman playacting. It's not Satanic," I said, determined to ignore any possibility of an uninvited guest making a sudden appearance and sweeping us all down to Hades. "And it could be useful, too. If you can keep from laughing, you might actually catch a response that means something to your highly trained eyes and ears."

He stared with great interest at his fingernails. "Then your aunt isn't seriously involved in spiritualism?"

"Let's see." I pretended to think. "I threw three fits today when she used my favorite t-shirt as a dish towel, and when I finished what I thought was a spectacularly clear expression of rage, she asked me if something was bothering me. So, not only is she not sensitive to vibes—spiritual or worldly—she can't even see what's in front of her face." I didn't mention that her blind spot only applied to me.

His shoulders relaxed. "So, what's the point of this evening?"

"Auntie thinks the suspects, I mean guests, might be thrown off balance by the thought of Elvira Jenkins naming her murderer through a medium. She also thinks your impressive presence might intimidate them, and she swears that's the right approach to get the killer to let something slip. Not a confession, but maybe a contradiction, or a bit of information they didn't mean to make public."

"The idea has merits." He took a step toward me, lowered his face next to mine, and said with a joking growl in his voice, "Do you really think I'm an impressive presence?"

No reason to mention that with him standing so close,

his cheek practically touching mine, I'd forgotten how to breathe.

Auntie saved the day. She whipped open the door. "There you are! Stop hogging the nice detective, Sissy."

Auntie grabbed Bowers' wrist and pulled him inside, and he looked over his shoulder at me and mouthed a silent scream. As I followed him in, I noticed my laughter was the only noise in my living room. The bright, friendly chatter stopped, for an obvious reason. The cop was here, and they were all suspects.

Catherine Jenkins broke the ice. She walked up to Bowers and took his hand in both of hers. "On behalf of the family, thank you for agreeing to come tonight." She motioned to include all those present. "We're all so grateful for the hard work the Wolf Creek police department has put into investigating the unfortunate death of my mother-in-law, and we're certain that you will find the person responsible and bring them to justice. And it's very, um, open-minded of you to come to a séance."

Catherine must have been very successful at her public relations job.

"Here, here," said Sonny, toasting the air with his drink. The rest of the guests murmured their agreement.

Bravo, Catherine. She'd succeeded in turning a room of potential suspects into a group of concerned citizens interested in justice. Not to be outdone, Heather Ozu came forward.

"The Baking Channel, especially *Blue-Ribbon Babes*, have full confidence in the Wolf Creek police."

Sonny joined the procession.

"We sure do. All of us want this tragedy behind us. It's hard to make people laugh if they're wondering about the corpse found on the set." He was the only one who laughed at his joke.

Bowers shook hands with everyone in the room as they each gave a short speech about how wonderful the police had been and what a huge hole the murder of Elvira Jenkins left in their lives. As the widower, Bull was allowed to simply shake hands and be done with it. Donna was the lone dissenter in the room.

"I'm just a tiny bit concerned about this—about tonight. There's already been a great deal of coverage in the newspapers about the murder, and they insist on mentioning names. When people type Donna Pederson into their Internet search engines, I'm worried that the top results will be about the murder. And while people can read those stories and see that I'm not involved in any way, I certainly don't want the second-highest ranked search result to be about a séance. People might get the wrong idea about me."

Bowers held her gaze, a keen light in his eyes. "Am I speaking to the new Blue-Ribbon Queen?"

Heather Ozu inserted herself into the conversation.

"That hasn't been officially announced yet." She turned an irritated glare on Donna. "And I'm not sure what you're so worried about. Anyone looking for the Blue-Ribbon Queen is going to search for just that term. No one would know Donna Pederson from Adam right now."

"Right now," Donna repeated. To Bowers she said, "I just can't imagine that having a séance is a good idea. I mean, some people actually believe in this nonsense. I think it's cruel to raise the hopes of Elvira's family."

Auntie was quick to deflect this criticism. "Elvira will not hesitate to speak if she has something to say. Since she was knocked on the noggin," someone gasped, "my apologies, but she was hit on the back of the head, she may not have seen who took her life and she may have absolutely nothing to say."

"She always had something to say," Tim said with a nervous laugh.

Now that Auntie had lowered the expectations of the group and couldn't be blamed when nothing happened, she herded us into a circle that included the couch and several chairs, including metal folding chairs we'd borrowed from the Women's Guild at St. Mel's with Penny's help. I hadn't anticipated the arrival of Bea, Jane, and Lola, so I retrieved a stool from the closet for additional seating.

The family was given the place of honor on the couch. Sharlene managed to squeeze in next to Bull. Auntie claimed my comfortable reading chair as her own, and there was a scramble for my kitchen chairs, which at least had cushions. I got stuck with a hard folding chair, and Bowers took the stool to my right.

On my other side, Donna sat ramrod straight, her lips pressed together in prim disapproval.

"Now, if we could all hold hands," Auntie instructed. "Sissy, you get the lights."

I flicked the switch by the hallway and then felt my way back in the dark. Bowers reached out a hand and directed me into my chair, so I could rejoin the circle.

Donna's clasp felt limp, clammy and cool, while Bowers had a firm grip. His fingers, wrapped around mine, were warm and strong.

Auntie took a deep breath and let the air out in a long hiss. "There are several non-believers here. That's alright, but I ask you to open your minds to whatever might happen. Don't repel the spirits intentionally."

Bowers leaned in and whispered in my ear. "You mean I

can put an end to this whole thing through sheer will power?"

His warm breath tickled. I shuddered. "Behave yourself."

"Ahem." Auntie cleared her throat. "I need silence." She made us wait a few minutes while she hummed and moaned, calling out to the spirit of Elvira. I wondered what she planned to do. Was she going to imitate Elvira's voice? That would be embarrassing.

"I sense a presence in the room."

"I counted thirteen," Bowers whispered, "including the dog." I squeezed his hand to shut him up.

"Elvira, are you there?" Auntie said in a raised voice. My eyes had adjusted to the dark with the help of peripheral light that came through the front window. Auntie's eyes were open but vacant, a look I'd seen her try out on tarot clients who probed too deeply with questions. In those instances, she had consulted her spirit guides and then said the information was not available to the Earthbound. If only we could be that lucky tonight.

Auntie closed her eyes. "We seek your counsel. I don't know if you recall, honey, but you were sent to the spiritual plane by an act of violence, perpetrated by someone with a bad attitude."

I leaned into Bowers and spoke out of the side of my mouth. "I wish Auntie's parish priest could hear this. It's worth at least ten Hail Mary's."

He snorted in response.

Auntie cracked open one eye. "Is that you, Elvira? I can't quite hear you. There's a distraction on my end."

Duly chastised, Bowers and I sat up and wiped the grins from our faces.

"That's better." Auntie's eyes were closed again. She

spoke her next lines in a lowered voice with rounded tones. She might have been imitating a television spoof on psychic rip-offs. "We need you to point to the murderer."

"How can she point if she's a spirit?" Sonny asked.

Catherine barked out a laugh, and Heather shushed him.

"Seriously. She won't have fingers."

Auntie gave him the look that used to send my cousins and me scurrying to hide out in the storm cellar. He bowed his head. There's nothing like an old woman's scorn to generate shame.

Again, she let the silence build.

People squirmed, and one of the metal folding chairs made a popping noise.

My nose itched. I let go of Donna's hand and scratched.

Suddenly, the room filled with shrill screeches. "Meow! Meow! MEOW!"

With the last shriek, an image of Emily leapt into my head. Her lips were curled back in a ferocious snarl, and yellow eyes gleamed with murderous intent. I felt Bowers go rigid.

Maybe I jumped back at the sudden, larger-than-life picture of my normally sweet kitty performing her role as demon cat, but it felt more like a hand grabbed my shoulders and shoved me, hard. My chair flew back and hit the floor, with me still in it, and the motion knocked the breath out of me.

Bowers was at my side in an instant. "Frankie." He tapped my face. "Frankie!"

I wheezed out a cough. "I'm not unconscious, so you can stop slapping me." I rolled onto my knees and he helped me up. Someone turned on the lights, and I saw everyone's expressions. If I could have breathed, I would have laughed.

Tim looked slightly curious but mostly irritated. Catherine cocked her head to one side and her eyebrows joined together. Sharlene looked around with wonder. Clearly, she thought this was part of the show.

Donna leaned as far away from me as she could get without tipping off her chair. Sonny Street studied me as if wondering how he could work something that attention-getting into his act without looking like an idiot. Heather thought I had the plague. Penny's hands were clasped together in delight, and Auntie looked like a bull about to charge. Bea looked uncertain. Lola was enjoying herself, and Jane disapproved. And Bull? He just looked concerned.

I gave a weak grin.

"I forgot to lock Petey up. My cat must have taken a shot at him, and it surprised the heck out of me."

All eyes moved to the covered birdcage in the corner of the room. Emily was nowhere in sight, but she moves pretty fast. She was probably hiding under someone's chair right now.

"I didn't hear anything," Sonny said. "Did I miss something?"

I grabbed the cage and took it to my bedroom, checked under the bed to make sure my cat wasn't in the room, and then closed the door behind me. Chauncey grabbed his chance to escape, and when I returned to the living room, he was doing his best to clean up the leftovers from abandoned plates. I shooed him away and threw away the ones he'd managed to lick.

The interruption ruined Auntie's great moment. The guests wandered from the circle to refresh their drinks and used the washroom. My aunt wasn't pleased with my interruption. I could tell by the gigantic frown on her lips and how she turned her back on me.

Assuming that Auntie wasn't the only one rattled by the interruption, I thought this might be a good time to check the pulse of the suspects. In the corner by the sliding doors that led outside, Heather poked away at the buttons on her cell phone, so I sidled up and waited until she hit send.

"I have a feeling that Elvira's not going to show up tonight."

She slipped the phone in her purse. "Did you really believe she would?"

"If anybody's spirit would have something to say, Elvira's would. Terrible how prone she was to make a fuss about things."

"What things?"

"I saw how Elvira acted at the taping of your show. Not using the sponsor's products." I shook my head. "Terrible. And all because *Blue-Ribbon Babes* couldn't honor the prize check."

Heather clenched her fists, gritted her perfect teeth, and growled out an argh noise. "One mistake and I'll never live it down! I told that old lady—I told all the contestants—that I'd forgotten to make the deposit. I had it in my safe, the money was all there, it just slipped my mind in the bustle of preparing for our show."

She held out her hand to show me a perfect manicure. "You think I do this myself? My appointment lasted an hour and a half. And I had a final fitting for my outfit—they practically sewed me into that dress—and then hair and makeup, last-minute changes." She curled her fingers into a fist. "One day. That's all they would have to wait for the check. One day! I could have given them the real check and then hoped I would beat them to the bank in the morning, but I'm not in the habit of kiting checks."

That seemed like a big price to pay for such a small mistake, if Heather was telling the truth.

"We happened to run into Jeremy. Such a shame he had to leave you over a little misunderstanding."

She narrowed her eyes. "Don't believe everything you hear. Jeremy's a big boy. He can make his own decisions, but he does have to pay the consequences."

"No offense, but he didn't seem that strong-willed when he was around you. He, um, fawned a lot."

That brought a smile. "People will do that if they think they can get something from you, but it's a waste of time with me. It takes more than being a kiss-butt to get into my good graces."

Did that mean Jeremy was lying when he said he wasn't really interested in show business? Did he hope his connection with Heather would lead to bigger jobs? Or was he after something else?

Sonny strolled over and patted my shoulder. "Was that part of the show? You should consider stunts, though I didn't get the point of it. You actually broke things up. Too bad. This is my first séance." He looked over at the abandoned circle of chairs and noted, "In movies, they always sit around a table."

"I'll remember that next time."

"And your aunt should have on one of those turbans. And really, no offense, but the medium should be someone sexy, like Heather. What about it, Heather? Are you up for a new career?"

I left the two of them mocking my aunt's production values and moved into the kitchen. Auntie was in conference with Bowers and Penny. She turned on me the minute I entered the room.

"I'll never be able to recreate the mood now."

"You were really doing well," Penny gushed.

"No more. I'm calling it," Bowers said. Little beads of sweat gathered on his forehead and upper lip. Funny, but I didn't think the house was that warm.

Auntie launched a protest. "I hardly got started. And maybe Sissy's accident will put the killer on edge. We might learn something. I have one or two things up my sleeve that will—"

Bowers held up a hand to stop the flow of words. "One attempt is good enough. And you're right. You'll never be able to achieve the effect you were going for, so that's that."

"You don't have to stay," she persisted. "I'm sure you've got important things to do. Why don't you go do them? I promise to take notes."

"My investigation. My suspects. My call. It's over." He stepped into the living room and waved a hand to get everyone's attention. "Ladies and gentlemen, it's been fun, but we're calling it a night."

The response was mixed. Most people headed for the door, some disappointed, some fleeing with relief. Bull wanted a word with Auntie, and she suggested they step out into my backyard.

"Behave yourselves," I hissed into Auntie's ear.

"I don't know what you're talking about," she snapped, following after him.

What was I talking about? Did I really think Auntie was tactless enough to play kissy with a widower before his spouse was even in the ground? With his son and daughter-in-law just yards away? She definitely liked him. I remembered her flushed face when she met him at the Baking Channel reception. And it seemed to me that she had been competing for Bull's attention when Sharlene dropped by the other day. Then again, Auntie was glad I invited Sharlene. Of course, she hadn't issued an invitation to my neighbor personally. Maybe I was giving it way too much thought.

"Thank you so much for including me," Sharlene said. She held up Mimi. "We really enjoyed ourselves. Your aunt is so impressive." She waved Mimi's paw at me before heading home.

Penny and the trio of ladies said they would stick around and help clean up. I accepted.

"You're going to stay with her for a while?" Bowers asked Penny.

"I told Kemper I'd call him around ten, so I have to leave at nine-thirty. Why?"

He put his hands in his pants pockets and scuffed the toe of his shoe against the floor—a stalling tactic if ever I've seen one. "Frankie might have hit her head. I want someone to watch—to look out for her."

"I'm fine." I gathered a few paper plates and tossed them in the garbage. "See? Eye-hand coordination working. No worries."

He seemed reluctant to leave, but when Bull came back in, Bowers left with the Jenkins's family. Auntie took her new friends into the living room for a chat, and she quieted their protests by insisting that Penny and I should have alone time now that she was engaged. The dirty look she shot me as she walked out of the kitchen told me Auntie's removal of our voluntary cleaning crew was in revenge for her ruined performance.

"That went well," I said, transferring the leftovers to containers. "Not."

"You couldn't help it," Penny said. "You lost your balance." She looked up through her bangs. "That's all it was, right?"

"Right," I sighed. "I'm a klutz."

"Your aunt's friends are nice."

"Makes you wonder what they see in Auntie."

Penny giggled and tossed the dishrag at me, and the kitchen somehow got cleaned in-between our goofing off. Penny left in plenty of time to make it home for her phone call with Kemper. The trio left the same time she did, thanking us for a fun evening.

My pajamas were in my bedroom. When I turned on the light, the first thing I saw was the covered birdcage, resting on top of my armoire. As I opened a drawer, I noticed a white feather on the floor. And another. I picked up five in all. Did cockatoos molt?

My muscles tensed, but I ignored the warning and slipped the cover up for a peek. A muffled cry escaped before I clamped my hand over my mouth, and I walked out of the room in a daze and picked up the phone. I dialed the number to Bower's cell phone. When he answered, I drew in a deep breath.

"I'd like to report a murder."

SEVENTEEN

Detective Gutierrez stood with her hands on her slim hips and studied the lifeless form of Petey the cockatoo.

"A dead bird does not qualify as a murder victim."

In the middle of my coffee table, Petey lay on the bottom of his cage, feet up, and his head turned to an unnatural angle.

"I'd say that bird had his neck rung. Used to do the chickens myself, when I was a girl." And with that pronouncement, Auntie handed me a glass of tequila, the strongest liquor in the house. I took a sip and grimaced.

"I don't understand why you're here," I said. "No offense."

Gutierrez said, "Bowers asked me to cover for him, but I don't know why he thought you needed the police." She pointed a slim finger at Petey. "I mean, it's a bird."

"Petey was Elvira Jenkins' bird. That's the lady who was killed at the Saguaro Studios. Maybe it was just a vindictive act, but maybe there's a reason why her bird had to go. It talked, you know."

Gutierrez turned a puzzled expression in my direction. "Talked?"

"Mostly it said Meow, but maybe it was capable of saying more, and the killer didn't want us to hear it."

"A trained bird." She blew out a steady stream of air. "I suppose that's possible. Did a particular guest show an interest in the animal or have the opportunity to slip into your bedroom?"

"People were in and out of the hallway to use the facilities after the, er, after I fell."

"Are you saying someone assaulted you?" The detective pressed her lips together to suppress her smile, but she didn't succeed. When I told her that wasn't a very professional response, she opened her notebook, the one she'd stuck in her back pocket the minute she'd seen Petey, though she didn't wipe the grin off her face.

I recalled the feeling that someone had pushed me, but it was an invisible force, not a person, and Detective Gutierrez had no interest in the supernatural. "Nothing like that. I just tipped over."

She gave a delicate snort, like a cat sneezing. "Klutz. Now, tell me about this party."

"It was supposed to be a séance to talk to Elvira Jenkins," Auntie offered, "but things were interrupted before they really got moving."

"A séance."

"All the suspects were here."

"She doesn't really want to hear about that," I said, squeezing Auntie's shoulder.

"Oh, but she does." The amusement left Detective Gutierrez' expression. "Who were your guests?" She readied her pen, and Auntie helpfully ticked them off on her fingers.

"Elvira's family. One of the other Blue-Ribbon bakers. Betty never showed, and Natasha and Bert couldn't make it. They said they were busy. Is that suspicious?"

"N-o-o-o. I'd say that was a healthy response." Gutierrez dismissed Auntie for the moment and turned her questions on me.

"Can you tell me how this doesn't qualify as interfering in a police investigation?"

"It was perfectly legitimate," Auntie cried. "Detective Bowers supervised."

I groaned.

Gutierrez' eyes lit up. "Bowers was here?"

I flinched at the zing that shot through the air, emanating from the lady detective. She obviously thought she'd hit the jackpot and found a way to embarrass Bowers.

"Just long enough to break things up and tell everyone to go home," I offered in a last-ditch effort to save his reputation.

"He was a spoilsport," Auntie agreed, and I felt my shoulders relax. "At least we know the murderer was here tonight," Auntie added.

"And you never left my sight," I said, "so at least we know you aren't the murderer. Ha-ha. Not that I really thought you were."

Gutierrez closed her book. "I'm glad to hear you've got it all taped up, because there doesn't seem to be anything else for me to do here."

"You're not going to dust the cage for fingerprints or look for clues?" Auntie offered the use of her face powder, since Gutierrez hadn't brought a crime scene team with her.

The detective opened her gorgeous brown eyes wide and blinked. "I'll send over our Animal Crime Scene Unit, Ma'am."

"I'll put on a fresh pot of coffee." Auntie scurried to the kitchen.

"Is there any such a thing?" I asked.

Gutierrez snorted. "What do you think?"

I didn't like the way she held my gaze as she said goodnight. Since Bowers had been to the séance, it would have been better if he had come himself. And I couldn't believe how he'd opened himself up to ridicule by allowing Gutierrez anywhere near my home. Had he had enough of séances and tarot readers and pet psychics? Was he washing his hands of the whole case?

I hoped this didn't mean that Gutierrez would be taking over the investigation.

EIGHTEEN

Auntie wore her new blue top and a denim skirt to Bull Jenkins' house the next morning when we delivered Petey to his final resting place. The shiny gold sandals on Auntie's feet were a jarring reminder of what now lie in the new shoebox, talons up.

I'd called ahead to warn Bull. He was waiting for us in the open doorway of his ranch style home when we arrived. He gently took the box from my hands.

"Oh, Bull. I'm so sorry," Auntie said, taking the opportunity to envelope him in one of her hugs. He turned his cheek for a kiss and patted her back.

"It's a mystery to me why anyone would kill Petey," he said, motioning us into the foyer. Once inside, I stopped walking and gaped.

"Wow."

He followed my admiring gaze through the living room, or what a decorator might refer to as the Great Space, to a back wall made entirely of glass. The view of the canyon was spectacular, with Saguaro cacti dotting a landscape of dry brush and dirt. A lone coyote trotted through the ravine carrying what I hoped was a jackrabbit. The houses on the opposite rim stared back. Thoughts of binoculars wielded by bored retirees made me take a step back.

"It is a nice view." Catherine Jenkins got up from a long, leather couch. "It was nice of you to bring the bird over here." She twitched her shoulders. "I don't think I could have, you know, handled the thing."

I noticed she was still in her pajamas—a light green silk pants set with cacti embroidered on the top. The material skimmed her curves, and when she curled her hands into fists and reached toward the ceiling in a full body stretch, I realized Catherine Jenkins had a hot body. Then I remembered her latest miscarriage and felt bad for being jealous.

"Do you live here?"

"Tim and I spent the last few nights helping out."

Bull jumped in and said, "There's plenty of room if the two of you want to stay longer."

"We'll stay as long as you need us, as long as we're not in the way."

From what I'd seen so far, Auntie and I could pretend to leave and take up residence in a nook and they'd never find us. The living room was larger than my entire house. Dark tile covered the floor, with a large area rug between the couch and chairs that looked like cowhide, minus the head and the hooves.

The dining room shared the open space. The centerpiece, a mahogany table, was long enough to seat an entire crew after the roundup, and they emphasized the rustic with a chandelier of lights housed in cowbells. A china cabinet held a collection of plates with birds on them—a cardinal, a robin, and something with a long beak that might have been a woodpecker. I didn't know much about birds except that they pooped a lot and I wouldn't want to own one.

Bull invited us to sit. Auntie sank down in a chair so wide and deep her feet didn't touch the floor. Catherine claimed the couch again and half-reclined with her elbow on the armrest like a centerfold. Okay. Not nice. I put my inner cat away and turned my attention to Bull.

Holding up the box, he looked around the room, obviously searching for the right place to set down Petey's dead remains.

"I buried all my animals in the backyard," Auntie said. "The kids made little crosses out of popsicle sticks. That was the secret. Calm them down first with a snack and then make a game out of decorating the grave."

"The backyard's out." I stood in front of a glass sliding door that led to a balcony. Outside, I looked over the railing just as a mother quail skittered by with her chicks, zigzagging their way down to the rocky canyon floor.

To my left, a detailed arrangement of ceramic containers filled with mini rose bushes, various flowering plants, and rows of herbs were displayed on aged, wooden crates next to two rattan chairs and a small stone table.

Bull joined me outside. "I'll have to bury him in the front yard." He led the way. The balcony circled around and put us back on the driveway. The front "yard" was a natural stone and pink gravel, with flowering shrubs placed in strategic spots to block the view of the front windows from passing traffic. Bull set the box down and retrieved a shovel from the garage.

"Gotta get this done before it gets hot." He chose a spot near a bougainvillea that he had recently watered. The ground, still damp, moved without too much effort.

"When did you last see Petey? I mean, did you take a

peek to see if he was doing alright when you were at my house?"

"Heck, no. You took him into a room and closed the door. That marks it as private, in my book. And besides, I never really cared that much for birds. Noisy critters. And Petey had a mean streak." He released a heavy sigh. "It would sure be nice if it turned out your cat got him. I hate to think of anyone killing an animal for fun."

"Until Emily grows opposable thumbs—and I'm sure she's working on it—she's not capable of strangling anything. It's too bad you weren't tempted to check on him. It would have helped me place the time of his death."

"I don't understand," he said as he dug. "It's like someone's trying to erase all traces of Vera from my life. First her. Then her beloved pet."

Erase all traces of Elvira. Interesting. "You still have your son. He's a reminder of your wife."

Bull nudged the box with his boot until it tipped the contents into the hole. "And it seems as if the family line is going to end with him."

"I heard about Catherine's trouble. I'm so sorry."

He replaced a shovel of dirt. "These things happen in God's time and to His purpose."

"She's young. She can try again," I said, hoping he took those words in the consoling spirit with which they were meant. They sounded kind of heartless once they were out. He caught my eye.

"I know what you mean."

"It's an uncomfortable thing to think about, but you're sure Elvira didn't have any enemies?"

He packed the grave down. "Not one. Sure, there were people who didn't like her, but they just avoided her. That's what normal people do. Not sneak up on someone and knock them on the back of the head with a frying pan." He nodded at the grave. "And then kill their pet bird."

Sneak up. He had a point. You wouldn't turn your back on a raving lunatic who was waving a frying pan around. The killer must have surprised her. Elvira was expecting the photographer, but who did she meet instead? Was it someone she knew? Or did she innocently pose for her picture, giving the killer time to retrieve the frying pan...no. That was stupid. She must not have seen her killer at all. She must have gone to meet the photographer, and as she waited, the killer, armed with the frying pan, snuck up and gave her a good whack.

When Bull bowed his head, we observed a moment of silence before he led the way into the house via the garage, so he could put away the shovel.

We entered the house by the kitchen and found Auntie leaning against the marble island and drinking from a mug.

"I hope you don't mind. I made coffee. Catherine went to get dressed."

We sat at a kitchen table that looked out over the part of the balcony that ran down the side of the house. Several kinds of birds fluttered around a hanging bird feeder, including a bright red cardinal. It was a peaceful view. I could get used to waking up to it every morning.

After a bit of chit-chat, we sat in uncomfortable silence. Instead of diving into a new topic, Auntie became uncharacteristically tongue tied. "Do you want me to—" She pulled a napkin from the holder in the center of the table and wiped down the tabletop in front of her, even though it was perfectly clean. "I wondered—that is, if you like—" She bunched up the napkin in her fist. "Oh, heck. Do you want my help to go through Elvira's things?"

Bull's pallor turned pasty gray. He sucked in a hiss of air. It was as if she slapped him.

"I put my foot in it again, didn't I. I'm sorry."

"No. Not at all. I just hadn't thought that far ahead. Once I do give her stuff away to charity or store it in the garage, it'll be real."

Auntie clucked. "That's how it was when Pitt died. I even wanted to hang onto his shaving kit. It felt like it was a betrayal to say goodbye to him."

I was a young adult when my Uncle Pitt died, at that age when death was something that happened to old people. That included anyone over forty. Uncle Pitt had been several years older than Aunt Gertrude—possibly decades—and that would have put him in his sixties. Still, the only thing I remembered about that time was that Mother spent a great deal of time at Auntie's.

"You just tell me when you're ready, and I'll come help if you like. I'll even fly back here."

"I'm grateful."

Bull's lower lip trembled, and he tried to cover it with a forced coughing fit. When Catherine swept into the room dressed in gray slacks and a white blouse, it provided a welcome distraction.

"I have some errands to run." She cocked her head at Auntie. "If I don't see you again, take care."

"Don't you worry. I'm not going anywhere until this murder business is solved."

"Really? Why not?" She moved around the table and put a hand on Bull's shoulder, almost a protective gesture. Maybe she thought Auntie planned to drop by frequently and bring the subject up, keeping Bull from having a quiet, family-only mourning period.

"Haven't you read the papers? Sissy and I are helping the police."

"Sissy?"

I raised my hand. "Right here."

She pointed at us one by one. "Sissy. Bull." She stopped at Auntie. "What do they call you? Your name is Gertrude, right?"

"Gertie."

Catherine shuddered. "I hate nicknames. I think they label people unfairly. Look at my father-in-law. He's as gentle as a lamb, but they call him Bull."

"It's an Andy Devine reference," I volunteered. Auntie had explained that Andy was Roy Rogers' comic sidekick.

"And Sissy?" She eyed me. "You don't look like a wimp to me."

"Short for Frances," Auntie said, "and I think it's a sweet nickname. Very feminine."

"Kids were cruel to me in high school." Catherine brushed a curling bit of hair out of her eye. "Kate, Kate, can't get a date. That's why I insist people call me Catherine."

"Anything for a rhyme," I said. "Besides, I can't imagine you had that particular problem."

She narrowed her eyes at me. "What's that supposed to mean?"

I was surprised that she took offense. Bull jumped in to the rescue.

"She means that you're a beautiful woman."

I fell over myself to say that was exactly my intent.

"Oh." Her cheeks flushed. "Thanks. Back then, I had braces, skinny legs, and freckles. I didn't feel beautiful."

"I just assumed you were born looking like that," I said.

She ran a hand over her hip. "Strict diet and exercise to lose the extra weight, braces to straighten my overbite. It takes work." She ran a critical eye over my makeup-free face, my jeans and black t-shirt. "If you ever want a change, give me a call."

After she left, I blew out a breath. "She's a little touchy."

"What can I say?" Bull said. "She's a woman."

"I'm a woman and I'm not touchy," Auntie said with a huff.

Bull grinned. "You just made my point." He lost the smile. "I meant that she's been having some woman problems lately."

"Speaking of women." I stood up. "I promised Penny I would sit in with her on a free consultation with a wedding planner."

"I planned my own wedding," Auntie sniffed. "People make too big a deal out of the party aspects and don't focus enough on the meaning. Not that Penny would ever do that."

Auntie hadn't moved.

"So, we'll just get going and leave you to it," I said to Bull, making another move to leave.

Bull scratched his chin. "I don't really have anything planned, except maybe trim back the rose bushes."

"I just adore gardening!" Auntie practically squealed. "Can I help?"

Bull seemed pleased to have the company, and he promised to give Auntie a ride home. That gave me an idea.

A peek at Elvira's personal things might give me a clue about the murderer's motive, but I hadn't thought the opportunity would present itself. However, while Auntie and Bull were working out on the balcony, I could slip into Elvira's room. It was a chance I needed to take, as I could hardly ask the man to rummage through his recently deceased wife's drawers.

I scratched my ankle, and while bent over, lowered my purse to the floor and scooted it under the table. If I got caught, I could say I'd forgotten it.

"I'll see you when I see you."

I'd made it all the way to the door before Auntie called out. "You forgot your purse!"

She brought it to me with the enthusiasm of a retriever, and as she handed it to me, I felt I might have to let her in on my plan.

"Keep Bull occupied for the next ten minutes," I hissed.

Off her startled expression, I jerked my head toward the balcony. "In the garden. Make sure he stays out there."

"Are we investigating?" Her pleasurable expression dropped into a frown. "Oh, but if anyone should go through Bull's private things, it should be me."

"I'm not going through his private things. I'm checking out Elvira's private things." I dug through my purse for my keys and passed them to her. "Leave these on the couch. If I get caught, I can say I came back for them."

Bull approached and held the door open for me.

Auntie grasped my hand in hers. "I don't expect I'll see you again for a couple of hours. At your house. After you're done with Penny, which is where you're going now."

I pulled my hand free. "Right. See you later."

"Much later." With the hand farthest away from Bull, she flashed me a quick thumbs up.

I marched out to my car, and as they watched, I realized I couldn't get into my car without my keys.

"Goodbye!" I called out. Auntie responded, still waving.

"See you later." Nothing. "Enjoy your gardening. Out back."

She got the hint and pulled him inside.

Since the front door was most likely locked, I gave them a few minutes and headed for the side door to the garage. Unlocked! Once inside, I pressed my ear against the inside door to the house and listened. Nothing.

I gently pulled it open, listened again, and then made my way on tiptoe through the kitchen, the dining room, and into a long hallway. All the doors were closed, so I cracked open the first and peered inside. The laundry room. I moved on to the next.

The second room must have been Tim and Catherine's temporary residence. There was a queen-sized bed that looked like it would have been a tight squeeze for Elvira and Stan, and an open suitcase rested against the wall. They weren't the intended target of my search, but as long as I was here...

One of them was a chocolate addict. The majority of the wastebasket's contents were candy bar wrappers. They kept the room and its contents neat. Even Tim's underwear was folded. Catherine's clothes were quality, but not new. Just well cared for, like her jewelry. I'm no authority on authentic stones and metals, but the few pieces scattered on the dresser were tasteful, if not real gems.

They owned matching white iPods docked in a charging station that was plugged into the wall behind a bedside table, and their magazines of choice were Auto Racer Weekly and Style Today.

That left one remaining door at the end of the hall, and

as I stepped inside the room, envy washed over me. Sheer white curtains draped over long windows, softening the bright midday sun as it filtered into a space eight times the size of my bedroom. To my left was a king-sized bed covered in a spread of orange and teal triangles, a more suitable size of bed for Bull and Elvira.

The dresser and armoire were Spanish style, made of dark wood and iron. The armoire belonged to Bull, judging by the cowboy hats on the top shelf, so I moved on to the dresser. There were six long drawers that turned out to be filled with clothes. I held back a shudder as I felt my way through bras that stood up on their own and underwear with enough material to provide me with a summer blouse.

On top of the dresser were a pair of white doilies on which a pair of turquoise earrings and a matching bracelet had been carelessly discarded, probably tossed there the last time Elvira Jenkins undressed. Next to them sat a large memory box topped with a red cardinal that was posed as if about to burst into song, probably because he'd never found himself in the underwear drawer.

If I'd been a first-class snoop, someone who wanted to know every deep dark secret Elvira Jenkins possessed, I'd have been disappointed. There were recipe cards—one for Never Fail Mini Cheesecake, and another for mint brownies. The index cards were decorated with candy canes, which meant Elvira gathered holiday clippings, put them someplace safe, and forgot about them, just like I did.

She had a flyer for a baking supply store, a few safety pins, and several mismatched buttons. I picked up a business card for Dr. Margaret Shaughnessy, OBGYN in Scottsdale. Bull said Elvira's doctor of twenty-something years was a Dr. Zimmerman. On the back of the card, written in big print, was the name Moira and the date June

12, 2001. On impulse, I copied the phone number on a piece of scratch paper in my purse.

The only other item of interest was a newspaper clipping about a protest against the Kitty Cat Club located in Reno, Nevada. The faces of the protester were blurred and faded, so I couldn't tell if Elvira was one of them. Without a date on the clipping, it could have been from last year or last decade. I hadn't a clue what made it memorable enough to keep. Maybe, while chasing Bull across the country umpteen years ago, Elvira had stopped off for a little protest. Ah, memories.

Her closet held blouses, skirts, suits and pants, just like one would expect. A row of wide shoes lined the floor, and on the shelf above the hanging clothes sat six clear storage bins filled with various craft items.

Disappointed, I slipped out to retrieve my keys from the couch. Auntie and Bull were bent over the balcony garden, deep in conversation. I made as little movement as possible as I searched for the keys. I should have been more specific about where to place them. Digging between the cushions and flipping back the decorative pillows, I finally found them underneath the spot where Catherine Jenkins had sat. Just as I pulled them out, the sliding glass door opened.

"Sissy? Did you forget something?" Auntie gave me my cue.

I held up my keys.

"You left almost fifteen minutes ago," Bull said. "You've been looking all that time?"

Auntie giggled and swatted his arm. "Have you ever tried to find anything in a woman's purse, Bull? They're like black holes."

It was the perfect thing to say. Women's purses have a reputation, and men like Bull give them a wide berth.

"Women." That summed it up for Bull. "We were just getting some lemonade. There's plenty."

I declined. "I'm already running late, but thank you."

And then I was off to an hour of torture for the sake of my best friend's wedding.

NINETEEN

Penny lived in a quaint, older section of Wolf Creek. Her home was a bright white Spanish-style ranch that made a nice contrast against the Peacock flowers and Hibiscus that lined the front.

The consultant had already arrived by the time I rushed in the door, and she perched on the edge of a leather recliner with a large book in her lap. She wore a lavender silk suit and matching high-heeled pumps, and her dark ash blond curls were swept into a loose ponytail and finished with a tasteful black bow.

I gave my t-shirt a tug and ran my fingers through my hair as I joined Penny on the loveseat. Introductions were made. Apparently, Tabatha Sellers' name was on the lips of every blushing bride-to-be in the Phoenix area, because her smile held the expectation that I would be impressed when I heard it. I made appropriate noises, and she returned the favor.

"Frankie Chandler. I'm not sure why, but that sounds familiar."

Penny leaned forward, eager to impress her guest. "You

might have read about her in the paper," she said with naive glee. "She solved a murder last month, and she's working on another murder right now. Solving it. Not committing it. She talks to animals."

Tabitha's smile froze. In her line of business, the woman was probably adept at handling family hostilities, financial worries and arguments along the lines of bridal party colors and invitation fonts. This had not prepared her for the appropriate response to death and dog psychics.

"How—" Her mouth opened and closed. "How unusual." She turned her attention to the book in her lap and opened it. "Shall we begin?" Pen at the ready, Tabitha said, "I have a few questions to ask before we get to the detailed planning stages. How many bridesmaids will you have?"

Penny didn't hesitate. "Frances is my maid of honor. Then Kemper has two sisters, and we have to include them. I have three cousins, and my mother would never forgive me if I didn't invite them all. Kylie is a junior bridesmaid. She's only fifteen." She counted off on her fingers. "Seven."

"That's some wedding party," Tabitha chuckled, and I wondered if she charged by the head.

Penny's smile dropped. "Do you think that's excessive? I thought it was a lot, myself, but Kemper insisted on his sisters, and I don't want to start off on the wrong foot with his family. I suppose I could drop the junior bridesmaid, but Kylie would feel left out."

"Whatever you want is fine," Tabitha soothed. "It's your wedding."

"Kemper's and mine," Penny added quickly.

Tabitha marked down the number in her binder. "Can I assume the number of men in the wedding party will match?"

"Yes. Though we're having trouble coming up with a last groomsman. But we'll think of someone."

"And is the wedding taking place here in Wolf Creek?"

I waited for Penny's yes, but it took the scenic route.

"It's complicated. Kemper's family is from New York, and mine are mostly in Wisconsin."

"So, the wedding will be in Wisconsin?" Tabitha readied her pen.

"We haven't actually decided."

"What happened to St. Mel's?" I asked.

"Kemper didn't like the idea. He said it was too impersonal because we haven't been parishioners there that long. Of course, he's right. And I understood when he said it would be difficult to get his entire family and all of his friends to Wisconsin. He wants them all there for our special day." She sang out *special day*, and gave a maniacal, tittering laugh before striking the air with one finger. "But it's not fair to ask my family and friends to travel that far, either. And there isn't any place in between, unless we have the wedding in the middle of Lake Huron."

Penny stopped laughing.

"Or everyone could head north to Canada," I said. "It could be one of those destination weddings."

"Canada? That's another country! Would our marriage be legal?"

I squeezed her hand. "Penny, honey. It's not another solar system. It's Canada. Our friendly neighbors to the north?"

She pulled her hand away and began twisting all her fingers together. "If we're going someplace foreign, we might as well go to New York! And what if I do and they have another hurricane? Wedding guests could die. We don't get hurricanes in Wisconsin. Or gangs. Isn't New York full of gangs? You read about people getting shot at weddings."

"Come on, Penny. Unless Kemper's family is the mafia, I don't think you need to worry. And I think even they call a truce for weddings." I shared this bit of wisdom culled from old movies, intending it as a soothing balm, but Penny wasn't listening.

"In fact, no one has ever died at any of the weddings I've been to in Wisconsin. Aunt Sybil had a heart attack once, but it turned out to be indigestion."

Tabitha set down her pen. "Are you sure this is a good time?" I noticed she directed the question to me and not to the bride.

"Wedding nerves." I smiled and leaned in to whisper into my best friend's ear. "Get it together, Penny. You're scaring the nice lady."

It was the right thing to say. Penny wouldn't dream of making other people uncomfortable, and once she looked up and caught sight of Tabitha's wide eyes and raised eyebrows, she blew out a long breath and said, "Sorry about that. I'm just a bit tense wondering how we're going to pull it off."

This was Tabitha's territory, and she picked her pen back up, gave it an authoritative click, and straightened her shoulders.

"There are many exciting ways that young couples are dealing with these types of issues. I have one client whose family is going to rent a large screen television, hook up a computer, and watch the whole thing on Skype! Think of the travel expenses they'll save."

"You can't exactly catch a garter on Skype." Penny's hard tone nixed the idea.

Tabitha's smile strained. "Why don't I just leave that

spot blank? Have you decided on a theme?"

"A theme? It's a wedding." Penny's eyes opened wide. "You mean like when ballparks have military night? Or flamenco dancers? Or give out free wristbands so you can eat all you want from the concession stands during the seventh inning? That doesn't sound very elegant."

Tabitha took a deep, centering breath and brushed her fingers through her hair. A few strands came loose from her ponytail and fell into her eyes. "You don't have to have a theme. It's a trendy thing people are doing now. But it's not necessary, or even, for some people, desirable. What about the food? Do you plan on a buffet or sit-down dinner?"

"A buffet is probably more in our budget."

"Excellent." I think Tabitha was just happy to fill in a box. "There are many creative things you can do with a buffet. And I recommend having servers walk around with crab puffs or shrimp rolls as people arrive, so they aren't ravenous when the buffet opens."

Penny's lip trembled. "My dad's allergic to seafood!"

Tabitha closed her book very, very gently. "Perhaps it's too early to put things in writing."

My friend almost knocked over her drink when she jumped up and grabbed the planner's hands in hers. "You're right. You're absolutely right. I need to think. By myself. Alone. That's what I need. Time alone."

I put a hand on her shoulder and pulled her back to give Tabitha some breathing room. "Pen? You're starting to sound like Sybil."

"Aunt Sybil?"

"No. The Sally Field version."

"Thank you for your time," I said to Tabitha. "We'll get in touch."

The planner didn't take the time to put her book back

into the matching leather briefcase. She grabbed her purse and briefcase, tucked the book under her arm and waved over her shoulder without looking back. "I'll call you."

Penny looked at me.

"That didn't go well, did it?"

I hugged my friend and asked her to explain exactly what happened between her happy announcement and now.

"We started out as one, unified couple, and then we broke apart into two raging monsters who want different things."

"I have a hard time imagining either of you in the monster role," I said.

"He wanted powder-blue tuxes. Seriously. I wasn't making that up. He said they would remind him of his prom."

"Okay. That's ghastly bad taste, but not so much monster material."

Penny buried her head in her hands. "What if we're not meant for each other? If we're just too different to be happy? What if we never agree on anything ever again?"

"You can still exchange Christmas cards." I kept a straight face until she cracked a smile.

When she half-playfully smacked me on the shoulder, her fist packed a wallop. This woman was under major stress. My optimistic, perky friend was battling forces too large to fight alone.

"You're coming with me." I picked up my purse.

"Where?"

"To Dot's. For my appointment."

It was like throwing a bucket of water on parched soil. It didn't soak in right away, but it was just what she needed.

TWENTY

Dot Truesdale lived in Fountain Hills, so Penny had time to decompress on the drive over. Cake, Dot's shih tzu, greeted us as soon as we walked in, and Penny and Dot exchanged greetings as if they were old friends, even though they only met once or twice before. Dot had that effect. Imagine a more dignified (and shorter) version of Carol Channing. Irresistible.

We followed her through a home tastefully decorated with Western accents and artwork and stepped outside through the back door where iced tea waited for us on the patio table. This was part of the ritual Dot and I went through on our appointments: I showed up, we drank iced tea and caught up on the local scandal, and Dot and I pretended she was using my services.

She retrieved an extra glass for Penny from the kitchen, and as soon as good manners allowed, she said:

"I heard about what happened to Elvira Jenkins."

As the former first lady of Fountain Hills, Dot employed an incredible information network made up of the various vendors who stopped by her house to do landscaping, cleaning, and every other service imaginable. She often ordered services she didn't need—like mine—just to meet the new business owners in the area, make new friends, and gather new sources.

We'd hit it off, and I kept a standing weekly appointment. Not that I ever read Cake's mind. He was easy to read without psychic abilities. His tail wagged constantly, he wore the standard shih tzu smile, and he stayed close to Dot's side. This was a happy dog. Besides. Dot insisted he should have his privacy. Our meetings were really social visits, but she insisted on paying. Until I became independently wealthy, I couldn't afford to turn down the checks.

From my position on the patio overlooking the canyon, I did a mental forehead slap and realized, had I been born a mouse, I never would have made it to the cheese. No sense of direction. On the opposite ridge, sunlight reflected off a wall of glass panes, making the Jenkins' house look like a blinding daytime star.

"They're practically your neighbors!"

Dot followed my gaze. "Not exactly, but I did know them by sight. I met Elvira when she tried to set up a homeowner's association. Thank heavens no one went for it. I can't stand committees, and no good ever comes from putting a group of people in charge of other people's lives. After that, she made a habit of dropping in every few months." She added with a wry smile, "Though I haven't seen much of her since Hal died."

Hal was Dot's late husband, and more importantly, the former mayor of Fountain Hills.

"Did Elvira work on any of Hal's committees?"

"No, but she liked to bend his ear over changes that she

thought would improve the area. Hal listened, of course, and sometimes she presented good ideas, but usually they were concepts one might agree with in principle, but you couldn't really do anything about. Like banning people from planting front lawns. It is silly and a waste of water to have grass in the desert, but people should be able to do as they please with their property and just pay a high water bill."

"What did you think of her?"

"She had a good heart. I'm sure of it. But people like to make their own mistakes, and they certainly don't want to be bullied, even if it's nicely. It can be dangerous to a person to be too helpful, if you know what I mean. She did ask me to sign a few petitions. Since I agreed with them, I did."

"Like what?"

"One was to keep an X-rated video store from opening up downtown. Another was to close an abortion clinic in the next county." Dot shuddered. "Thank God both were successful. So, you can see that she had a good heart, but you can also see how she made enemies."

"But I don't see activists coming to the Blue-Ribbon premiere to kill her. Wouldn't they prefer to off her at a protest site to make their point?"

"Frances' Aunt Gertrude grew up with Mrs. Jenkins," Penny said. "They were best friends until they fought over Mr. Jenkins."

Dot raised a brow at me. "That I did not know. And here I pegged Elvira's son, Tim, as the murderer."

"Why?"

"Money. He's always been a bit of a gambler—both literally and figuratively—and some of those risks didn't pay off, although he makes good money now as an RV salesman. Of course, people are hanging onto their money right now, so his income might have dropped. I can't imagine that an inheritance wouldn't be welcome."

"Does he inherit anything? I just assumed any money would go to her husband."

"My sources aren't that good," Dot laughed. "It was really just a wild guess, because anything else just seems so improbable."

"Catherine Jenkins said she and Tim were staying with Bull for a few days."

Dot nodded. "After you lose your spouse, it's lonely. I can tell you that from personal experience. Of course, you're so shocked you don't notice right away."

"Catherine said she met Tim out east, when she was working. It's a good thing they live around here now, so they can be here for Bull. That's Elvira's husband, Stan," I added, just to be clear. I should have known the most connected woman in Fountain Hills would be way ahead of me with information.

"Tim and Catherine have been in Arizona since they first married, about seven years ago. Tim sells luxury RVs in Scottsdale, and he's good at it. You don't sell a product, you sell an experience, and Tim has a way of creating a vision of rebellion, or freedom, or adventure. Whatever he thinks the buyer is looking for. He almost talked Hal into one, and Hal wasn't an emotional buyer."

"Tim sounds good at his job."

"He is."

"At least he has something to occupy his mind."

"You mean because of the murder?" Penny asked, and I explained about Catherine's most recent miscarriage.

"That's too bad," Dot said, and it occurred to me that she and Hal hadn't any children. "I know it wasn't her first. I learned that from my grocery delivery boy, John." She chuckled. "Everyone's a boy at my age, but John's a married man. He and his wife were having trouble getting pregnant, so he sympathized with Tim and Catherine when he met them at the fertility clinic. Do you have any idea how expensive fertility treatments are? It's incredible."

"You don't know who their doctor is by any chance?" I thought back to the business card I found in Elvira's bedroom.

"A good, Irish name."

"Shaughnessy?"

Dot gave me a sharp look. "That's it."

"Lucky guess," I murmured, averting my eyes. It looked as if Elvira had been poking her nose into her son's very private affairs, but what could that have to do with her death?

"It's too horrible to even think about," Penny said, but her expression showed that unhappy marriages were on her mind. The conversation had become too somber for my taste, so I changed the subject.

"Catherine said she ran a public relations business. I wonder why she doesn't set up shop here. I heard she was very successful, and it might help ease her mind to keep busy."

"It must be hard to start a business right now," Penny said.

"Tell me about it." I thought about my lack of animal behavior clients. "But it sure keeps you occupied."

"Have you come up with any suspects we can grill?" Dot asked, a devilish grin crinkling her face. Dot helped out with my amateur investigation last month by pretending to need the services of a landscaper and pool guy. I needed an excuse to interview them, and Dot seemed to enjoy her involvement. She turned out to be quite the actress.

"There are several people who could have wanted her out of the way." I counted off on my fingers. "She made Heather Ozu, host of *Blue-Ribbon Babes*, angry."

Dot grinned. "I saw the show."

"There are the contestants who lost out to her, especially Donna Pederson. That woman is ambitious, and being Blue-Ribbon Queen will be an asset to her new bakery. At least she thinks so. I guess it's possible that Elvira's husband, Bull, may have another woman on the side."

"Frances!" Penny shrieked.

"I know he doesn't seem like the type, but it's possible."

I did catch him holding Auntie's hand when he first came to my house, but that could have been a friendly gesture. Was he actually hitting on her? Did he flirt with other women? Was there one in particular? A special lady? Not that I'd seen. It might be worth thinking about, but I moved off family members for now in order to please Penny. "Natasha Young, the director, has bigger plans, and it would be to her benefit if *Blue-Ribbon Babes* failed."

"Movies?" Penny asked.

"Charity work."

Penny snorted. "Hardly your selfish killer type."

"It's an opportunity that might not be there if she doesn't grab it now, but she's got a contract that won't expire for another year."

"Kill to do charity work?" Penny turned her gaze on Dot. "What do you think?"

Dot squished up her nose and shook her head. "Not my favorite motive."

"Back to Heather Ozu. She said she simply forgot to make a deposit, and that's why the winner would have had to wait to cash the prize money check, but what if she's mismanaged funds? What if Elvira was going to make a fuss about the prize money, and that would lead the Baking Channel folks to take a closer look at the books? Heather could have lost her job or even gone to jail if it was not mismanagement but embezzlement."

"That sounds better," Penny said doubtfully, "but Heather seemed so together when I met her at the séance. I have a hard time seeing her as a disorganized diva."

"She said she was distracted by a nail appointment." I looked at my barren fingernails. "That's not something I would know about."

"Did you say séance?" Dot raised her brows. "What have you two been up to?"

"Nothing. It's all Aunt Gertrude."

"You haven't met her yet, but she's a very talented psychic," Penny gushed. "The real deal."

Dot's eyebrows inched up even farther.

I couldn't very well explain Auntie to Dot without hurting Penny's feelings, so I moved the conversation in a new direction.

"I give up. No one killed her. She was holding the skillet above her head, got distracted by her bird, and dropped it. The whole thing was an accident."

"People are so disappointing," Penny said. "They have dark sides you don't even know about. You marry someone hoping you'll have a nice life, and that they'll at least be able to take care of you, say, if you decide to raise children. But you never know, do you? I mean, what if Bull did kill his wife? What if he was having an affair? Can you ever really know anyone?"

Dot looked at Penny, surprised at her gloomy outlook. "Not completely, no. But you can know enough. Most people I know who suffered through an affair had warning signs. They just ignored them. For instance, one husband ignored his wife for years because he was preoccupied with his job. She did everything to get his attention until a sympathetic party filled the gap. I'm not condoning an affair, but it certainly shouldn't have been a complete surprise."

"Penny's getting married, and I think she's got a case of jitters."

"Congratulations!" Dot leaned in and gave her a hug. "Marriage is a big commitment, but it's worth it. Tell me about your young man."

As Penny listed Kemper's qualities—his kindness, his patience, how hard he worked at his job, her face lit up. She practically glowed with satisfaction.

"I've been an idiot," she said. "Could you take me home? I want to call Kemper."

We said our goodbyes and promised to keep Dot updated on any developments.

Auntie hadn't yet returned from bonding with Bull over his garden, so I took the opportunity to have some peace and quiet in my own bedroom. Emily and Chauncey joined me on the bed, and I propped up the pillows, leaned back, and dug through the pile of stuff on the bedside table for my latest novel.

Auntie was interested in the classics. There was a well-thumbed copy of Dracula and a worn hardback of Anne of Green Gables. Interesting combination. She had lifted the menus from several restaurants we'd dined at, which was cheaper than buying postcards for memories. They included one from the Prickly Pear. Should I tell Penny?

Nah. My friend would have given it to her had my aunt asked.

A few loose pages slipped out of the pile, and I gathered them up. Auntie had made use of my computer and printed off the pictures she'd taken so far. Most were surreptitiously taken on the night of the *Blue-Ribbon Babes* taping. Since the studio banned audience photography, Auntie hadn't been able to set up the shots. One caught my attention, and I switched on the bedside lamp and studied it.

My aged relative must have fumbled with the zoom button, because the photo was a close up of the set during a break. Heather stood to the side, and Auntie caught her in an unguarded moment, looking bored. I could guess that Betty had been the last guest to appear because an employee carried her cast iron skillet, and he was headed for the side of the counter where they stashed the used utensils. A face was framed in the fake window, and I squinted and held the photograph close. Sonny Street's features were contorted in anger, but I couldn't make out who he was talking to.

Oh, how I longed at that moment for the fancy equipment they used on television shows, the magical computer programs that would allow me to close in on a specific spot, or at least a magnifying glass. Then I noticed that Auntie had left her reading glasses on the bedside table. I held them in front of the picture, angling them to magnify the photo. I could make out a finger pointed at Sonny's face, and on that finger sat a large yellow bird. I'd seen that ring before. Sonny was arguing with Elvira Jenkins.

That bird ring wouldn't be enough to interest the police, but it proved why Sonny Street had been late for his performance between Betty and Elvira. It hadn't been a potty break as Auntie suggested. He'd been busy arguing with

Elvira Jenkins. Or maybe she'd insulted him and ticked him off. The point was that he didn't like her very much at that moment, and that moment was shortly before Elvira took a nosedive onto the spill mat on the *Blue-Ribbon Babes* set. Sounded like a certain comedian belonged on my suspect list.

TWENTY-ONE

"They haven't called you in," Howard said, checking the list of names cleared to come onto the Saguaro Studios lot.

This morning, while Auntie sang Old Smokey at the top of her lungs in the shower, I'd slipped out of the house, leaving a note on the kitchen table that I'd be right back. A spring sun sparkled in the sky, the air was permeated with the sweet scent of new blooms, and the invigoratingly crisp morning temperature raised my spirits. A wasted trip to Saguaro Studios would ruin my mood.

"Isn't Sonny Street here today?" I asked, feigning surprise and hoping Howard would think we had a prearranged meeting.

"He got here an hour ago. He's practicing his warm up for *Time Flies When We're Baking Pies*." He tapped his clipboard. "But he didn't call you in."

"It will only take a minute," I pleaded. "I have something very important I need to ask him about Elvira Jenkins's murder."

"No can do. I got reamed by Ms. Ozu for letting you

and your aunt on the last time. It would be my job if I let you past the gate."

I didn't want that on my head, but then I thought of someone else on the lot I would like to have a chat with. Fiona Flynn.

"Could I at least drop by the makeup department? Fiona lent me a lipstick, and I've got to return it."

"No can do."

I was about to plead, but Howard cut me off.

"Fiona cleared out. Left her job yesterday. You can probably find her at her grandma's."

"Her dead grandma's?"

Howard's face fell. "I had no idea. No wonder she was in such a fussy mood."

"She gave me a business card with her grandma's address written on the back, but I can't seem to find it."

The car behind me honked, and I took advantage of Howard's impatience to get rid of me.

"Maybe it's in here somewhere." I pulled some wadded tissues out of my purse and placed them on the passenger seat. Then a pen. Then a cough drop. I wanted to give the impression I would clear out my entire purse, item by item, unless he helped me.

The car honked again.

"She lives in Mesa. Somewhere near Pioneer Park. Now you've got to get moving."

"Thank you so much, Howard. You are the best."

He motioned me through the gate with a stern warning to make an immediate u-turn. By the time I made it to the opposite side of his booth, Howard hung out the window and waved.

"Sonny has lunch most days at the Brew and Grill on Ambrosia Street, but you didn't hear it from me."

I gushed some more and drove back home, stopping for bagels so Auntie wouldn't question where I'd been. I didn't want her anywhere near Sonny Street. Auntie reminded me a tad of Elvira Jenkins, and I didn't want Sonny clamming up because she brought back memories of his fight with the bossy Blue-Ribbon Babe.

I held up the bag of bagels as I walked into the kitchen.

"Where'd you go for breakfast? Wisconsin?"

I tossed the bag on the counter. "Har-de-har-har. I went into Scottsdale to a place that's really good. It's a treat."

I'd purchased them at the corner minimart, and they had the texture of old footballs. When Auntie declined, saying she had already eaten, I stuck them in the freezer so there would be an excuse for how hard and dry they were when we finally ate them.

"What are your plans for the day?" I asked, feeling guilty that I hoped she had plans. My aunt had flown all the way to Arizona to see me, well, me and the *Blue-Ribbon Babes* premiere, and we hadn't really spent any quality—or quantity—time together. But really. Murder took precedence over family bonding.

"Bull was going to take me to the botanical gardens, but I can cancel if you want to do something together."

Her willingness to alter her own plans made me feel worse, but I was still happy to wave goodbye as the couple drove off in Bull's silver SUV.

I showered and changed and made it to the Brew and Grill by eleven o'clock, because I didn't know what time Sonny Street ate lunch. I entered a cute, rustic place, with brown leather benches, dark red tables, and a wooden bar that stood between the dining room area and the waitresses' pickup window.

When the waitress led me to the back of the room where

they probably hid single diners, I told her I'd prefer something by the window. I took my time studying the menu, partly to kill time and partly because it offered an amazing selection. Every style of burger I could imagine had been concocted and named to match the theme: the Amber Onion Patty Melt, the Cure What Ales You Bacon Cheddar Burger, the TransPorter to the Future Burger with everything on it.

The Stout Burger caught my eye. It boasted the best of all worlds, with bacon, blue cheese, mushrooms, grilled onions, layered over a quarter pound of Angus beef. The waitress recommended the garlic fries, and I added a cola. I stressed that the burger should be well done and congratulated myself on killing a few more minutes.

I took tiny bites to stretch out the eating process, and I buried my face in the paperback I'd thought to bring along and hoped that the waitress would forget about me.

Around a quarter to twelve, the lunch crowd showed up. The waitress set down my bill and asked me if I'd like anything else. When I asked to see the menu again so I could review their dessert selection, she slapped it down and tapped her foot. I put a five on the table—over thirty percent of the bill—as a hint that she wouldn't miss out on income if I remained.

By two o'clock, I'd replaced the five with a twenty, and Sonny Street still hadn't made an appearance. The waitresses were huddled by the pickup station along with a few busboys, and the chef leaned out the window to the kitchen. They all looked my way as they whispered, and I'm sure they expressed some choice comments about single ladies who sat and read through the entire lunch rush.

I left my payment, grabbed my purse, and who should hold open the door for me as I exited but Sonny Street. His mouth dropped open and he stepped back, but he recovered nicely.

"Nice to see you again. Sorry to hear about the bird. Maybe somebody thought it was a chicken. HA!"

I motioned back into the restaurant. "Do you mind if I join you for a minute? There's something I wanted to ask you."

His smile never even slipped. "Lead the way."

The same waitress who'd endured my long lunch greeted us. She took one look at me and said, "You've got to be kidding," which was hardly fair considering the size of my tip.

Fortunately, Sonny thought she was ribbing him about his job as a comedian, and he laughed up a storm.

As a regular, Sonny waved off the menu and said, "The usual."

Her pen trembled in her hand as she asked for my order.

"Nothing for me, thank you."

She snapped the book shut and took off before I could change my mind.

Sonny wore jeans and a red t-shirt, and it occurred to me that he was a good-looking guy—something that didn't come across as he told lame jokes to amuse the Baking Channel crowds. He gave me a dimpled grin and said, "What did you want to talk about? Are you thinking about going into show business? Because you've got the looks, if you play them up better. You know, pushup bra, makeup, a better cut of clothing."

I assured him I didn't harbor any show biz aspirations. "The night Elvira died, I couldn't help but see you arguing with her. I wanted to know what about?"

The dimples did a disappearing act. "None of your business."

His quick and accurate reply made me rethink my approach. He wasn't intimidated by me. He didn't seem to have heard about my alleged role helping the police. Or maybe he didn't care.

"I just thought it would be easier to talk to me about it instead of the police." He didn't immediately spill his guts, so I tried a friendlier approach. "My aunt knew the victim, and from what I've heard, she was a hard lady to get along with. Kind of judgmental and nosey."

"Got that right," he muttered. "Still, I think I'll wait for the police."

"Are you Sonny Street?" A middle-aged woman with two young daughters beamed at him from behind stylish glasses. "I visited the Baking Channel last year, and I remember how funny you were!"

He turned into Mister Charming, asked the girls how old they were and admired their sparkly tennis shoes. He had a way with the kids, and they giggled a lot—both the girls and their mother. After he sent them off with autographs, I targeted his weak spot.

Reaching for my purse, I casually mentioned *The Wolf Creek Gazette*. "I have to prepare something new for the reporters. They're so persistent, always looking for fresh information. Your fight with Elvira might be the answer to a prayer. And, since we haven't actually discussed it, I won't be limited by tiresome facts." I skirted around the fact that the modern reporter didn't rely on the verity of information provided.

When I moved to leave, he made a grab for my purse and tugged hard. I fell back into the booth.

"You could ruin my career," he hissed, keeping his voice low enough that no one outside our booth could hear.

"I don't want to. It would be a shame, because you actually seem like a nice guy."

I thought I'd make it easy for him. "Were you hitting on an underage page? Hitting on any page might be unethical, since you'd kind of be her boss. I can see where Elvira might chew you out for that."

That made him laugh. "The pages are usually hitting on me. And I'm very careful not to date employees. I've seen too many relationships not work out, and then all of a sudden there's a sexual harassment lawsuit. No thank you."

"What then?" I gasped. "Drugs?

He gave me his profile. "Does this face look like I have a substance abuse problem? Wrinkles. Puffy eyes. Broken capillaries. Rotten teeth. Again, no thank you."

"What's left that could possibly get Elvira worked up?"

He sulked for a minute or two. "She saw me paying off Brandon."

A payoff? Thinking back to the racing forms I'd found in Heather's office, I gasped. "Your bookie?"

"He's a little young for a bookie," he said. "He's sixteen."

"You weren't—" I narrowed my eyes. This could put a whole new spin on how nice he had been to those little girls.

It took him a minute to catch on, and he pressed back against the booth in horror. "Ew! That's disgusting." He moved forward so fast that it was my turn to jump back. His hands on the table, his face a few inches in front of mine, he said, "I pay him to advise me on jokes."

I cocked my head in disbelief. "The stuff you were using at the *Blue-Ribbon Babes* taping?"

"Heck no. I can write those in my sleep, but I don't plan on working for the Baking Channel forever. I've got plans. And if you want to appeal to a younger crowd, you've got to keep up with the slang. It changes every five minutes. These kids have the attention span of a five-minute egg." He dug in his pocket and pulled out a notebook. "That's good. The old ladies will love it." And he proceeded to capture his brilliance on paper.

"Anyway, I usually mail him a check, but he came down the night of the taping because he wanted his money right away."

"Why?"

"I don't know. Prom. A new video game. Who cares?" He seemed to deflate. "There. It's out. I'm ruined."

"What does that have to do with Elvira Jenkins?"

He snapped his book shut. "That's exactly what I said. It's none of your business. But she started citing child labor laws, and tax evasion. She said what I was doing was a crime and she would let the Baking Channel know. And she was serious!"

"That does sound a little extreme."

"He's a kid, for goodness' sake. Teens should be able to earn a little spending cash without having to fill out a tax return. I mean, talk about sucking the motivation out of ém before they even get started. Look. It would have been embarrassing, but I doubt I would have been out of a job, because it had nothing to do with the Baking Channel. I didn't have a reason to kill her."

I remembered the teenager who cut in front of us in line outside the stage. He urgently wanted to speak to Sonny Street. I asked him to describe Brandon, and it matched the kid who asked for him that night.

The waitress arrived with his burger, and I got up to go. "No worries. No one will hear your secret from me."

His dimples were back. "Say, you're alright. Thanks." He toasted me with his burger and took a huge bite.

Under my breath I added, "Unless you're guilty," but I gave him a matching smile and headed for Pioneer Park.

The Grandma Flynn who answered the door was a sturdy woman who didn't look as if she had been sick a day in her life, let alone dead. She wore a solid green apron over a print housedress. Assuming that she'd been hard at work in the kitchen, I apologized for interrupting her.

She looked over her shoulder at the television set. "It's a commercial break, so talk fast. Whatever you're selling, I'm not interested." She narrowed her eyes into tiny slits. "Why are you staring?"

"Fiona mentioned you were, um, under the weather." Or underground. "You look very healthy."

She sniffed, and her long nose twitched. "Allergies. I'm surprised Fiona bothered to mention it. They're not the end of the world."

"I'm actually a friend of Fiona's, from the studio. Can I talk to her?"

She held open the door and jerked her head toward a hallway at the back of the room. "Last door on the right."

Grandma Flynn reclaimed her spot on the couch in time for a hemorrhoid commercial.

Now that I was here, I wasn't sure how to begin. I didn't want to scare her by bursting into the room and demanding to know who she recognized at the premiere or why she lied about her not-so-dead grandma, so I thought I'd start with a little bit of truth and tell her that I'd been to the studio to see Sonny and heard that she'd left. I merely wanted to offer my congratulations, and by the way, who was it that she recognized and why did she lie about her grandma?

The walls of the hallway were crammed with photos of Fiona—from her birth to a picnic that must have taken place within the last year. She'd been a natural redhead, a bright carrot red that made her face look huge. Now I understood the bleached-blond look.

I knocked on the last door to my right and said, "Fiona? It's Frankie."

She didn't respond, so I knocked again and put my ear to the door. Things were very quiet in there. Maybe she had frozen in place in the hope that I'd leave if she didn't say anything.

I cracked open the door. The first thing in my line of site was a pink, decorative pillow lying on the green shag carpet. Then my gaze moved to a quilted coverlet sprawled in disarray on the bed. We were kindred spirits. Fiona was a slob. I peeked in further and gasped at the statue of the Blessed Virgin, tipped over onto its side. She lay on the dresser, watching me, her expression still serene. I crossed myself in reflex.

"Fiona?" It came out a strangled whisper.

White cotton curtains moved gently in the breeze that came through the open window. Maybe Fiona had scrambled through the window to escape me, though I couldn't imagine such an extreme reaction was necessary. She could just tell me to bug off if she didn't want to talk.

I crossed the room to lean out the window, and I found Fiona Flynn. Her fingers clutched at a pink silk scarf that was wrapped tightly around her neck. Her swollen tongue stuck out between pink lipstick-covered lips, and her eyes bulged out. The last thing I noticed before the room went black was that, though her cheeks were wet from tears, her tattooed eyeliner hadn't run.

TWENTY-TWO

"And then I hear this one screaming her head off. Almost gave me a heart attack."

My head rested between my legs as I sat in Grandma Flynn's kitchen, and in my dazed state, I was impressed at how her green tile floor shone. Maybe she'd share her cleaning secrets.

I could hear people moving through the other rooms in the house and knew it must be the police.

"Why did she kill my Fiona? Why?"

My head shot up at this accusation, and the room spun. I lowered my forehead to my knees and muttered, "She was dead when I got there."

"Calm down, Mrs. Flynn," Detective Bowers said. "Frankie, can you talk yet?"

I lifted my head, slowly this time, and felt the blood rush out of it. After a moment's dizziness, the room stopped spinning and I could clearly see the furious face of Grandma Flynn. She wanted to kill me.

"What were you doing here?" Bowers' hard tone, barely controlled, was like a green light to Grandma Flynn.

"Yes, Missy. Why were you here? Why did you kill my Fiona in the prime of her life?"

"I came by because I heard Fiona left the studio. She'd been talking about opening up her own beauty shop."

"And she was going to make a success of it," Grandma Flynn said. "She had a natural talent for beauty. Anyone with eyes in their head could see that."

I guess it's hard to break the habit of praising the grandkids, even when they're dead.

"I knocked on her door, but she didn't answer."

"Maybe she knew you were going to kill her where she stood, and she froze, silent as a mouse, because she was afraid."

Her description was eerily similar to the one I'd envisioned as I waited at Fiona's bedroom door, though in my version, she was paralyzed with the fear of talking to me, not of losing her life.

"Go on," Bowers said.

"I peeked in and saw the Blessed Mary statue tipped over and knew something was wrong."

Grandma Flynn crossed herself several times, pulled a rosary from her pocket and kissed it. "Attacking the Virgin. I've never heard of such filth."

"I didn't see her, but the room was pretty messed up."

"Fiona always kept it neat as a pin."

"The window was open, so I went to look out—"

"Thought you'd catch her running for her life, did you?" Grandma Flynn's sneer showed me what her opinion was of people who followed other people out of windows.

"That's when I found her."

"Did you recognize any of the cars parked out front when you got here?" Bowers asked.

"I wouldn't even know what to look for. I assumed they belonged."

He took me by the elbows and stood me up. Then he hooked a finger under my chin and lifted my face, so he could look me in the eye. His knit brows and blue eyes showed more concern than anger. "Can you drive?"

My shaky nod wasn't encouraging, but he handed me my purse and keys.

"I want you to go straight home. I'll come by later."

Grandma Flynn sputtered. "You're not arresting her?"

"Not yet."

"She waltzed into the house, friendly as you please, and disappeared down the hallway. Now Fiona's dead. What more proof do you need?"

"When's the last time you actually saw Fiona alive, Mrs. Flynn?"

"I vacuumed her room right before *Pizza with Tony* came on." She clutched her hands together in a prayerful position. "I know it's not a Baking Channel show, but I always made sure to flip the channel during commercials to see the wonderful job my Fiona did on the faces of the hosts and guests." Tears ran down her sturdy cheeks. "She specialized in hair."

Bowers looked at his watch. "That was about an hour ago." He bent his head to look me in the eye. "And how long ago did you get here?"

Grandma Flynn answered for me. "She interrupted me during the second commercial break."

"The killer had about a twenty-minute window."

He turned me toward the door. "Home. Now."

When I returned to Arrowhead Drive, I was relieved to find that Auntie hadn't returned from her outing. Let her enjoy her gardening date with Bull. In the time it took me to drink a glass of cold water and splash my face in the bathroom sink, Bowers made the drive to my house. The control he'd shown at Grandma Flynn's? He left that behind. He stormed through the living room, dragging me by the hand, and then flung me onto the couch so hard my bottom bounced when it hit the cushion. He sat on the coffee table facing me, and his jaw twitched as he ground his teeth.

"What business did you have going to Fiona Flynn's? And don't tell me the two of you were pals."

"Okay. Here's the truth."

"It better be."

"When I was at the reception after the *Blue-Ribbon Babes* show, Fiona acted like she recognized someone, but she didn't have a chance to say who. Then, when I asked her about it at the memorial, she said she'd made a mistake."

Bowers didn't say anything, but his left eye twitched.

"Come on, Bowers. She suddenly comes into enough money to open her own shop? And Grandma Flynn looked pretty good for a dead woman."

"What do you mean by that?"

"Fiona said she'd gotten the money from her dead grandma. Since she only mentioned one grandmother living in the area, it had to be the same woman."

"Maybe she didn't think it was any of your business where she got the money."

"True, but she didn't have to lie about it."

"What exactly did she say about recognizing someone?"

"She was talking about how she got her start at a beauty parlor, where she was doing such a good job with the makeup and hair of some women in the show—"

"What show?"

"She didn't say. But then she came back to Arizona to live with Granny and work on the Baking Channel."

"Back from where?"

"I don't know. Do you want to hear what I do know? She looked over at this group of people and said something like how interesting or it couldn't be."

"Who was she looking at?"

"Who wasn't she looking at? The entire cast of *Blue-Ribbon Babes* had just come in, including Bert the producer and Natasha the director. Guests were walking up to talk to them, and their family members were there. It could have been anybody."

He thought about this for a minute, and then he said, "I want to know everything that you or your aunt have been up to. Everything."

Bowers was being a bossy pants again, and that raised my verbal hackles. "Auntie bought some new shoes the other day." I probably shouldn't have been a smart aleck at this moment, not when Bowers had steam coming out of his ears. His expression didn't change; his eyes remained on my face, disconcertingly steady. His body stayed rigid and tense, his hands on his knees. It would have been less intimidating if he said something nasty or yelled at me.

"Okay." I let out a big sigh to show him his request was unreasonable. "Where to start. First Auntie and I went to Saguaro Studios to have a word with Heather Ozu."

"Now why would you do that?"

"Auntie pitched Heather an idea for the show and she was following up. At Heather's invitation."

Crossing his arms, Bowers kept his voice neutral. "And what did you ladies talk about?"

"Well, it's more interesting what we found on Heather's desk before she got there. Not that we were snooping, but there wasn't a receptionist and we just walked into her office and these papers were just sitting on her desk." Okay. That did sound like snooping.

"And what kind of papers were they?"

"Past due notices."

"So, the woman's late on her credit cards."

I hadn't really noticed who the invoices were from. "She's not just the star, you know. She's a producer."

"That's listed in the credits."

Oh.

"But did you know her assistant—former assistant—said they didn't have enough cash in the bank to cover the prize money?"

"And how would he know?"

"Because...he was her assistant?"

"He managed the bank accounts for her?"

I didn't have an answer to that one. "But Jeremy said he hadn't been paid in three weeks, so there must have been money problems."

Bowers pressed his lips into a grim smile. "Not exactly true. Heather advanced him his paycheck a couple of weeks in a row and refused to do it again. Then he decided to take a personal loan from petty cash."

"But...but..." Actually, what I was thinking was butthead, as in Jeremy was a lying butthead. "But what about Heather's gambling problem?"

He drew his brows together. "Who says she has a problem? The angry assistant?"

"She had a racing form in her desk drawer. Maybe you should check out if she suffered any recent losses at the track. Maybe that's what happened to the prize money. She blew it at Turf Paradise the day before the premiere."

He stared. His mouth drooped at the corners in an unhappy frown, but perhaps he was unhappy because I was finally making sense and had beaten him to the solution to the crime.

"Don't you see? Heather Ozu would be the perfect person to kill Elvira. It matches up with that conversation I overheard. That's confidential information. And the threatening response, The truth is the truth, honey. Jeremy said the prize money wasn't there. That the check was a fraud. That's illegal, you know."

"Heather Ozu explained the situation to me. She quite fairly told the contestants in confidence before the show that there was a glitch and they'd have to wait twenty-four hours for the money." He held up a hand to stop my protest. "And it's been confirmed by the other contestants."

"Okay. Scratch Heather. Donna Pederson is now the Blue-Ribbon Queen. That will help her get her new bakery on its feet. Pretty convenient, huh? And Sonny Street was seen paying off a teen who was updating his jokes."

"What?"

"Elvira threatened to report him to the tax bureau or the president or something. That's a motive. And Natasha Young has a motive. She'd rather be working on a charity show, but her contract is for a year, so she might miss an opportunity to live her dream. If *Blue-Ribbon Babes* went under, she'd be free to pursue the job. And Elvira's family could have wanted her dead...just because."

"That's all you've got?" He shook his head. "Not a very good case. I've got a better one. Old rival travels from Loon Lake to Wolf Creek to carry out old threats and then lies about her past to the police."

I scrunched up my face. "It's funny how unworldly older people are, don't you think? They come from a time when privacy was respected, and you didn't just blab your entire personal life as if you were a guest on the Jerry Springer show."

"I can appreciate that, but your aunt wasn't being demure. She lied to me."

"I wouldn't call them lies."

"I would. When the murdered woman's husband was once an object of your obsession, that's important."

"You know about that?"

Bowers smiled, but it lacked warmth. "We police are actually pretty good at our jobs. And to show you how impressive we really are, I already know about the financial condition of *Blue-Ribbon Babes*. And I didn't hear it from a ticked-off ex-employee. And it's not anything to kill over. They're slow at paying their bills, but that's not a crime."

He checked his watch and stood. "I've got work to do, although I might have a better shot at catching the killer if I stay here."

I struggled to gain the upper hand. "Listen to how you phrased that bit about my aunt. Obsession. No wonder she didn't want to mention anything. You put a negative spin on everything, and it was probably embarrassing to her. Think of the things you did when you were younger. Imagine if you had to strip them bare in front of an unsympathetic audience?"

Even though his smile hadn't qualified as a friendly grin, it was better than the scowl that now replaced it. "You think I'm unsympathetic?"

"If the shoe fits."

"You think I don't care. Unbelievable."

The dazed, hurt look in his eyes made me rethink my blunt comment. Grandma always said that words could be like blows, but who knew Bowers was so sensitive? And I'd said unsympathetic, not uncaring. Big difference.

"Of course, you care about your job," I said in a placating tone. "That's what makes you good at it."

"My job? You think all I care about is my job?"

He pulled me to standing, cupped his hand behind my neck, and brought his mouth down on mine in a rough kiss that hurt my neck. When I didn't struggle to get away or pound on his shoulders with virtuous feminine fists, he took that as a good sign, and the kiss turned soft and sensual. When I started kissing him back—I didn't want to be rude— he wrapped an arm around my waist and pulled me to him in a tight grip.

His phone rang, and we broke apart, each struggling to breathe at a normal rate.

He pulled out his cell phone, pointed it at me and said, "You and I are going to have to talk after I wrap up this case." Then he answered the call with an abrupt, "Hello."

After I wrap up this case? That statement was a tad arrogant, not to mention kind of cold after the hot lip lock we'd just shared. Was he able to turn off his emotions so easily? My vision was still swimming, and my breathing hadn't returned to normal, yet here he was sounding all professional and detached on the phone.

Was he really so confident he had the murderer pegged? And was it Auntie? Bowers might have meant his comment about finding the killer in my house as a joke, but it occurred to me that, tickle or no tickle, I might be able to find out how seriously he suspected Auntie if I took a peek inside his head. It might be worth a shot. And he was distracted by the phone call.

I took a deep breath to clear my mind. Bowers hand shot out and grabbed my wrist. After our intimate moment, I was startled by the lack of warmth in his eyes. He rested the phone against his chest, and in a deadly calm voice, said:

"Frankie, if I have something I want you to know, I'll tell you. Okay?"

He wasn't asking.

I blinked at him and said, "I don't know what you mean." I sighed, as if that's all I'd been doing a minute ago. "This whole thing has been so trying."

He wrapped up his call and left without another word to me. I had a feeling I might have crossed a line.

TWENTY-THREE

As soon as he cleared the driveway, I ran a comb through my hair and applied some tinted lip gloss. Looking at my reflection in the bathroom mirror, I noticed a healthy glow to my cheeks, though I wasn't wearing blush. As I remembered that kiss, the blushed deepened. I wondered if Bowers would give it a second thought? I wondered why I cared?

I grabbed my purse and headed into Scottsdale. My suspect list was as gaunt as a mangy dog, and my clues were so lame they couldn't withstand the interrogation of a four-year-old. I needed something solid if I planned to impress Bowers with my aunt's innocence. That discrepancy between Elvira's own doctor's name and the contact information on the business card I'd found in her memory box might mean something, and it might have been overlooked by Bowers. I planned to find out.

Dr. Margaret Shauhnessy's practice was located in a large, white medical office building. Three floors of offices surrounded a center courtyard, with tables and benches set against a waterfall and surrounded by green foliage. It provided a relaxing atmosphere for patients as they waited for appointments, test results, and good or bad news.

I exited the elevator on the third floor, and as soon as I walked in the glass office doors, I realized I should have brought a date. The patients came in couples, and as they checked out the newcomer, their expressions all seemed to reflect incredible sadness or tenuous hope.

"Can I help you?"

The receptionist had plain features but an expression of kindness and sympathy. The name on the business card read Moira. Not Dr. Moira. Just Moira. I looked into the curious expression of the receptionist and said, "Are you Moira?"

A nurse in a white uniform had been flipping through folders in a drawer. She plucked one out, snapped the drawer shut, and approached the window. She had ebony hair and the complexion of a teenager, but I put her age around mid-thirties because of the lines around her eyes.

"I'm Moira," she said.

"Is there somewhere private where we can speak?"

Her gaze drifted toward a hallway that I assumed led to the examination rooms. "We're pretty busy right now. Do you have an appointment with Dr. Shaughnessy?"

"This has to do with Elvira Jenkins."

Nurse Moira paled, clutched the back of the receptionist's chair, and swayed.

"Are you alright?"

She handed the file to the receptionist and murmured instructions. Then she came out into the reception area and held open the front door. She didn't speak until we made it to a corner of the walkway that was left in shadow from the awning above.

She wrapped her arms around her waist in a posture that was both defensive and self-comforting.

"Who gave you my name?"

"I didn't mean to startle you—"

"Who-gave-you-my-name." The words came out in a rat-a-tat, as if they were fired from a gun.

"Elvira." That was sort of true.

"She wouldn't do that. She swore our conversation was confidential."

"And our conversation will be as well." I rested a hand on her arm, but she shook it off. "I'm just trying to find her murderer, and what you talked about may have a bearing."

"It couldn't. I didn't tell her anything."

"So, she just showed up, introduced herself, and you didn't talk about anything? I find that hard to believe. You're awfully upset."

"I could lose my job!"

Her hand shook as she wiped away tears. "I was young and stupid, okay? I made a mistake."

"Malpractice?" I asked, thoroughly confused by now.

She coughed out a harsh laugh. "I guess you could call it that. I took a job at an abortion clinic." She gripped my arm with surprising strength, and I felt uneasy, even though I outweighed her by twenty pounds.

"I was naïve. I thought I was helping people, and then I saw—" She closed her eyes and looked sick.

"And Elvira wanted to know about it? Did she plan to use you at one of her protests?"

"No. And that's all I'm saying. I've paid for my mistake, and I'll keep on paying for the rest of my life, every time I go to sleep. Nightmares."

"Was it at a clinic around here?"

"That's not how she found me." Her sharp tone warned me that the discussion was over.

Nurse Moira dried her face, assumed her professional demeanor, and said, "Don't come back here." She headed through the clinic door without looking back.

What could Moira's job at an abortion clinic have to do with Elvira Jenkins murder? Did Elvira threaten to hold the nurse up as an example at one of her protests? Did Moira lash out to protect her job? That might have provided her with a motive for murder.

I drove until I found myself in front of Granny Flynn's house. Unless Granny had calmed down, I was the next to be murdered.

The police cars were gone, so I made my way to the front door. I knocked lightly, almost hoping she wouldn't answer, and when she did, Granny Flynn seemed bigger than I remembered. Maybe it was the broom in her hand, which she raised above her head, ready to deliver a whack, as soon as she recognized me.

"Why aren't you in jail?"

"Because I didn't kill your granddaughter."

I stuck my foot in the door before she slammed it on my face. "And I would really like to find out who did and bring them to justice."

She eyed me and probably saw a wimp who never worked out, and realizing she had forty pounds on me, she held open the door.

"What do you want to know?"

She let me into the hallway, but she made no move to invite me to sit down. I didn't blame her. The woman was in mourning. The television was off.

"Fiona recognized someone at the Baking Channel the other day. Did she mention it?"

"No."

"She was going to open a shop in Tucson, I understand."

She rested the broom against the wall and took a hankie out of her apron pocket to dab her teary eyes. "To make all the college girls beautiful. Yes."

The furniture in the house was well cared for but worn. The couch cushions were depressed from the weight of too many bottoms over too many years. The doilies on the end tables couldn't hide all the spots where the sheen of the wood had dulled. All the knick-knacks looked old, if not antique. The newest thing in the room was probably the magazine on the coffee table.

"That must cost a lot of money."

"She was thrifty, my Fiona."

Thrifty probably wouldn't pay for a new shop. "She didn't come into a large amount of cash recently?"

Granny's eyes narrowed, and she stepped forward. "Are you accusing my sweet granddaughter of doing something wrong?"

I held up my hands. "Not a chance." Blackmail was wrong last time I checked, so I ended that line of conversation.

"Fiona mentioned that she worked at a club before she moved to Arizona. Do you know where?"

"She lived in Nevada."

That didn't narrow it down, much. "Do you know who she worked for?"

"She wasn't big on keeping in touch. The young never do. They have their own lives."

"What type of club was it?"

"Entertainment. Probably a cabaret. She did the

makeup for performers, some of them pretty famous, she told me." She smiled and puffed out her chest.

"Did she ever mention the name of the club?"

She knit her bushy brows together, puzzled. "It was a candy bar."

"Rolos?"

"I never liked those."

"Reese's?"

"No, but something like that."

I paused, remembering Petey's constant meow, meow, meow. "Kit Kat?"

"That's it!"

Petey *had* held a clue, only it had been too obvious for me to see.

TWENTY-FOUR

Aunt Gertrude's visit had certainly added to my social schedule. First the premiere, then the reception. Visits to Bull's house and visits from him, not to mention from my neighbor, Sharlene. I was maxed out on my personal contact limit, but Auntie insisted we accept the invitation we'd received from the mayor's wife.

Mike and Toni Haskell lived in a deceptively simple home on Eucalyptus Circle on the west side of Fountain Hills. From the outside, it appeared a simple gray stone house with an arched entryway. The driveway sloped down on the right side of the house and led to a large, circular area for outdoor parking. A winding iron staircase led to the first-floor balcony and a sliding glass entrance into their home.

The living room, dining area and kitchen were all open, and the same burnt orange tile joined the rooms together into one, big mingling area. Buena Vista Social Club played in the background under the chatter of guests.

I stopped walking when I reached the marble island in the kitchen.

Canapés covered with a variety of cheese spreads,

brochettes, fruit bouquets and chocolates were just some of the sumptuous finger foods begging me to try them. I loaded up a plate and followed Auntie to our hostess.

"I'm so glad you made it," Toni said in a low voice through a smile that didn't move when she talked. Toni isn't exactly a social butterfly, which makes her duties as first lady difficult to bear. "I don't know half the people here. When they come up and say how nice it is to see me again, sometimes I freeze."

"When I'm at a party, I just call everybody Honey," Auntie said. "Makes them feel special and keeps me from feeling the fool."

The host and producer of *Blue-Ribbon Babes* hovered near the appetizers, probably choosing a single item to add to her plate for show. "Is Heather Ozu a big supporter of Mike's?"

Toni laughed. "She probably drops by every candidate's parties. Smart celebrities don't get political. It's like slapping the faces of half your fans."

"Clever girl."

Bert accompanied Heather into the living room and they slipped into mingling mode like professionals. Unlike me, Heather didn't have awkward moments. I usually spent the first half hour at get-togethers looking for a guest who looked like they wouldn't bite. I spent the rest of the time debating whether to say hi, since I assumed either they would be repulsed by me or I'd never get away from them.

"I heard about the makeup girl," Toni said. "If I were you, I'd stay home more. Finding bodies can't be much fun."

"You got me there."

Auntie was doing her card trick on some guests. With the image of Fiona's poor, dead face still fresh in my mind, I found it difficult to feign interest in the light-hearted conversations taking place around me. When Toni asked if I'd like to see her latest weaving project, I jumped at the chance to go somewhere private.

In a back room, probably a former bedroom from when her kids still lived at home, a large loom rested at an angle, surrounded by shelves of yarn every color of the rainbow.

"This is so soft," I said, running my fingers over a fluffy black skein.

"That's alpaca. They're like miniature llamas. So cute, you almost feel guilty taking their fleece. I'm using that in my latest project, along with these."

Toni picked up several balls of yarn in neutral colors and held them up one at a time.

"This is mohair." She held up a mossy green.

"Doesn't that come from rabbits?"

She gave the ball of yarn a squeeze and giggled. "Close. Angora goats. They look kind of like my mother-in-law's sheep dog, with curls falling in their eyes." She picked up another ball of yarn. "I have this off-white worsted wool on the weft."

"What's a weft?"

"Do you really want to know?"

I paused. "I probably wouldn't understand, anyway. I'm craft impaired, but I can recognize beauty when I see it, and this is beautiful," I said, looking over the block of fabric she'd woven so far.

"Yeah. Too bad I have to take it apart."

"The whole thing?"

"Just back to here," she pointed to the spot. "I broke a thread—the mohair, naturally. It's so difficult to work with. The darn stuff catches on everything. When I tied up the new strand, I didn't notice it was a shade off."

A shade off. That was a term I could apply to the

murderer. Bull's family, the contestants, Heather, Sunny. They all seemed like ordinary people, but one of them had the will to kill.

"You can hardly tell. It seems like so much unnecessary work to start over."

"It's a gift for my mother-in-law. She'll notice." She sang, "One of these things is not like the other." Then she covered her mouth with her hand. "I didn't mean it to sound like she's snooty. She's a fabric artist, so she's attuned to colors. It's intimidating making her gifts. I don't know why I torture myself."

I admired a few decorative yarns with sparkles and flags, and then my hostess suggested we get back to the others. With one last longing look at her loom, Toni turned off the lights.

The party was in full swing. Auntie came up and said, "Where have you been? People have been asking me about the investigation. I told them we were *this close* to cracking the case, with the help of the police, of course."

"You what?"

"I was just making conversation, and it really helped. People actually *wanted* my business cards. I ran out." She beamed at me as if increasing her client base was the reason we came.

Across the room, Sonny Street broke into laughter at something whispered by a woman I recognized as a city council member.

"If one of these people is the murderer," I whispered, "you may have given them a reason to strangle us with our scarves or whack us on the head with a frying pan."

"Don't be silly," she said without lowering her voice. "You haven't got any cast iron in your kitchen. The worst that could happen with that cheap cookware you own is we'd get a big headache. And my neck is too short to wear scarves, so I don't have any."

"What a relief."

But I wasn't relieved. Standing not twenty feet from me was a pretty nice group of people: Natasha, with her dreams of helping the poor; Bull and his family who, in different circumstances, would probably have made good friends. Okay. Acquaintances. Bert was your average guy trying to get ahead in a competitive business, and Heather... I didn't think I could ever feel warm and fuzzy about Heather.

The not-so-nice part was that one of them most likely murdered an old lady in cold blood. One of them snuck into Fiona Flynn's bedroom and strangled the life out of her, putting an end to her beauty business dreams. And one of them, an invited guest, had the nerve to kill a cockatoo in my own home. Just like Toni's troubling mohair, one of these people was a wayward thread, seeming to fit into the group, but on closer examination, not what they seemed.

An image of poor, dead Fiona flashed in front of my eyes, and I reluctantly conceded that I was going to have to do something so awful, so against nature, that I'd probably spend eternity being shunned by my fellow guests in Hell.

Bull jumped at the chance to give Auntie a ride home when I told him I had a migraine. I slipped out of the party and into my car and set out for the Jenkins' home.

God help me, I was going to dig up that bird and try to read poor, dead Petey.

TWENTY-FIVE

Outdoor lighting strategically lit up the shrubs in the Jenkins' vast front yard, which was inconvenient. The Bougainvillea bush where Bull buried Petey showed in the spotlight like a trampy starlet soaking up her fifteen minutes of fame.

I'd pulled the tire iron out from under the spare tire in my trunk, because I didn't have a handy shovel or spade in the car. The ground was still soft from the evening watering, and the knees of my pants were soon soaked through. Jabbing and pulling with the iron only loosened the ground into a pile of sifting dirt. If I wanted to get to the corpse under that dirt, I was going to have to use my hands.

Two cupped hands at a time, I removed stones, sand and earth and dumped them next to me, working slowly, because I didn't want to suddenly touch stiff feathers or, please no, maggots. I wished the idea of squirmy, grubby worms hadn't come into my head, because I went back to using the tire iron, and it was taking forever.

Finally, with a soft thud, I hit something solid. After removing the lid to the shoebox, I leveraged the iron under

Petey's corpse and gave it a shove. He flipped up onto the edge of the hole and then slowly rolled back in. Good enough.

I leaned back on my feet and closed my eyes, taking two deep breaths to steady my nerves. I willed my mind back to the night of the *Blue-Ribbon Babes* show and invited Petey to come along for the stroll down bad-memory lane. I remembered the moment when I discovered Elvira's body and could hear his wings flapping, and the repeated squawks of "Meow!" as he tried to escape his cage.

Tell me what happened, boy. Tell me who did this.

Nothing.

I imagined how it might look from his point of view on the counter of the *Blue-Ribbon Babes* set: a dark form sneaking up on his former mistress, skillet raised above the victim's head, ready to strike.

Give me a face, honey. Just a peek.

What if the bird had chosen that exact moment to clean his feathers, and with his face turned away from the set, actually missed the whole murder? What if Petey had nothing to tell? What if I was out of my mind, kneeling in the dirt, expecting a dead animal to talk to me?

"What are you doing?"

I scrambled to my feet and brushed off my knees. Catherine Jenkins stared at Petey, then me, her brow wrinkled as if wondering what possible explanation I could have for messing with a dead bird. I thought fast.

"I was driving by and saw a coyote digging up Petey." I picked up the crowbar. "I scared him off with this, and, well, I was just trying to decide if it would be worth it to rebury him in the same spot, or if I should...I hadn't really made it past that point."

She made a face. "I wouldn't want to have to touch that thing. Come on inside."

"I don't want to bother you."

"You're a mess."

I held up my hands. There was sand up my nails, and I'd cut my index finger on a stone. Blood had mixed in with wet soil, and it looked as if I'd been mixing chocolate cake batter with my hands.

"If you don't mind, I'll just wash up real quick and get going. Auntie is going to worry if I'm not home when she gets there."

"She was still at the party when I left, so don't rush."

Catherine unlocked the garage door and switched on the light. We passed through into the kitchen. I was still clutching the tire iron in my grip, so I rested it against the cabinets. It was too dirty to put on the table. I turned on the faucet and let warm water run over my hands.

"Better her than me," I said. "I don't like parties."

"I know just what you mean. I'm not that social myself."

A loud flutter passed by my ears and I ducked down and searched the ceiling. Catherine stepped back and followed my gaze.

"What is it?"

"Didn't you hear that noise?"

"What noise?"

"I think you might have a bat in the house."

Catherine covered her hair with her hands and frantically searched the kitchen. "I don't see anything. Are you sure?"

I listened. "I swear I heard something fly by my head." Unnerved, I scrubbed my hands with soap, rinsed, and searched for a paper towel.

"Under the sink," Catherine said.

I opened the cabinet and rummaged around. "You're out."

The fluttering noise came so close to my head that my ears popped, and with that pop, I was on the *Blue-Ribbon Babes* set. Elvira bent over the kitchen sink and scrubbed her mixing bowl. She rinsed it, turned off the water with her elbow, and went in search of a dish towel to dry her hands. A shadow pulled the cast iron skillet from under the counter, crept up behind her and raised the weapon high. With one crashing movement, Elvira Jenkins dropped like a rock, and her daughter-in-law, Catherine Jenkins, stood over her, a satisfied smile on those thick, gorgeous lips.

Startled, I lost my balance, and landed on my butt, just as the tire iron swung past my head and crashed to the floor.

"You!" I gasped.

She raised the iron again, and I scrambled around the island and ran into the living room. She was close on my heels, and in a repeat of my performance with Petey, I jumped the coffee table to put the piece of furniture between us.

"Why couldn't you leave it alone?" she said, her upper lip curled in a snarl. "I deserve my privacy!"

"Privacy?"

She swung the iron and brought it crashing down on the coffee table. I fell back onto the couch and looked at the ugly gash left behind on the wooden surface of the table. She headed right, so I went left.

"You thought you were so clever, dropping little hints. Your career will lead to exotic places. And meow, meow, meow. Rubbing it in my face."

I rolled out of the way just in time to escape the next blow. My brain worked furiously, and though it begged for a rest, I forced it to explain why it hadn't connected the clues with Catherine Jenkins. Exotic? Meow? What did she think I knew? And then it hit me.

"You worked at the Kitty Cat Club!"

Her eyes narrowed, and a low growl rose in the back of her throat. Her fingers tightened around the iron and she lunged forward, but I was ready for her this time. I grabbed the iron before it could connect and yelped at the pain in my palm. We struggled, her face so close I thought she might bite me. I reared back and gave her a head butt that clacked my teeth together. Her grip loosened, and I jerked back and forth until I wrested the iron away, but I pulled too hard, and it flew out of my hands and under the couch.

As I held my side and panted for air, I took in her fit body and flaming red hair. "Oh my gosh! You were an exotic dancer?"

"Don't act so surprised. I knew what you were up to." She threw up her hands, waved them girly style, and launched into a mocking imitation of me. "Let's play the nickname game. I'm Sissy and this is Gertie. What's your nickname, Catherine?"

"I didn't actually ask. You brought it up, and you said they called you Kate."

"Any moron can figure out Kit is short for Catherine. Even that idiot Elvira figured it out. She knew I owned my own business in Reno."

"You said out east."

"Reno is east."

"Not from here."

She threw back her head and shrieked. "You're just like my mother-in-law. So superior. She'd been to the Kit Cat Club to protest with her busy-body group. The old gas bag is one of the reasons I had to close down. No one wanted to pass by a group of screeching old ladies to get into the club." She added in a reasonable voice, "It ruined the ambiance."

"And then you met Tim?"

"He was one of my best customers!"

I gasped. "Did Elvira know?"

She smirked. "I assume he didn't share that with his mommy."

"So? Why did it matter?"

"It didn't. Not exactly."

She clenched her fists and started to cry. "It wasn't her business!"

"If Tim knew about it and it didn't bother him, why murder Elvira?"

"Because she found out about the abortion."

The tears turned into sobs, and she dropped down onto the coffee table. "God help me, I had an abortion." She looked at me as if pleading with me to understand. "I didn't know it would affect my ability to get pregnant. I didn't know there would be any consequences. I believed what the nurse told me. In and out and it's all behind you. And for a while it was. I didn't think about it, and everything was fine. I met Tim. We got married. And then we wanted a family."

By now she was sucking in deep breaths of air.

"It took forever to get pregnant, but I thought it was my age, and when I was finally expecting, we were so happy." Her voice went dead. "And then the first miscarriage. And the second." She wiped her nose on her sleeve. "Elvira started nosing around. She was going to help make things right, like she always did." She barked out a laugh. "I don't know how she found out."

I had my suspicions, but I didn't think Nurse Moira meant to let it slip. Maybe she just mentioned she met Catherine before, in Reno. Elvira seemed to have done a bit of protesting in Reno. Maybe she saw Moira when she protested at the clinic, and recognizing her at the doctor's office, put it together.

Catherine's eyes blazed. "And then that self-righteous witch said she was going to tell Tim. He had a right to know. It would have killed him. Actually, it would have killed our marriage. Tim wanted a child so badly. If he found out we couldn't have children because I'd—I don't think he could have handled it." She stopped crying. "So, I killed her instead."

"I understand the bird, because I mentioned he'd been talking. Quite frankly, I'm not that sad about Petey. He was pretty annoying. But why Fiona?" My face muscles, wrinkled in thought, then relaxed as I figured it out. "Oh. She did hair for the girls at the club. You're the old boss she recognized. And then she suddenly had money. She was blackmailing you."

Before me sat the most dejected woman I'd ever seen. Her eyes were rimmed with red from crying, her hair stuck out in a wild mess from our tussle, and her shoulders slumped in defeat. She looked vulnerable. Her heartache over the loss of her children touched me, and before I'd thought things through, I said, "I'm so sorry."

She met my gaze. "Me too. Nothing personal."

Catherine had gotten her wind back—surprising, considering all the talking she'd done—and she launched herself through the air and tackled me. I hit the ground hard, and even though the wind was knocked out of me, when she wrapped her fingers around my throat, I fought back. I pushed her shoulders hard, but her grip held tight.

"Don't—want—another—murder," I gasped.

She didn't like my advice and squeezed harder.

In the distance, a voice called my name. Was it God? Or

my dead grandma? No offense, Granny, but I wasn't ready for a reunion. I jammed one knee between us, but the room started to swim.

I heard a loud thump, then another, then a crash of glass. A rattan patio chair flew over our heads and rolled across the rug.

Bowers wrapped his arms around Catherine's shoulders and pulled her up. She still held my throat in her grip, and she dragged me to a sitting position. When he finally shook her loose, she kicked and struggled like a spitting cat.

"Okay. Calm down."

Bowers jerked her arms behind her back and shoved her to the ground. With one knee between her shoulder blades, he pulled out his cuffs. I crawled over and watched while he cuffed her hands. I wanted to make darn sure she was helpless before I let down my guard. When he had her properly restrained, I fell back on the floor to catch my breath.

Bowers leaned over me and took my chin in his hand. "Are you alright?"

I coughed a few times, still trying to get my breath. "Just dandy."

"Catherine?"

I looked up to see Bull, Auntie, and Tim staring in open-mouthed surprise. This was going to take some explaining.

TWENTY-SIX

Bowers insisted that a patrol officer drive my car home, and he drove me back to Arrowhead Drive. Auntie remained behind to comfort Bull, while Tim got busy looking for a criminal attorney. The ride was uncomfortable and silent, and when the car pulled up in front of my house, I reached for the door.

Bowers took my arm in a firm grip. "Not so fast."

"It wasn't my fault. I just went there to read Petey."

He blew out a sharp breath. "Petey, as in dead Petey?" He let go of my arm.

"Which was crossing a line, I know, but too many people had already died. What were you doing there?" I asked.

"I was waiting to arrest Catherine Jenkins, because I didn't want to crash the mayor's party."

"You knew she was the killer?" I stared. "I don't believe you."

"That's what the police force does. Solve crimes. What we don't like to do is waste time saving people who get in our way."

"Sorry to be such a problem."

"That didn't come out right." He slammed his palms against the steering wheel. "Why are you such a pain in my side?"

"If you hadn't been interested in Auntie as your favorite suspect, I wouldn't have felt the need to be a pain in your side."

"My investigation was none of your business. It's not as if you'd been hired as a consultant to the department. You and your aunt are just two people who capitalize on people's fixation with the occult."

"Ah. So that's what I am. An opportunistic con artist. Glad we got that cleared up."

Bowers slammed the palm of one hand on the steering wheel again. "Just because I care about you doesn't mean you get special consideration. And yes. You are opportunistic. When people have problems, instead of directing them to a priest or a psychiatrist, or even a priest psychiatrist, you take advantage and mess around with things you have no business going near."

He put a hand on my shoulder and turned me to face him. "Frankie, I'm out there every day looking at the worst of human nature. Evil is real, and it doesn't need you skipping around offering it free fries with every order for a reading. It doesn't need another way in."

"What do you mean *a way in*?"

He cleared his throat a couple of times. "This is going to be harder than I thought."

He reached for my hand and seemed to think better of it. "I saw it." He dropped his head in his hands. "I can't believe I'm admitting this, and if you repeat it, I'll deny it, but I saw the...it."

"I don't understand."

"Right before you flipped back in your chair at the séance, there was this horrible image of your cat."

I sucked in my breath. "You saw what I saw?"

"It was as if it was your cat, but it wasn't your cat. I've never seen Emily look so ferocious."

"How?" I whispered.

"I wish I knew, because it's something I never, ever want to experience again."

He shifted his position to lean against the car door, which was as far away from me as he could get and still remain in the front seat. I could tell he blamed me, as if I were some harpy running around and intentionally handing out bad dreams to the kiddies.

"I don't know how it happened."

"The bird said—it's just too stupid to repeat, but I'm sure it said—meow."

I nodded. "Three times."

"The Kit Cat Club?" he asked, a dazed expression on his face.

"Yep. And you got that right away, so you can see it would have been better if we had worked together on this."

"You're not suggesting that I ask the neighborhood cat for the name of the culprit the next time I'm investigating a murder." His eyes popped open. "You're not, are you?"

"It's not that simple. What do you think? That animals talk to me in complex sentences? That they draw me pictures and explained things in clear terms?"

The tears were getting ready to flow, but I scrunched up my eyes to force them back. I was not going to have a pity sob in front of Bowers. A deep breath helped steady my voice.

"When animals decide to invade my personal space, they throw me images, energy signatures, feelings. They don't talk. Except Petey did know a few words. Mostly meow. On the night of the séance, you saw exactly what I usually get. That image of Emily was a typical message, and they usually come uninvited." I threw my hands up. "Why do you think I stopped doing the pet psychic readings?"

He rubbed his face with his hands, as if he were trying to wipe the image away.

"Wow. I had no idea."

"Now you do."

He stared ahead of him, his fingers tapping the dashboard in a nervous rhythm.

"That's awful. I mean really, really awful."

"Tell me about it." I sighed, relieved that someone finally understood that a psychic connection with animals wasn't a fun thing to experience.

"And weird."

"Oka-a-y. I'm not sure I like being described as weird."

He turned to face me. "What does Auntie think?"

That made me laugh. "Let's get something clear. Not one member of my family knows. They think I dabble in theatrics like my aunt, and it's going to stay that way." I shook my finger at him. "So, if you ever feel the need to call my mother, which was a pretty low thing to do without telling me first, don't even think about mentioning it."

"Mention it?" Bowers said. "I'm going to pretend this never happened." He nodded his head several times. "I warned you about dabbling in this crap."

"Maybe you didn't hear me, but I don't dabble. I don't seem to have any control over it. It's like they take possession of my mind at will. I've even been visited by a dead dog."

He cleared his throat. "Maybe you should see a priest.

They seem to know a lot about spirits and possessions and, well, stuff."

"I already did," I snapped. "But not because there's anything wrong with me. I just kind of ran into him."

Bowers took my hand. "And?"

"I'm not possessed, if that's what you're wondering. My head doesn't spin around, and I don't levitate, and I haven't vomited green since I overdosed on Halloween candy when I was eight."

"That's good." He waited. "Did he have any insights?"

"I learned it's a no-no to sacrifice my children to strange gods."

"You have children?"

"No, but it's a good point to remember if I ever do."

"I meant did he have any advice."

"He seemed more concerned about Auntie's tarot card business."

"We're going to have to work on that," he said, nodding again.

"We?"

Bowers leaned forward and clutched my hand in both of his. "Frankie, I really care about you, and I'd like to see more of you."

I felt a flutter in my chest. "You do?" I thought back to his kiss and decided I'd like it, too.

"I'm just—well, I don't want to worry that you're in my head."

I looked at his hands, holding mine, and an idea occurred to me. "Bowers, do you remember the first time—IT—happened last month? When I was trying to communicate with Sandy and get him to release the lock on the door and I sort of wound up reading your thoughts?"

"How could I forget?"

"We were holding hands. Just like we were holding hands the night of the séance."

He didn't just let go of my hand. He threw it away from him as if it were a bomb set to go off any moment.

I grabbed my purse from the car floor. "Well. I guess that's that."

"I—" He stared out his window. "You can't expect me to date a woman I can't even touch. I'm not a lecher, but that's asking too much."

I softened my voice. "Bowers, I don't understand what's happening, but I'm sure we could work it out. Just don't ever touch my hands." I added a weak grin, but my chest tightened because I guessed his answer.

He cleared his throat, but his voice still cracked when he said, "I don't think I can do it."

I gave a short nod, said goodnight, and saw myself to my front door. By the time Auntie came home, I'd already made up the couch, and I pretended to be asleep. She whispered my name a few times, gave up, and crept into my room. I didn't want her to see I'd been crying.

"You're sure you've got everything? You don't want something else to read or a snack for the plane?"

Terminal Four of the Sky Harbor Airport bustled with travelers setting off on adventures, returning from business trips, or in Auntie's case, heading home. I had a strange reluctance to let Auntie pass through security and out of my life. Well, not out of my life. Just out of the vicinity. It wasn't as if I'd enjoyed having a roommate, but what can I say? She smelled of home.

"If I have another coffee, I'll have to tinkle before I get

to Wisconsin, and I read about some woman whose insides were sucked out by the airplane toilet. No thank you."

"Good to know."

She reached for her carry on. I hung it over her shoulder and kissed her cheek.

"No regrets about your visit?"

"I had a wonderful time, Sissy. I could have done without the murder, but we don't get to choose what life throws at us."

"Um, when you get home..."

"Not a word to your mother. I figured that one out myself."

"And you're not sorry to leave Bull?"

"Heavens, no! I'd forgotten how bossy he was. Besides. Once he has time to get over Elvira, I wouldn't be surprised if he gave Sharlene a call. Widowers don't live long unless they find another wife. That's what statistics show. And it would be nice if those two got together."

That was a relief. I might be missing Auntie now, but if she took up permanent residence in Arizona... I shuddered.

"The air conditioning is a little cold in here. You should get back out in the sun. I've got my book, so don't worry about me."

Before she left, I wanted the answer to a question that had nagged at my brain over the last week. "What's the deal with Sharlene? You kept hinting there was something wrong with her?"

"Nothing but loneliness. Promise me you'll drop in on her once in a while."

I agreed, and then I hugged her tight and didn't let go until she pulled away. We both had tears in our eyes. I stood, watching, as she placed her bags on the conveyor belt and took off her sandals. She gave me a final wave after she passed through security, and I stared down that hallway long after she'd disappeared.

"You look a little lost."

An elderly man, one of the Navigator volunteers, gave me a kind smile and offered to assist me.

"I'm feeling a little lost right now."

"Where are you headed?" he asked.

Where was I headed? Good question. The pet communication lines were back open, but I wasn't sure if that was a good or a bad thing. With Penny set to walk down the aisle, I saw the end of my social life. Seamus had abandoned any thoughts of romance with me for a new love, but that didn't bother me as much as I thought it would. Bowers was another matter, but I couldn't do anything about the fact that he had dumped me before we started dating.

On the flip side, I could take a few pet psychic appointments, see how it worked out, and maybe increase my bank balance. It wasn't as if Penny were dead. Or Seamus. Or even Bowers. And I still had Chauncey and Emily.

"Time will tell." I reassured him with a smile.

"You're in the airport but you don't know where you're going?" He looked over his shoulder at the Navigator counter, probably hoping for backup in case I started to drool or demand that he bow to the queen of Mars.

"'It's alright. I'm alright." I took a deep breath and blew it out slowly.

"I'll be fine."

And I almost meant it.

A NOTE FROM JACKIE

I've never thought of birds as cute and fuzzy, but since many people love their pet birds, I tried to see them as something other than modern day dinosaurs. Little dinosaurs, but just as scary.

I went to Pet Supply, the local, family-owned pet store, and visited with their resident cockatoo, thinking this touch of familiarity would take away my fears. The owner was kind enough to share many tidbits about these intelligent creatures. Great, I thought. Dinosaurs with brains.

Jackie

Don't miss out on Frankie's next adventure!

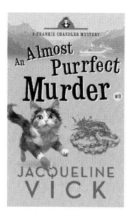

When Frankie Chandler's boards an Alaskan cruise ship for her best friend's wedding, she's hardly a cheerful advertisement for sailing the ocean blue. Her best (and only) friend is getting married, which means the end of impromptu girl's nights. Her only consolation is the all-night buffet, but even that can't make up for the body she discovers below her balcony.

The only witnesses are a troupe of performing cats. Just when things can't get any more bizarre, Detective Martin Bowers joins the cruise in Juneau, and the investigation isn't the only thing about to heat up.

ACKNOWLEDGMENTS

Albert & Beverly Voirin brought home my first and only pet bird – a parakeet. It did not end well.

Many thanks to Chris and Zack at Pet Supply, Santa Clarita—the best pet store around—for their many insights, both for my dog, Buster, and this book.

Many thanks to my support group of brave souls willing to read proof copies and give me feedback and advice, especially Mary Grant, Andrea Voirin, and Gayle Bartos-Pool.

Thanks to Foster for his unwavering belief in me.

Finally, thanks to my Readers Group, a community of readers who love mysteries and laughter as much as I do.

BOOK CLUB QUESTIONS

A Bird's Eye View of Murder

Frankie is back, and this time she's billing herself as an animal behaviorist. Is she hiding from her psychic "gift"? Should she embrace it warts and all?

Aunt Gertrude is messing up Frankie's home and her routine. When Frankie gets irritated with her, she usually keeps it in check. Should Frankie stand up to her aunt? Or does it show more strength of character to respect her elderly relative?

Bowers suggests that Frankie may be messing with things she shouldn't when she takes part in a séance. Is Frankie traveling on dangerous ground, or is the occult not a big deal?

Aunt Gertrude, known for reading tarot cards, tries her hand at a séance and palm reading in an attempt to generate

BOOK CLUB QUESTIONS

business. Why do you think people are willing to pay for these services?

Catherine feels guilt over her inability to carry a child to term. Should she have been honest with her husband about the possible cause? Or is her abortion strictly her business?

Aunt Gertrude and Elvira had a falling out years ago when Elvira pinched Auntie's Lemon Blueberry Buckle recipe to win the heart of the boy they both loved. Is Auntie jealous over a lost love, or is the stolen recipe the real source of her ire?

Several characters experience broken dreams. Are there dreams you've had that were not as sweet as you had hoped when you achieved them?

Did you think that Bull was a chauvinist?

The Blue Ribbon Queen is a coveted title offered by The Baking Channel. Why do you think women like Elvira and Aunt Gertrude are drawn to this type of competition?

Frankie and Bowers run into a relationship hurdle that they can't get over. Should they have tried to work it out no matter what the cost?

ABOUT THE AUTHOR

Jacqueline Vick writes the Frankie Chandler Pet Psychic mystery series about a woman who, after faking her psychic abilities for years, discovers animals *can* communicate with her. Her second series, the Harlow Brothers mysteries, features a former college linebacker turned etiquette author and his secretary brother. Her books are known for satirical humor and engaging characters who are reluctant to accept their greatest (and often embarrassing) gifts.

Visit the author at jacquelinevick.com.

Made in the USA
Columbia, SC
27 June 2024